Jungle Passports

THE ETHNOGRAPHY OF POLITICAL VIOLENCE

Series Editors: Daniel J. Hoffman, Tobias Kelly, Sharika Thiranagama

A complete list of books in the series is available from the publisher.

JUNGLE PASSPORTS

Fences, Mobility, and Citizenship

at the Northeast India-Bangladesh Border

Malini Sur

UNIVERSITY OF PENNSYLVANIA PRESS

PHILADELPHIA

Copyright © 2021 University of Pennsylvania Press

All rights reserved. Except for brief quotations used for purposes of review or scholarly citation, none of this book may be reproduced in any form by any means without written permission from the publisher.

Published by
University of Pennsylvania Press
Philadelphia, Pennsylvania 19104-4112
www.upenn.edu/pennpress

Printed in the United States of America
on acid-free paper

10 9 8 7 6 5 4 3 2 1

A catalogue record for this book is available from the Library of Congress.
ISBN 978-0-8122-5279-8

For Anima, Nilima, Rakesh, and Neel

CONTENTS

Timeline   ix

Introduction   1

Chapter 1. The Rowmari-Tura Road   23
Chapter 2. Rice Wars and Nation Building   42
Chapter 3. Cow Smuggling and *Fang-Fung*   67
Chapter 4. Kinship, Identities, and "Jungle Passports"   93
Chapter 5. Fear, Reverence, and the Fence   119
Chapter 6. Bangladeshi "Suspects" and Indian "Citizens" in Assam   145

Afterword   170

Notes   173
Bibliography   187
Index   203
Acknowledgments   211

TIMELINE

1822	Regulation No. 10 of 1822.
1826	British annexation of the Kingdom of Assam.
1875	Construction of a road from Tura leading to Brahmaputra's eastern banks.
1897	Great Earthquake
1905	Partition of Bengal (British India).
1912	Revocation of the Partition of Bengal (British India).
1930s–1940s	Evictions of "illegal migrants" and agricultural expansion programs in colonial Assam.
1946	Petition to the Bengal Boundary Commission for the inclusion of *Adibashistan* within India.
1946	Foreigners Act of India.
1947	Partition of the Indian subcontinent and the creation of two new states, India and Pakistan.
1950	Immigrants (Expulsion from Assam) Act.
1964	Prevention of Infiltration of Foreigners Scheme for Assam and setting up of Assam's border police.
1965	India-Pakistan War.
1971	Formation of Bangladesh after a prolonged war of liberation. The geographical territory that was formerly East Pakistan became Bangladesh.
1975	Assassination of the first president of Bangladesh.
1975–1977	Kader Bahini Rebellion.
1979–1985	Assam Movement.
1983	Illegal Migration (Determination by Tribunals) Act (IMDT).
2001	Boroibari border conflict between India and Bangladesh.

2005   India's Supreme Court strikes down the IMDT as
                unconstitutional. In Assam, all existing cases under
                IMDT transferred to thirty-two foreigners tribunals.
2011   Fifteen-year-old Felani is shot to death by an Indian
                border troop.
2014   BJP-led India government proposes amendment to Indian
                citizenship to include non-Muslims from Afghanistan,
                Pakistan, and Bangladesh.
2015   Updating of the National Register of Citizens in the state of
                Assam begins.
2019   Updated National Register of Citizens excludes 1.9 million
                people in Assam.
2019   India's Citizenship Amendment Act is passed.

Introduction

"Hallo, hallo—signal clear? Line clear? Shall I send them? Okay!"
    The three-year-old Badshah screamed in excitement, holding a
    mobile phone.
Pretending my tape recorder was a phone, I responded: "Hello,
    hello, is everything all right?"
Badshah (giggling on the bed): "Hello, hello, shall I cut the wire?"
Me: "Who were you speaking to?"
Badshah: "Business."
Me: "What business?"
Badshah (playing with the mobile): "Goru" (cows).[1]

As Badshah jumped around, his father, Alibaba, a Muslim landless laborer
in his mid-forties, hurried about preparing himself to smuggle cows from India to Bangladesh.[2] He would physically drive the animals across the *chars*
(riverine islands) situated along the India-Bangladesh border. The English
words "line," "signal," and "clear" were a part of the *borderi* lexicon used in
this remote *char* in the Indian state of Assam—one of the many volatile silty
depositions in the mighty Brahmaputra River.[3]

In April 2007, I began fieldwork along the border, living on the *char* next to
the one where Alibaba's modest one-room house stood. His house was a mile
away from the border. At that time, India had just started building a new multilayered fence to control unauthorized Bangladeshi migration and the threats
of Islamic terrorism, smuggling, and political separatism. The new fence
sought to replace the earlier boundary that comprised old fences and fence-
like structures. In some stretches, bamboo signposts with plastic flags marked
the international boundary. Often the borderline was a mud path between rice
fields or a tarmac road that divided agricultural land. Changing tides toppled
floating pillars that were markers of international water boundaries.

The India-Bangladesh border is 2,545 miles long. It is longer than the combined length of the Israel-Palestine and U.S.-Mexico borders.[4] At the geopolitical level, this border is not a warring one such as the Israel-Palestine or India-Pakistan borders—and yet it continues to be a site of land and identity conflicts and gross human rights violations.[5]

Indian sources estimate that twenty million unauthorized Bangladeshis reside in India.[6] Indian troops especially suspect Muslim cattle workers such as Alibaba who rely on the border for their livelihood.

A little less than half of the India-Bangladesh border cuts across Northeast India, a region that is geographically isolated from the rest of Indian territory and heavily militarized.[7] India's militarization of states in Northeast India is seen as a prerequisite for containing armed struggles for sub-nationalism and self-determination.[8] The Armed Forces Special Powers Act (1958) protects the Indian armed forces from prosecution for crimes, suspends democratic functioning, and exposes people to constant state surveillance.[9] Protracted conflicts between the Indian military forces and ethnonationalist militant groups have generated a "frontier culture of violence."[10]

At the Northeast India-Bangladesh border, groups demanding independent nations and homelands take refuge, negotiate passage to Bangladesh, and procure arms. These struggles amplify border militarization as well generate unintended alliances in the odd-shaped zone that straddles Assam and Meghalaya, Northeast India and the five bordering districts of Kurigram, Sherpur, Jamalpur, Mymensingh, and Netrokona in Bangladesh where I conducted ethnographic and historical fieldwork. Despite boundary pillars and the newly fortified structures, the Northeast India-Bangladesh border region is not well-defined. Unlike many boundaries, the landscape of *chars,* hills, foothills, and rivers itself is shifting. Rivers frequently flood and constantly change course, inundating low-lying plain regions and pushing silt for new settlements. Border societies laboriously reclaim the wetlands for cultivation and settlement—the forces of nature dictate life in these shifting regions.

This book is about an in-between period when India started replacing old boundary structures with a new multilayered fence along its borders with Bangladesh. It specifically explores the diverse mobilities of people, goods, and animals amid political, historical, and ecological forces at play in the Northeast India-Bangladesh borderland. I retrace my steps in time to resituate and contextualize the fence in histories of road-building and rice wars that goes back almost two hundred years. In an era of global nationalistic rhetoric, this book seeks to foreground how the ubiquity of border infrastructures that seek to resolve issues of national citizenship and migrant "illegality" establishes their indeterminacy of purpose. The shifting and twisting ecology of the terrain, along with the complex exchanges, continues to defy contemporary visions of homogeneous nation-states.

Old trade routes, territorial animosities, and circuits of smuggling and migration join shifting *char* landscape in Assam with the neighboring Indian state of Meghalaya and five bordering contiguous districts of Bangladesh. The border cuts across similar societies. Here, the dense black earth of the *chars* gives way to red hills. Speeding buses are packed with passengers and poultry; trucks carrying cement, gravel, and stacks of barbed wire compete for space on the dilapidated roads. The arrival of engineers, building materials, and migrant laborers to build India's new border fence transformed the remote villages into bustling hubs. This reordering of the terrain and the construction noises disrupted elephant corridors; elephants descended from the forests, trampled upon the newly laid pillars of the fence, and destroyed rice harvests and houses.

Amid all the din, Garo Bangladeshi Christian women traders briskly crossed the border with sacks of export surplus clothes to sell in India. They described their journeys as using "jungle passports," alluding to their moral claims to a shared indigenous landscape and the camouflaged use of forest cover of the region. Other laborers and transporters relied on secret routes, skillfully crawling under old border fences clutching amulets and depending on trees from which angels were said to guide lost travelers. When I arrived in Bangladesh's border villages for fieldwork, rumors circulated: "Is India building a wall like the Great Wall of China?" Everyone believed that India would electrify the new wall and that anyone who came into contact with it would die. Indian border troops never put these rumors to rest.

From 2007 until 2015, I closely followed the Northeast India-Bangladesh border's shapeshifting and its implications for border societies. The emergent infrastructures, routine floods, and distraught animals reminded the villagers that they could not take for granted the land, the border, their relationships with each other and with border troops, or even the actions of animals. On days when crossing was impossible, traders, transporters, and their families went hungry.

Despite these difficulties, the division of sovereignties and distinct regimes of mobility pushed Alibaba and others like him to undertake perilous journeys in order to make a living. Badshah's excitement as he ran out to join his kite-flying friends—all screaming "line clear, signal clear"—reminded me

Figure 1. India's new border fence with Bangladesh under construction in the states of Meghalaya and Assam, Northeast India. (Photograph: author)

Figure 2. The Indian Border Security Forces patrolling the India-Bangladesh border during floods in Assam, Northeast India. (Photograph: Shib Shankar Chatterjee)

again and again that borders are not just sites for studying the imprints of state violence. The *hurmuri jatras* (rushed journeys) and travel by "jungle passports" maintained transborder livelihoods, kinship, and religious life amid nationalism, disasters, fears, and despair. Here, people forge meaningful relationships beyond the lines of nations, religions, and ethnicities.

The Border as Life Force

What is it that propels life to continue to revolve around a heavily fortified fence amid violence, scarcity, fear, and uncertainty? How have longstanding socioecological histories and territorial conflicts severed emergent political topographies of mobility, nationalism, and citizenship? What do the forces that shape the lifeworlds of deportees, refugees, farmers, smugglers, migrants, bureaucrats, lawyers, clergy, and border troops in this region tell us about reciprocity and exchange and the enforcement of state violence, illegality, and border infrastructures in general? And what might border societies and their relationships to infrastructures—longing, nostalgia, fear, and deference—convey about the unfinished business of nation building, identity, and insularity or about the hardening of borders that is globally evident in the twenty-first century?

This book seeks to answer these questions. I show how borders continue to gather life's promises even when walls and checkpoints brutally divide nations and societies. Despite the attendant risks, borders propel lifeworlds of mobility, identity, and citizenship that are perennially in the making. The powerful forces that regulate the fragile balance of life and death at the nation's margins compel people to cross borders again and again.

Today, more than ever, attention to these shifts may help scholars think about the life forces that connect divided landscapes. Over the past decade, the world has been experiencing a resurgent politics of nationalist authoritarianism that locates borders on the frontline of debates on globalization, unauthorized migration, and citizenship. In 2019, state repression and severe economic, political, and climatic changes led to over seventy-one million people becoming either stateless refugees or internally displaced.[11] These events have reversed the euphoria that accompanied the crumbling of the Berlin Wall and the end of the Cold War in the 1990s, which inspired scholars to study transnational belonging as an extended social field stretching across national geographies.[12] In contrast, contemporary political events generate more attention to "power geometries" and antagonistic borders. While people may physically move more, such movement may, paradoxically, be more violent and precarious than before.[13]

Interlocked webs of relationships shape border societies, but borders are also sites where a sense of being uprooted and rendered less than human continually lingers. By virtue of their location, the loyalty of border residents to the nation continues to be in doubt, and ethnic and religious minorities and the rural poor who reside here are wrought even more marginal to the projects of the nation-state. The very vitality and tugs and pulls that hold people together across national territories and beyond the lines of blood simultaneously result in an enduring sense of danger and loss.

In this book, I situate four elements—ecologies, infrastructures, exchanges, and mobility—showing how they work in tandem through permeable boundaries to shape the force of life and loss at the Northeast India–Bangladesh border. Ecologically, this region stands at the confluence of *chars* (riverine islands) and partly forested hills and foothills. Historically nature's fury shaped the rhythms of life—as forest fires that impeded British colonial mapping and earthquakes that crafted political subjects. Rivers continue to destroy and create *chars*, and the floods that continue to devastate agricultural land and cattle impinge upon national citizenship and belonging. Relentless climate change exacerbates these, and deforestation and denudation have led to the disruption of elephant corridors in the forests. Furthermore, as agricultural production becomes volatile, people increasingly rely on the border for their livelihood. Yet, rivers and forests are also passageways for making a living from smuggling.

The second element—infrastructures—and people's relationships to these continue to gather uneven stories surrounding old maps and new roads, and new fences and old identity papers. These associations push anthropology's engagements with marginal histories far beyond the material remnants on which India and Bangladesh revive their past and structure the present. I show how border infrastructures are perpetually unfinished projects, which ensures their routinization as well as their menace. While India's new border fence, outposts, and growing digital surveillance impede people's access and thereby their ability to make a living from the border, other infrastructures such as old trade routes enable people to express notions of neighborliness and friendship across national territories.[14] As political authorities and states refashioned territories, rural societies fought for the very borders within which their lives came to be gradually enclosed. The exchange of goods—rice, cattle, and garments—attests to both the border's violence and its genera-tive potential for sustaining kinship, and livelihood. Risk-taking and enter-prising smugglers rely on duplicity and amorality as a way of life as well as relationships of trust and reciprocity with border troops beyond monetary gains and bribes. In the final pages of the book, I show how the urgency of border crossings redefines life, migrant "illegality," and national citizenship. As these elements weave in, competing notions of space and sovereignty are mediated by the fractured, shifting, and contingent experience of time. Rural societies that rely on the border for making a living negotiate their claims to the borderland in ways that mitigate and transcend the totalizing nature of state violence. These four elements, as this book will show, are fundamental to the anthropology of borders and border societies.

Even in the face of the sheer force of state violence, deadly ecologies, and incursive infrastructures, borders remain permeable. Such porosity is hardly generative of failed projects of nationalism and border militarization; instead, it attests to how border societies constantly recalibrate the nation's power of territorial regulation in their lives. Eric Beverley argues that frontiers not only signify edges that function as spatial limitations but also as sites of creativ-ity, power, and resources. He shows how fragmented sovereignties along fron-tiers enabled people to move between territories and partake in different regimes of authority; frontiers are productive sites for marginal people because social and legal governance had limited impacts there.[15] Borders work in a similar way, making the brutal performances of sovereign authority most visible while showing how the territorial regulation of sovereign power is far from complete at the nation's edges.[16]

Scholarly discussions on life in unstable borders and times are especially critical today.[17] The present offers a decisive political moment, in which ef-forts to fortress territorial boundaries and ultranationalism are forcing people toward uncertain border crossings and violent encounters with increasingly hostile nation-states. The hardening of borders in the twenty-first century shows how force and life become enmeshed, where their productive tensions can be read as will and erasure and where they mutate the ephemeral and precarious into the durable.

The dual logic of force as momentum and stasis unfolds through the bor-der's life-giving and life-taking properties. In his reading of Nietzsche's "will to power," Deleuze says, "We will never find the sense of something if we do not know the force which appropriates the thing, which exploits it, which takes possession of it or express in it" and "a plastic force . . . [is] a force of metamorphosis."[18] If we shift our engagement with force from the meta-physical domain that also formed the locus of Nietzsche's interventions and yet retain its essence of malleability, we learn how life's unevenness and its propulsive energies drive people to live and move amid constriction, danger, and violence. At borders, the more insidious workings of violent national-ism and arbitrary state power reveal life's relationship with a range of forces: forces that destroy life and forces that enact the constructive potential of life. Borders generate decisive moments that establish the margins of precarity and prosperity, as well as forge the boundaries of death and life.

As an essence of life force, vitality imbues borders with productive im-plications. João Biehl reminds us that people's struggles and visions unleash dynamic plurality, motion, and ambiguity that are irreducible to a single nar-rative. These bring to the surface the ongoing, antagonistic conversations between the plasticity of life and death.[19] The suppleness that defines human and nonhuman interactions attunes to the role of power and knowledge to form bodies and identities, without reducing people to the mere workings of such forces.[20] As Bhrigupati Singh asserts, life forces lie in the potency and ephemerality that shape life as a whole. People's capacity for action are constantly in flux and movement, including the progression toward death and loss.[21]

This book shows how the vitality and political salience of borders trans-fix some people in fear and nostalgia while simultaneously push others to move. The border shapes people's experience of risk and time as they recali-brate the violence perpetrated by nation-states, and in turn, people reshape the border. While the use of force establishes the "nation's fragments" as mar-ginal political subjects,[22] I suggest that even dangerous margins are vibrant centers of relationality and exchange. In the pages that follow, I show the workings of the border as an assembly of life force and the risks and uncer-tainties that surround fences and walls.

Fence Building

The ambition of building walls to divide the United States and Mexico, the checkpoints that delegitimize mobility between Israel and Palestine, and the construction of India's new fence with Bangladesh reveal how nation-states are invested in building barriers. Territorial sovereignty, as expressed in ro-bust spatially delineated boundaries and unambiguous regimes of national citizenship, ensures that national security mandates easily conflate unauthorized migration with loss of jobs, crime, and terrorism to sustain and justify border militarization.[23] The twenty-first century has proved that political and social instabilities are neither momentary nor exceptional; rather, borders provide the foundation to rethink space, politics, and collective life. Borders will continue to play a critical role in influencing national sovereignty, citizenship, and identity;[24] nation-states will continue to barricade borders against the flows of refugees and undocumented migrants in spectacular ways and erode ordinary people's use of borders for earning a livelihood.[25]

India first proposed the creation of a new border fence with Bangladesh in 1986.[26] Land acquisition issues between India and Bangladesh, as well as between the various Indian states and the federal government of India—in addition to local land disputes—delayed the start of the construction work.[27] Bangladesh did not object to India's fence per se but instead objected that the location of the fence violated the 150-yard demarcation area that had been bilaterally agreed upon in 1974. In April 2007, a multilayered structure comprising two outer rows and one inner row of ten-foot metal pillars interlaced with razor-sharp barbed wire started making an appearance in the *chars* of Assam and the foothills of Meghalaya that bordered Bangladesh. Unlike the old single-layered fence, the new barrier was similar to India's border fence with Pakistan.[28]

Border walls and fences are the locus of sovereignty; these infrastructures emplace nationalism. The barbed wires, concrete fortifications, and militarized checkpoints evoke the poetics of contemporary nationalism as much as its politics.[29] Infrastructures comprise both the material and emergent terrains of political authority that make and unmake political subjects.[30] When infrastructures break down, they further attest to the unstable relations—rather than certainties—that hold together these material and political assemblages.[31] Wendy Brown asserts that, far from reflecting the escalating sovereignty of nation-states, the proliferation of border walls across both rich and poor nations actually symbolizes declining national sovereignty and a shift in the locus of sovereign power from the nation-state to capital and religiously sanctioned violence.[32] Sankaran Krishna ascribes India's graphic displays of violence—in particular, the ways the nation-state abstracts, disciplines, and abuses its border residents to serve the interests of nation building—to the postcolonial predicament. His formulation of "cartographic anxieties" renders the postcolony as a distinctive political form that is trapped between "former colonies" and "pre-nation[s]."[33]

Border walls and fences are perennially unfinished projects of national governance and rule. As projects that are continually built, uprooted, and demolished only to be rebuilt, such infrastructures displace scholarly preoccupations with border fortifications as uniform artifacts expressing sovereign losses or violent narrations of the postcolonial form. Peter Andreas argues that even robust infrastructures, such as those that divide the U.S.-Mexico border, and border enforcement function as political and symbolic gestures; they struggle to reduce smuggling and unauthorized migration. The U.S. border policies only trigger more sophisticated ways of moving people and commodities, which in turn spiral into more militarization. Border militarization compels undocumented immigrants to rely on human traffickers and increases risks to life.[34]

Yet unlike other infrastructures, border fences do not "break down," even when their structures do. Instead, even as metal pillars rust and barbed wire becomes brittle, border patroling continues to intensify the nation's unsettling presence. Even broken walls and fences establish the anxious domestication of lethal infrastructures in lives and livelihoods through the armed forces that surveille border crossings. In other instances, states mobilize harsh landscapes to serve their goals. Jason De León's powerful grounding of border policing in desert ecologies reveals how the harshness of nature amplifies migrant deterrence in the U.S. Here, state policies and bureaucratic actions even draw upon on the agency of vultures to render invisible the decapitated bodies of border crossers. In doing so, these ecologies make the work of border agents possible in ways that absolve them of the violence they enact.[35]

India's border building and enforcement disrupted elephant corridors and cow smuggling routes along the Northeast India-Bangladesh border. Traders and transporters crossed the border with increasing risks to their lives and bodies and to that of the animals they cohabited with and traded in. The dispersal of sovereignties between nation-states and local and transborder authorities generates its own logic of human and animal mobility. Both state agents and locally powerful elites, armed, well organized, and enjoying immunity against the law, function as sovereigns who perpetrate violence.[36] They also feed off commercial exchanges and transactions. As the nerve centers of collective life, the distinctions between the legal and the illegal are constantly subject to adaptation and manipulation at borders.[37] Varied legitimacies, regulations, and value conversions reorder state rule and control in such zones.[38] Here, the gap between enforcing official mandates and regulating everyday life on its own terms makes borders "sensitive spaces."[39]

Figure 3. A border *char*, a river island composed of sand and silt, situated in Assam, Northeast India bordering Kurigram district of Bangladesh. (Photograph: author)

Figure 4. Garo Indian women cross a river border carrying sand in their baskets for India's border fence construction along the state of Meghalaya, Northeast India and Mymensingh District, Bangladesh. (Photograph: author)

The forms of value conversion evident at the Northeast India-Bangladesh border reshape the relationship between notions of the sacred that guide notions of religiosity and nationalism, as well as ideas of economic exchange that impinge upon kinship and gendered identities. In this book, I show how India's new border fence mediates the highly lucrative business of cow smuggling across the borderland *chars* by abruptly shutting some routes of passage between India and Bangladesh and opening others. The uncertainties that define cow smuggling find expression in the frequent invocation of *fang-fung*, a common word in the *char* borderland that denotes the amorality that shapes duplicity and dependency. *Fang-fung* is also rooted in masculine debates about power, influence, and profits in riverine regions where land and male employment cannot be taken for granted. Smuggling creates a border that is imagined and projected by traders and transporters as "running"—another English word domesticated in the *borderi* lexicon to mean open for business and brimming with life.

In contrast, India's new border fence retreats into a backdrop for Garo women's "jungle passport" journeys. Bangladesh's nation building and export networks facilitate reasonably profitable border crossings by Garo Bangladeshi Christian women, who belong to the Garo indigenous community and trade in export surplus garments. Their relationships of trust and dependence with Indian border troops, as well as the varied ways in which nation-states and market forces reshape social boundaries, disrupt the cyclical narrative of national security, risk, and state control over illicit economies and mobility. As Willem van Schendel states, the interplay of geographic scales and the web of social relations that structure border societies and economies, as well as shape notions of community and belonging, productively exposes the complexities of space.[40] The elements that make the force of life—like their "jungle passport" journeys—also remind us why the dust from old maps and new fences will never settle at borders.

The Northeast India–Bangladesh Border: An Overview

The ecological and political uncertainties that people experience in the India-Bangladesh borderland are underscored by the resilience of British colonial and postcolonial cartographies. The border itself cuts across a spatially and ecologically diverse terrain.[41] This includes border enclaves that are territories of one state surrounded by the other.[42] The southern deltaic border

regions are divided between India and Bangladesh.[43] The drawing and redrawing of British maps, the partition of the Indian subcontinent, and postcolonial conflicts have unfolded through the imposition of boundary lines
that aimed to divide but could not entirely segregate similar societies.

In British India, from the nineteenth century until the partition of the
Indian subcontinent in 1947, the borderland that I write about in this book
comprised the dissident frontiers of the Garo Hills and the adjoining plains
of the provinces of Assam and Bengal. The partition of the Indian subcontinent led to large-scale violence and displacement. Agrarian land, forests, and
rivers that comprised contested British provincial territories transformed into
the warring nations of the newly independent India and Pakistan. Pakistan's
territory was bifurcated, with one part of Pakistan (known as East Pakistan)
separated from the other part of Pakistan (known as West Pakistan) by India. In 1971, with the independence of Bangladesh from Pakistan after a protracted Liberation War, the territory of East Pakistan became Bangladesh.
Since 1971, India's eastern and northeastern boundaries have bordered the
new nation-state of Bangladesh, and the India-Pakistan border is confined
to the west and north.

The British East India Company, later the British government, and the
states of India, Pakistan, and Bangladesh all classified this region's various
inhabitants as "rude savages," frontier "land-hungry" peasants, spies, and
traitors who needed a combination of paternalist protection and violence to
be made into loyal subjects and citizens. By virtue of their fraught location,
their loyalties and attachments to multiple territories, the complex ecologies
that rural societies inhabited, and the emergent quality of the nations whose
borders peasants and traders battled for and whose boundary lines they came
to be placed within, these border societies have been marked as Bengali Muslim frontier peasants and Garo "tribes" and Christian ethnic minorities
since the nineteenth and twentieth centuries. All of these classifications reflect histories of this region that were always in flux, even as political authorities and nation-states sought to demarcate rigid ethnicities and territorial
distinctions. Furthermore, India's efforts to contain political dissidence, insurgency, and the demand for independent homelands in the states of Assam and more recently Meghalaya has intensely militarized these states.

Although colonial and postcolonial conflicts over land, resources, and
the mapping of identities have ensured that the border's location, traditional
boundaries of arable land, and religious and political delineations were
often at odds with one another, the frictions transcended prior boundaries of

religion, kinship, and nationality. In other words, longstanding animosities did not overdetermine the border's violent ability to create uniform spheres of difference and rule. Rural societies have resisted the changing forms of border rule, continuing to forge complex alliances that move across and re-order the uneven geographies into national territories. Amities and conviviality continue to be critical forces along the Northeast India-Bangladesh border. And yet, the Northeast India-Bangladesh borderland has received relatively little attention in the study of border societies in South Asia.[44]

In this book, I follow the lives and struggles of Bengali Muslim householders who live close to the border in Bangladesh's *chars*. They belong to Bangladesh's dominant ethnicity (Bengali) and religion (Islam). Just across the border from them, in a very similar landscape in Northeast India, I follow the lives of rural societies comprising Muslims of Bengali origin in the state of Assam who depend upon the border for a living. Their presence close to the border is suspicious for the Indian state as they are an untrusted religious minority. In Assam, their presence is controversial, and they are suspected to be unauthorized Bangladeshis and older settlers who grabbed land on account of a long history of contested migration between the British provinces of Bengal and Assam. Indian political parties have exploited undocumented Bangladeshi migrants by using them as a cohort of underclass voters for decades. Aided by shared language, culture, and religion, they are suspected to easily slip into Indian citizenship. While corrupt Indian politicians offer them identity cards in exchange for votes, the politicians have done nothing to ameliorate the poverty and legal ambiguity enveloping migrant lives. Since 2015, the National Register of Citizens—a massive bureaucratic exercise implemented in the state of Assam aimed to detect unauthorized Bangladeshi migrants—has excluded 1.9 million people from Indian citizenship in this state. This register was implemented with the intention of addressing questions of land loss, language, and ethnic conflicts but has further compounded problems and human misery. Those excluded from the register live in conditions of statelessness.

When I write about the Garos in the context of the Rowmari-Tura road, I situate their predicaments in the nineteenth and early twentieth centuries in Tura, which became a British frontier outpost. Today, Tura is located in the state of Meghalaya in Northeast India, and the Indian Garos are constitutionally classified as a "scheduled tribe," which draws from British colonial classifications.[45] In the late colonial and early postcolonial period, I write about the Garos who lived in the foothills and plains of the Mymensingh district, which was a part of East Pakistan and, since 1971, Bangladesh. In the context of contemporary "jungle passport" journeys, I am specifically referring to Garo Bangladeshi Christian traders who live and travel between Mymensingh and Netrokona districts in Bangladesh and Meghalaya, Northeast India. Among Garo families on the Indian side who are today Indian citizens, many were displaced from East Pakistan and Bangladesh. Lowland Garos of Bangladesh, writes Ellen Bal, who have greater contact with Bengali culture, distinguish themselves from the hill Garos and call themselves *Mandi*, meaning human being, while Indian Garos call themselves *Achik*, meaning "hill person."[46] While the Garos have distinct histories and political identities in India and Bangladesh, I show how political transformations in this region have reshaped notions of ethnicity along the borderland. All the Garo families and traders I lived with and write about are Christians. In present-day Bangladesh, the Garos increasingly prefer *adibashi* and "indigenous" to "tribe" or the Bengali term *upojati* (subnation), which holds pejorative connotations for them.[47] I have retained the generic term "Garo," the term by which the Garos refer to themselves for outsiders.

Sensing Borders and Paper Trails: Fieldwork and Archives

From 2007 to 2015, I lived on both sides of the border in remote villages divided between India and Bangladesh. I initially conducted fieldwork for almost a year from 2007 to 2008 as a part of my PhD dissertation. Here, I followed the building of India's new border fence for approximately 200 miles on both sides of the international boundary and conducted fieldwork in villages in Northeast India and Bangladesh situated within 5 miles of the border.

I returned to the field after completing my PhD in shorter phases of three months each between 2013 and 2015. Although my intention was to revisit the field, my fieldwork exposed the breadth of new issues and interweaving of many aspects and struggles, in particular with regards to citizenship issues and the impact of the gradual completion of the new fence, that I have elaborated in this book. Most of my time was spent in villages and along the border construction site in lower Assam and the Garo Hills of Meghalaya and the adjoining Kurigram, Sherpur, Jamalpur, Mymensingh, and Netrokona districts of Bangladesh. In between my fieldwork in Assam and Meghalaya, I conducted participant observation in two foreigners tribunals in Assam where suspected "illegal" Bangladeshis were being judicially tried.[48] The

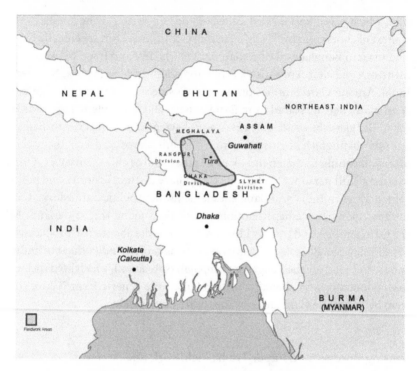

Figure 5. Map with fieldwork locations. The location of the Foreigners Tribunals are intentionally concealed. (Photograph: author)

households where I resided included teachers, priests, politicians, transborder traders, transporters, brokers, and migrant workers. My early acquaintance with Alibaba, in a cattle market on a *char* in Assam in April 2007, led me to a large transborder network extending into Bangladesh.[49]

In this borderland, most villagers were bilingual. People spoke Goalparia, Rangpuria, Assamese, Bengali, Garo, Sylheti, and Hindi. In addition to Bengali and Hindi, languages I knew, I was able to follow conversations in Goalparia, Rangpuria, Assamese, and Sylheti. I spoke to the Indian border forces in Hindi and in Bengali with members of the Border Guard Bangladesh. Interviews with bureaucrats, police officers, lawyers, and judges in India were conducted in English. In Assam, I conducted interviews with members of the Assam Movement (the largest civil society agitation on immigration in postcolonial India) and the All Assam Students Union (the largest civil society pressure group in Assam advocating against Bangladeshi immigration). In writing this book, I have used the *borderi* lexicon, which includes both English words and expressions from other languages. One such instance is the borderland expression "*jongol* passport" (jungle passport), which combines English and Bengali-Garo words. Another is *fang fung* in Bengali or *bung bang* in Garo, which implies deceit and duplicities that shape border crossings. Similarly, the terms *kacha bebsha, pakka bebsha*, or *du nombori bebsha* referred to the moral compass of smuggling—the first expression related to small-scale and subsistence trade, while the second and third referred to bulk smuggling and trade in contraband, respectively. Their meanings are slightly different at the borderland compared to conventional meanings of the terms, in that these words are not used to demarcate informal and formal economies.

Borderi not only fundamentally shaped lives in this zone but was also central to my survival. Villagers taught me to discern how borders turned into hotspots for a variety of reasons—not just national security—and then cooled down. These forces were so palpable and present that they even shaped three-year-old Badshah's game: "Line clear, signal clear!" As the building of India's new border fence and roads progressed, villagers lived with extended periods of uncertainty. They did not know how but anticipated that the fence would drastically change their lives. India's militarization of Assam and Meghalaya to contain political dissidence and the presence of Assamese and Garo groups demanding independent homelands also disrupted access to the land adjoining the border for both farming and transborder trade. Although they are not a part of the national armies, instead being termed "federally recruited paramilitary forces," the border forces of India and Bangladesh are entrusted with military-like functions.[50] Traders and transporters frequently told me, "We fear the troops and their guns." The fear of death at the border haunted our conversations.

Sometimes, I had permission to see the border fence, to walk with patrolling officers, to observe the proceedings of judicial tribunals, and to look at official records. At other times, each of these activities became impossible. During periods of high security and alerts, the border was *gorom* (hot and dangerous): no one could come into contact with the border fence. The border was sealed even in places where there were no fences. Traders in India held, "Even ants cannot crawl under the fence" at such times. In contrast, the most obvious visibility of goods and people were during periods of low anxiety about national security in Northeast India, when all of the "lines" were cleared (i.e., when passage was granted for the movement of people and goods). Bureaucrats and border police frequently used two unique words that

India and Bangladesh have coined—"pushbacks" and "counter-pushbacks." These refer to the extralegal but frequently implemented physical pushing of people who are suspected to be migrants and refugees across the border. During such events, it is common for people to remain stranded in the dividing line between India and Bangladesh for days without shelter and food.[51]

At border outposts, both Indian and Bangladeshi state agents indicated that they were responsible for my safety as a woman in crime-infested backwaters. This did not reduce the intensity of their interrogations or intelligence gathering, however. In India, border troops provided me access to the border as an Indian national but suspected my intentions as an outsider who might be involved in politically dissident activities or as a journalist intending to report their corruption. Given the Indian state's militarized gaze in Northeast India and along its borders with Bangladesh, Indian intelligence agents stalked me for days without speaking to me. When I confronted them, they hesitated to answer my questions or reveal their identity. At nights, I was watched by cap-wearing men who stood next to my window as I slept. When I woke up and flashed a torch in their face—as I did twice in the middle of the night—they fled. Meanwhile, in Bangladesh, I was familiar as a Bengali but also a foreigner as an Indian national. The Border Guard Bangladesh (BGB) and intelligence officers attached to the border camps routinely checked on my movements. However, the Bangladeshi intelligence agents openly interrogated me rather than stalking me.

My location close to the border and the biweekly markets meant that my presence could never be innocuous: even as I needed protection, I could also endanger traders and transporters. Sometimes they entrusted their wellbeing—and indeed their existence—to me, and at other times, some tried to control my fieldwork and kept track of my movements. Given the heavy militarization and corruption, multi-sited fieldwork transformed from a methodological necessity into an existential precondition. The labor of ethnography at militarized borders entailed not only the ability to see but also the constant pretense of "not seeing." My fieldwork occupied a hovering zone between the routines of rural life and following the disruptive trails of border construction and smuggling; the almost frenzied movement between different border locations was fundamental to my survival and safety. Soon I became geographically disoriented. Sometimes, when I was confident that I stood within Indian territory, I had unknowingly intruded into Bangladesh.

When groups seeking independent homelands bombed and blocked roads in Guwahati and Tura—where I traveled to recharge my digital recorder and camera, and rest—and I was unable to return to the border villages, the state and district archives and libraries offered refuge. I sat in dimly lit, dusty rooms, intending to marshal at least a sense of the area's visual history by poring over old maps and newspapers. However, my sense of well-being in the archives was short-lived as I progressed to files of official correspondence and police reports. These documents laid bare the violence associated with map-making, conscriptions, ethnic cleansings, and deportations—processes that were foundational to crafting regions into British colonial and later India, Pakistan, and Bangladesh.

English terms such as "disturbed areas," "rude savages," and "infiltrators" leapt out from the archives. Official correspondence between India and East Pakistan mirrored the words used in reports of the British colonial state. As David Ludden underscores, such state-directed and sedentary vocabularies obscure human mobility. Scholarship reflects official reports of territorial practices in ways that privilege the sedentary at the expense of the mobile. As a consequence, Ludden writes, "We imagine that mobility is border crossing, as though borders came first, and mobility, second."[52]

I also located important documents in various churches in remote villages in Bangladesh where I was conducting ethnographic fieldwork. The Christian priests who were mandated to chronicle daily events within the church premises, notes on proselytization, and the activities of their laity in general, meticulously inscribed state violence, in particular religious persecution directed at Garo Christians. In their detailing of the fears and anxieties that their laity experienced, these records further erased any temporary sense of relief from ethnographic fieldwork that I may have felt in sieving through old papers. I continued archival research until 2018, in the National Archives of Bangladesh at Dhaka; the Heritage Archives at Rajshahi, Bangladesh; the International Institute of Social History in Amsterdam; and the British Library in London.

While in the first few months of fieldwork, guns, border outposts, and stalkers seemed to belong to the landscape, in the later months, they appeared more conspicuous than ever. Those I lived and traveled with asked, both facetiously and with concern, if I was insane to come to a such remote and a dangerous region. By the time I concluded my first year of fieldwork, I started disbelieving people's intentions to protect me from harm. I also no longer believed myself.

Although I left the border in 2008 after almost a year of fieldwork, the border continued to linger in my body and mind, resurfacing in trauma dreams. My ethnographic obsession with the new infrastructure, which I edged toward but did not yet dare to touch, would ultimately produce a total loss of control over my own body and mind. I was immobilized with fear. The tactility of violence—always emergent near a lethal border—had rendered my skin nontactile. Yet, its pores continued to expose my nerves and organs to the border. Registering in my nerves the two nations whose rough edges I sought to study, my pen constantly failed to give meaning to their dangerous margins.[53]

My trauma dreams made me retrace my steps back to the borderland from 2013 to 2015. By this time, India had fenced off extensive stretches of the rice fields and forests. By 2015, the rains and floods had rusted the barbed wire of the new fence. The border villages still resembled disaggregated construction sites. The Bharatiya Janata Party–led Hindu nationalist government in India had ensured troop escalation, which had completely disrupted the border's rhythms. Everyone—villagers and troops alike—seemed to be perennially on edge. As convoys of patrolling jeeps whizzed past in far-flung villages, red dust spiraled from the surface of the broken roads enveloping me as I walked from one village to another, moving from India to Bangladesh and then back again. The spiraling red dust rendered hazy the forests and the fields adjoining the fence, investing the infrastructure with an appearance of more power. My heart pounded; like before, I feared that I would encounter either marauding elephants or angry border troops.

From the initial months of fieldwork until its end, the meaning of the words "prevent," "protect," "guard," "control," and—above all—"life" and "death" shaded into one another. I have lived with but never got accustomed to the partly visible and partly camouflaged presence of guns and uniforms, the occasional screeching of sirens, constant frisking and interrogation, and the sense of being perennially watched. The danger and protection that emanate from border walls and guns continue to heighten my consciousness of the state apparatus even today.

The Road and the Fence

This book begins its arc in Rowmari, a border town in Bangladesh, where people's recollections surrounding an old trade route—the Rowmari-Tura road—animates historical discussions. Today, Rowmari and Tura are situated in two nation-states—Bangladesh and India—and yet they belong to a border-land. The road is a metaphor for disruption, mobility, connection, identity, and longing—themes that this book engages with. It provides the foundations to transcend the most obvious religious dichotomy of this region into Hindu and Muslim (the two majority religions of India and Bangladesh, respectively), as well as conventional understandings of ethnicity and gender. I started searching for the road in old maps. Instead, I found its traces in the heliotropes of British colonial surveyors as they battled forest fires, in a devastating earthquake, and in the making of the Garos as a tribe. I continued journeying on the road through time, locating its changing forms through rice harvests raided and lost. Unknowingly, I traveled on the road with bull smugglers and transporters. I left the road temporarily to follow Garo women's "jungle passport" journeys and judicial trials of suspected Bangladeshis while carefully attending to questions of identity, legitimacy, and mobility that informed their lives. The road makes a return in the book through India's new fence, fears, and recollections of a war. I had a final look at road through the lens of an Indian soldier's binoculars. As I held the binocular to my eyes, Bangladesh seemed so near. This, even as Indian villagers arrived at the outpost seeking permission to see the new barrier—a majestic structure standing between rice fields and forests—and pointing toward Bangladesh as a "new" foreign land.

The book is not about just another barricade. Instead, I show how the Rowmari-Tura road and India's new fence continue to stand at the confluence of national fault lines that continually reshape border lives. It is precisely the struggles that make life possible at the "thin edge of barbed wire," as Gloria Anzaldúa writes, that unsettle the linear narrations of nation building that attempt to seamlessly connect the present and the past.[54] Anzaldúa's poetics of difference from the nation's margins restate why understanding the social foundations upon which national territories have historically been crafted is important for the interrogation of place and power in the contemporary moment. She attributes contemporary border violence to its intrinsic relationship to histories of conquest, land loss, and dispossession.[55] I read her relocation on race and culture to the border as one that reinforces anthropological endeavors to investigate contemporary ethnic, gendered, religious and national identities beyond bounded territories and categories and to strengthen its productive engagements with marginal histories.

Although the occasional shadow of my stalkers and ghosts may seep into these pages, my sensibilities do not eclipse the power of borders as a life force for those who live along it and who continue to endure and overcome violent nationalism, scarcity, corruption, manipulation, and fear. Most important, I advocate for carefully attending to the forces that shape border lives and are in turn shaped by borders.

I hope readers find the forces and lives in the subsequent pages meaningful and that this book in a small way shapes the way we think and write about borders and beyond.

CHAPTER 1

The Rowmari-Tura Road

A broken asphalt-and-mud road connected Rowmari, Bangladesh, with Tura, a town in the state of Meghalaya, Northeast India. For over six decades, Ali's oxcart had traveled the almost fifty-mile distance between Rowmari's marshlands and Tura's hills. "In British times and even later," the eighty-year-old cartman told me, "except for the bustling frontier markets that the road led to, our journeys were silent. From Tura and onwards to Bhutan and Tibet, we did not see anyone for miles." Traders flocked to Ali's doorstep carrying fuel and cooking utensils for the long journey, returning from Tura with precious timber. A mile away from Ali's house, Rowmari's retired postmaster pointed out the sturdy wooden beams supporting the post office's roof, telling me that the wood to make them had also traveled downhill from Tura.

Ali and his neighbors romanticized Tura's inhabitants, describing them as the "friendly" hill Garos. Mahfuz, the retired Imam (clergy) whose daughter Khairun I was staying with in Rowmari, stated that for decades, the Garos used to journey downhill from Tura to Rowmari to hunt turtles with spears in the Jinjiram River. The river often flooded, washing away villages and spreading silt into other locations, creating new *chars*. The river's changing form made and remade Ali and Mahfuz's lives as *nodi bhanga manush*, whose lives were entirely dependent on rivers.

Although my arrival from Tura to Rowmari in the winter of 2007 prompted our initial conversations, soon stories about the Rowmari-Tura road gathered their own momentum. These tales, across time, unevenly connected Ali's oxcart journeys along the river with the "turtle hunters."

Mahfuz guided me as we walked the Rowmari-Tura road, starting at the erstwhile Rowmari-*ghat* (quay). Raising his voice so that I could hear him over the sound of speeding buses, Mahfuz described how during the era of British rule, steamer boats had sailed from this dockyard, which was then in the British province of Bengal, to the neighboring province of Assam. Stopping to catch his breath at the side of the road, he silently indicated a pillar. Time had reduced this cemented pillar, hidden in a patch of grass, to a nondescript stone stub. It stood by a shallow lake. Slowly circling a shaky finger, Mahfuz drew invisible lines in the air, sketching the sturdy ropes that had once chained the boats to the pillars.

The loud honking of buses interrupted the momentary silence that had descended. It jolted us to the present, diverting our attention away from the pillar to the busy road. We continued walking eastward in Tura's direction. Soon, we reached a busy intersection where the tarmac road forked in three directions. One led to the national highway that connected Rowmari with Bangladesh's capital city of Dhaka. On this stretch, imported air-conditioned buses raced trucks packed with smuggled Indian bulls bound for Dhaka and other locations where they would be slaughtered for beef and leather. The second road was a mud path leading to the border villages. On this road, oxcarts such as the ones that Ali had once owned continued to trundle. The final road was wide and continued past hardware stores and tea stalls in the direction of Tura, India. Along this stretch, vans with loudspeakers moved at a slow pace, the announcements enticing villagers to work in Dhaka's garment factories.

Conversations in the local market affirmed Rowmari's connections with Tura. At a tea stall, elderly householders spoke excitedly about Bangladesh's plans for a new culvert that would connect Rowmari and Tura. When in 2012, the directors of the Dutch Bangla Bank inaugurated a new 144-foot bridge costing more than U.S.$75,000 and replacing the older bamboo structure, Rowmari's newspapers carried reports about its renewed connections with Tura.[1]

Despite the promise of increased connectivity, India's new border fence with Bangladesh—under construction when I first started fieldwork in Rowmari in 2007—was gradually dividing the landscape. Sandbags shielded a Bangladeshi border outpost. Bangladesh's border troops stood at the outpost's gate with guns strapped to their chests. Mahfuz and I walked on again, stopping at a distance from the angular metal pillars of India's new barrier. Mahfuz pointed in the direction of Tura, describing it as "the land of the Garos." Earlier, I had conducted fieldwork in Tura, a dusty town that India's federal security forces had heavily militarized. Except for the un-

documented Bangladeshi laborers from Rowmari and its adj
who worked in Tura, no one had ever mentioned the Rowmari-

Road and Race

The Rowmari-Tura road's presence in Rowmari where border villagers my-
thologize it and its absence in Tura queries the relationship between Bangladesh's marshes and the adjoining hills of Northeast India. The British colonial
archives had consigned the road to obscurity. The disjuncture between the
contemporary ubiquity of an old trade route in Rowmari, its relative lack of
acknowledgment in Tura, and its historical incomprehensibility in British
records probes why the remnants of the road gather impetus as an ethnographic force. Who constructed the Rowmari-Tura road and why? Where did
the road begin and end? Who were the inhabitants of Rowmari and Tura? In
seeking to answer these seemingly simple questions, we have to reckon how
in nineteenth-century British India road building was intrinsically tied to the
making of tribes and the marking of borders in regions that came to comprise British India's northeastern frontiers. Jungle passages and roads were
fundamental to British territorial incursions that came to bear upon frontier settlements and identities. In other words, roads were border fences and
walls. What is today romantically recalled as a trade connector in Rowmari
was in effect a disorderly passage for appropriating land and conscripting
labor in Tura and its surrounding regions. In fact, as I propose to show in
the following pages, the Rowmari-Tura road functioned as a disruptive seg-
regator, both in its territorial forms as well as in its human implications.

As geographical, instrumental, and political designs, routes enabled access to unexplored terrains that the British East India Company and later the
British state came to control as frontier territories.[2] South Asia's frontier histo-
rians have demonstrated how routes were arteries of commerce and warfare;
roads especially possessed strategic importance since they provided access
and passage for military interventions. Road connections realigned borders
and communities; their material formation made the "borders of maps" real.[3]

In regions that came to comprise British India's northeastern frontiers,
roads were sites of territorial contestations between the colonial officials who
desired access to territories and societies who rebelled against aggressive demands for passage. In 1826, in the Khasi Hills that adjoined the Garo Hills,
David Scott, the first commissioner of Assam, negotiated with the Khasi chief

Tweerat Singh for road construction through Khasi territory into Sylhet. However, in 1829, when the Khasis suspected that their lands would come under taxation by the British as in the plains, they revolted and killed two European officers and sixty guards. Military operations continued until 1933, when the Khasi chief surrendered. Official records depicted the Khasis as "misguided and infuriated savages" who perpetrated "diabolical cruelty" on officers.[4] The "savage" recurs as a trope to describe resistance to road building in the region. In the Naga Hills, British officials had to engage with existing political structures in order to build roads in the northeastern frontiers. When administrators came to appropriate the skills and labor of frontier dwellers for road construction, these groups often opposed British efforts and used the constructed roads for their own purposes.[5] In these rich historical accounts of territorial alliances and resistances, tribes emerge as prototypes of cultural specificity and social structure. In the pages that follow I hope to unsettle this recurring motif.

This chapter traces the Rowmari-Tura road's current existence to its emergence in the form of the first printed map of the Garo Hills, an event that established Tura as a British frontier outpost. British administrators mobilized both "primitivism" and nature as political forces to reorder territories and make the Garos a tribe. The production of ethnological knowledge that glossed over bonded labor for road building was central to territorial consolidations. If colonial cartographies and road construction irrevocably reversed the geographical and racial tentativeness that surrounded the Garo Hills, they still failed to completely bring this region under centralized British control. As segregating stratagems, maps and roads have created "settled" frontiers such as Rowmari and "savage" frontiers such as Tura. When British administrators mobilized race as a way to enforce spatial distinctions, they discursively transformed Tura's "savages" into governable British subjects. Representational and development processes that rested on punitive expeditions, civilizing missions, and resource extraction in the hills of the northeastern borderlands of the British Empire came to forge the identity of the Garos as "primitive" in comparison with other "ethnic" inhabitants of the British provinces of Bengal and Assam that adjoined it. In addition, nature's fury—forest fires, haze, and earthquakes—anchored political tensions to nervously hold together uneven territories while pulling people apart in competing directions. In the nineteenth and early twentieth centuries, natural disasters along with the imposition of racial boundaries to gain territorial control and resistance to these incursions made British India's northeastern frontiers volatile.

Adeline Masquelier's ethnography of road building in Niger seamlessly joins contemporary and historical violence. Niger's postcolonial roads recall the colonial brutality of conscription, finding expression in sinister registers through which the Mawri make sense of their contemporary dislocation as marginal farmers in a global economy. Their memory of the historical violence surrounding road building further explains the ambivalence toward roads and mobility in general.[6] Along the Greek-Albanian border, people historically reconstruct roads in their daily lives to express competing notions of nationalism and intercommunity conflicts.[7] Yet roads continue to energize "infrastructural promises," including the possibilities and anticipations that surround the building of connectors.[8] Even Ali and Mahfuz's expansive geographic sensibilities and villagers' excitement that the new bridges on the Rowmari-Tura road will connect Rowmari with Tura make this evident. The road's presence in Rowmari glosses over historical and spatial uncertainties as well as political disconnections; its absence in Tura underlines these. Contemporary narrations inadvertently reproduce circuits of difference between Rowmari and Tura, as well as between Bangladesh and Northeast India. Even today, when undocumented Bangladeshi migrants cautiously navigate this road that cuts across the Bangladesh-Northeast India border, they experience threats, torture, and death at the hands of Indian border troops.

In the remaining pages, I foreground three spatial events relating to boundary demarcations, geographical surveys, and a devastating earthquake that occurred in sequence from the early nineteenth to the early twentieth centuries. These make evident the tribulations that undergird the promise of connections. All these events related to the lives of the hill Garos. Today, this region is a part of the state of Meghalaya in Northeast India. India constitutionally recognizes the Garos as a "scheduled tribe."[9] This group is different from the Garos who reside in the plains and foothills of contemporary Bangladesh, who Bangladesh regards as ethnic minorities and who I write about in the next chapter. Let me begin, then, with the British imagination of the Garos as "rude mountaineers," a motif that was central to mapmaking and road building.

"The Rude Mountaineers"

In British official records of the early nineteenth century, the Rowmari-Tura road did not feature. But the Garos who resided in Bengal's northeastern frontiers did. In the precolonial and the early British colonial period, the Garos, who produced cotton—an important fiber for export—controlled the low-lands and the passes in the hills as gestures of territorial power but not necessarily settlement of land.[10] In 1788, Lord Cornwallis, the governor general, sent John Eliot, the commissioner of Dhaka, to the Garo Hills. Eliot, the first European to have visited this region, described its inhabitants as "savages" who ate "all manner of food" and the "blood of all animals." His descriptions of Garo men as "well shaped . . . hardy; their color [is] of a light or deep brown" and Garo women as "ugliest creatures . . . short and squat in their feature" set a racialized tone that would recur in British official records.[11]

For the officials of the British East India Company, the Garo inhabitants of Bengal's Rangpur district, where Rowmari was located then, were racial misfits in Bengal's civilizational landscape. At the same time, the hills did not appear to belong to Bengal, by then a taxable and revenue-generating province. In a landmark legal decision, Resolution X of 1822 officially placed the Garo-inhabited regions outside the province of Bengal. The racial stereotype of the Garos derived from head hunting expeditions in response to Bengali landlords' aggressive encroachments into Garo territory in pursuit of its rich forest resources. The new regulation intended to protect the "Garo mountaineers" from intrusions by predatory Bengali landowners, as well as to establish a direct tributary relationship with them. The British interpretation of local animosities emphasized that the settlements and levies that the landlords had imposed on the Garos had neither resolved the border disputes nor served to "civilize" them.[12] Emphasizing the importance of customary Garo social structures, the 1822 regulation included provisions to appoint British officers to administer a special system of civil and criminal justice. British administrators recruited Garo chiefs to claim rents from frontier markets to bring them under partial control.[13] They coerced 155 Garo chiefs to pay nominal tributes.[14]

An important boundary-making device, Regulation X harnessed racial distinctions as markers of geographical governance and in the process further established the Garo Hills as an uncivilized enclave. As a consequence of making the Garos "governable" subjects, the hills that had been situated within the province of Bengal now came to surround it. If ethnological classifications accorded Bengal's residents a higher position in civilizational hierarchies, in geographical terms, the new regulation flattened the province into a plain.

British ethnological sketches established the geographical remoteness of the Garo Hills. Records fearfully depicted the region as "above all *jungly*

countries in India . . . the most fatal one for a European to visit. Few or prob-
ably none, have penetrated one day's journey into the interior, and escaped
without a severe fever: and three fourths of those who have done so, have
fallen victims to its baneful climate."[15] They described the region's matrilineal communities as fierce headhunters who treasured "as many human skulls
as their houses could contain."[16]

Writing about the forested areas of Bengal, K. Sivaramakrishnan argues
that British governance intentionally created such "zones of anomaly."
Imagined as predatory locations, officials regulated these resource-extractive
zones through tribute-based relationships rather than through taxation. Agricultural taxation, he states, was both impossible and obstructed in such
zones.[17] The regulation of forests as zones of distinction set an important
precedent for administering the frontier regions in British India. By the end
of the nineteenth century such regulations would reorder people's relationships to land and labor. Ali and Mahfuz's descriptions of the Garos as
distant "turtle hunters" speak to the social and political distance that shaped
notions of neighborliness.

The union of race and geography, however, did not stabilize provincial
borders. Land disputes between the Garos and Bengali landlords ensured that
boundary lines constantly shifted. By the mid-nineteenth century, British administrators recorded that 121 Garo villages had acceded to British mediation in border disputes along the borders of Bengal's Mymensingh district
and the Garo Hills. Garo chiefs irregularly paid tribute to the British in exchange for protection against Bengali landlords, who persisted in aggressively
claiming Garo territory, forest resources, and elephants. The British record-
keeping of border disputes makes it evident that a willingness to share levies
derived from frontier markets, which administrators misinterpreted as acts
of submission, did not in fact lead to Garo acceptance of British border-
making. In 1848, for example, the Garos, who resided along the foothills,
vehemently opposed the new line which placed their territory in Bengal and
compelled British survey officers to redraw the border. Bengal's landlords objected to the redrawn line and retaliated by intruding into Garo territory,
forcibly claiming large sections of the Garo Hills.[18] The Garo opposition to
British reordering of the foothills shows how colonial administrators had
limited territorial control, even in a jurisdictional sense.

In the mid-nineteenth century, this border dispute reached a deadlock.
After passing through the local revenue and civil courts, it reached the higher
courts. In 1868, by which time the British administrators served directly

under the British Crown instead of the British East India Company, the courts passed a partial decree that favored Bengali landowners. In 1869, the British state completely excluded the Garo Hills from the jurisdiction of Bengal's civil, revenue, and criminal courts. The new borders that made the Garo Hills into a distinct administrative unit canceled any rights that Bengal's kings and landlords had exercised over forests and elephants, important resources for warfare and transportation. In exchange, British administrators offered financial compensation to Bengal's landlords.[19]

Cartographies of Conquest

Unlike Bengal, where the British had deeply entrenched territorial command, legal mediation of border disputes neither extended nor served to enable territorial control in the Garo Hills. Despite the establishment of a frontier police force to control the border, British administrators were barely able to consolidate their authority.[20] Even in the late 1860s, the geographical understanding upon which British territorial expansion was being crafted was still limited. After conquering the neighboring kingdom of Assam in 1826 and surveying and mapping land in Assam's valleys for over fifty years, the 2,300 square miles that comprised the Garo Hills were disconcertingly opaque for administrators. There were no roads to Tura.

Hence, in the mid-1860s, British officials turned their attention to the Garo Hills in earnest. Geographical and ethnological endeavors combined to create scientific spectacles.[21] While there is nothing distinctive about how militarized cartography provided a renewed understanding on the Garos, the colonial gaze in this instance was fashioned in alliance with natural disasters—forest fires, haze, and earthquakes. Mastering nature was central to making the Garos legible as a tribe. Officials chose Tura as the seat of British political authority in the region for strategic reasons: the hilltop at Tura was fairly even and large, and its ridges ensured good protection against attacks. In early 1868, a road that was six feet wide was completed. Several roads were also constructed from Tura downward toward the Brahmaputra plains. British officials also started regulating the capture of elephants and charging hefty amounts for their capture to increase revenue.[22]

In the autumn of 1869, Major Goodwin Austen and Lieutenant Beaven of the Trigonometrical Survey of India led a cartographic expedition to the

Garo Hills to remedy the absence of geographical knowledge of the region. Armed with a heliotrope—a reflecting instrument popular for military signaling and forest surveys—and accompanied by a retinue of local porters, they attempted a triangulation survey. Austen and his armed surveyors traveled uphill on elephants until they finally located a suitable spot from where they attempted a triangulation survey to sketch the zone between the foothills and the summit. The subsequent journeys uphill were tedious. The surveyors were anxious about encountering the inhabitants of "interior" villages, who regarded the expedition as a territorial intrusion and refused to aid the surveyors or accept bribes. In the days that followed, during which Austen and his team attempted to measure land from the Nokrek peak, villagers described as belonging to "outer villages" resisted the survey team. The surveyors faced difficulty in recruiting local guides, as the village headmen refused to cooperate with them. When the surveyors finally managed to find the correct route to accomplish the measurements, they recorded their victory in words that shamed the Garos, further testifying to how this geographical endeavor was simultaneously a disciplinary expedition. In a sudden turn of events that remains unexplained in the British records, the "interior Garos" agreed to form amicable alliances in ways that facilitated subsequent surveys. After traveling to and measuring the furthest point westward on the Tura mountain range—in the center of the Garo Hills—the survey team retraced their steps eastward. The inroads that enabled administrators to meticulously trace the geographical coordinates did not lead to a stable alliance with the Garos. Fears of Garo resistance finally led Austen to shift the expedition downhill. In the spring of 1870, when the troops once again attempted to climb uphill, they encountered a forest-fire haze that prevented them from calculating supplementary angles to measure the land.[23]

Despite these setbacks, his superiors regarded Major Austen's expedition as highly successful. It encouraged the British state to dispatch another topographical survey team to the Garo Hills from 1871 to 1872. Administrators asserted that by this time, Garo sympathies were divided: while some villages accepted British jurisdiction, sixty villages fiercely resisted. To bring these dissenting villages under British jurisdiction, three detachments of police and infantry battalions were sent to the Garo Hills. The British armed forces overwhelmed the Garos. British documents note that the Garos surrendered skulls captured in previous headhunting expeditions as gestures of submission. Surveys progressed until March 1871, when an autonomous

Garo village resisted the arrival of two Bengali survey porters. The records also state that the porters entered a dormitory for unmarried men during a festival where the villagers offered them liquor. Subsequently, the headman reportedly ordered that the porters be captured, after which a struggle ensued and one of the porters was killed. The other fled to Tura. British officers speculated that the survey porters may have annoyed the Garos by interrupting their festivities and drinking, apart from demanding their labor for clearing the hill. They also suspected that the inebriated porters may have been easy targets for "head hunting."[24]

British administrators framed Garo responses to the Bengali porters in terms of distinctly violent sensibilities. The officials used this to justify brutal territorial intrusion, and the placement of a police outpost in Tura in March 1872. Finally, in May 1872, the police captured the Garo headman of the village where the porter had been murdered. In retaliation, the Garos once again attacked the frontier police, but additional police battalions crushed their rebellion.[25] British expeditions continued until the western and northern fringes of the district were conquered, and additional police forces were deployed in Tura.[26]

Major Austen's incursions quelled dissenting populations, enabling new forms of geospatial knowledge that established British territorial control in Tura. Commenting on the final form of the trigonometrical surveys as the first printed map of the Garo Hills, the statistician for the government of India, William Hunter, wrote, "The Garos in all their attempts to resist the authority of the British Government, had relied on our ignorance of their country. . . . This has all been cleared up now and the administration of the District generally facilitated by the publication of the map, which may be regarded as one of the great gains of the expedition of 1872–73."[27] This attests to Thongchai Winichakul's astute reminder about how mapping and militarization mutually reinforce each other as technologies that restructure space to create geo-bodies.[28]

As a cartographic feat, the map of the Garo Hills is a testament to the fragmented military tactics required to bring the hills under British command. In unifying Garo territory, the map represented a coercive assemblage of military expertise rather than a concerted military achievement. The new geographical knowledge of the Garo Hills reinforced narrow visions of race. The ethnological terrain on which cartographic knowledge rested, like the precise measurements of the complex terrain, glossed over

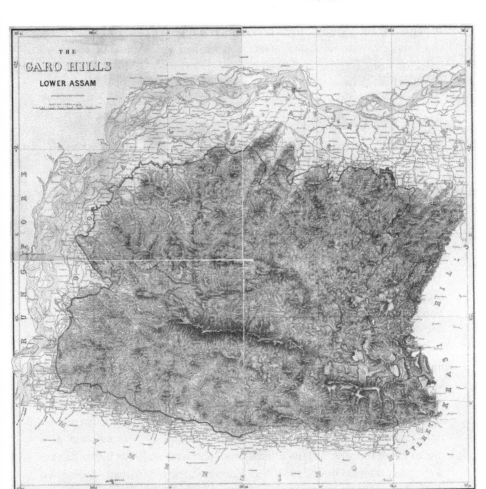

Figure 6. Map of the Garo Hills. Reproduced by permission of the National Library of Australia, Canberra. Collated and compiled by Deboleena Majumdar.

prior political arrangements between neighboring Garo villages and other territories. Rather than acknowledge the Garos as a cluster of social groups embroiled in land disputes with their neighbors, administrators polarized political practices. Thick descriptions of cartographic feats further misrecognized vacillation between granting and refusing territory as inconsistency rather than as a form of political assertion in its own right. Cartographers disregarded that Garo notions of territory and territoriality were far more than static primordial attachments and unified expressions of resistance based on lineage and shared habitat.

Road Building

It was this context of political strife and the ethnological imprints of militarized cartography that made roads—such as the one that Mahfuz, Ali, and others in Rowmari refer to as the Rowmari-Tura road today—visible. Soon after the printing of the Garo Hills map, the road from Tura that went downhill toward the Rowmari *ghat* finds mention in British records. The road's visibility in the archives progressed alongside records of the increasing reliance on bonded labor for road building in the Garo Hills.

Although the printed map showed a neat outline around the Garo Hills, the border was unsettled. In 1873, the new Bengal Eastern Frontier Regulation reinforced the segregation between the hill regions and plains that British administrators had initiated in 1822—which itself largely rested on the stereotype of the "Garo mountaineer." Unlike the previous legislation, the new one placed Mymensingh's foothills, which included Garo populations bordering the Garo Hills, outside Bengal's jurisdiction. When Assam became a separate British province a year later, casting off Bengal's shadow, administrators incorporated the Garo Hills into Assam. Assam's tea plantation economy provided new impetus for exclusionary jurisdiction as a means of preventing the land alienation of planters. As Bodhisattva Kar asserts, such internal boundary lines—known as the inner lines—segregated the hills from the plains, the sedentary from the mobile, and forests from cultivable land. Inner lines gradually came to function as temporal barriers that placed the hills outside the domain of capital and development.[29] They restricted mobility by conferring enormous powers to British administrators and military agents to regulate entry into this region.[30] British border arrangements flattened Bengal into settled revenue-generating plains and simultaneously made the neighboring province of Assam more mountainous, forested, and far more "primitive" in comparison—a feature that explains why and how the Garo Hills were so easily incorporated within Assam's territory.

In a quick turn of events, the Garo Hills were placed outside the inner line regulations surrounding regional mobility and trade in 1875.[31] British extraction of forest resources in the Garo Hills and the region's proximity to and trading links with Bengal quickly overrode prior exclusionary regulations. However, this opening neither remedied the racial distance that coded this landscape as an exceptional space nor redeemed its inhabitants of their "primitiveness." In fact, the region's forested mountains persisted as an arena of aberration from where British administrators could aggressively claim "primitive" labor.[32] Records of road trade between Tura and Rowmari that register traffic in commodities from Tura downward to the Brahmaputra's eastern banks gloss over this extraction. Instead, these records provide accounts of two-way trade traffic, noting that timber, cotton, vegetables, and bamboo were channeled downhill from Tura, while from the riverside, traders supplied rice, cattle, poultry, dried fish, weapons, and iron implements to Tura.[33] Imported bulls from northern India, which were regularly driven between the hills and the riparian landscape, shrank the distance between the flood-prone plains of the Brahmaputra and the Garo Hills. Carts such as the one belonging to Ali, Rowmari's retired cartman, traveled with traders and goods and larger convoys of pack animals.[34] The unnamed road between Tura and the eastern banks of the Brahmaputra, where Rowmari was situated, was maintained and widened for wheeled traffic.[35]

By this time, Edward Dalton's ethnological descriptions had represented the Garos as the residents of Assam's hills who had come to colonize the land as early settlers. Unlike the Garos in the valleys and plains, who had come to be "Hinduised and dispossessed by Mech and Koch landlords," the interior tribes of the Garo Hills were represented as "uncivilized and unconverted."[36] Garos resistance to renewed British demands for conscription for road construction, repair, and porterage only reinforced their uncivil image. For instance, in 1881, the road between Tura and Bangalkatta became a bone of contention between British authorities, who demanded village headman provide Garo laborers for road construction. Eighteen Garo villages revolted. Threatened by the scale of this revolt, administrators deployed 150 armed police constables in the area. When protracted negotiations and armed tactics failed to compel the Garos to surrender, the British contingent burnt two large villages to quell the revolt. Subsequently, the entire district was placed under British control. Quelling Garo resistance to conscription, by 1882, British administrators had ensured that 68 miles of roads were constructed.[37]

The Great Earthquake

Frontier roads did not necessarily make military surveillance easy. The Brahmaputra's marshes were barely visible from Tura's mountains. With great difficulty, the military police battalion stationed in Tura found one specific location from which they could view Rowmari. From this location, they regularly practiced heliotrope signaling to maintain contact and ensure disaster preparedness.

On 12 June 1897, a disastrous earthquake, the worst in two centuries, affected an area of 150,000 square miles. It claimed 1,500 lives. In Tura, the disaster killed twenty-seven people. It submerged several villages, destroyed cultivated land, and wrecked granaries. A timber bridge was pushed up to eight feet above its usual level, disrupting Tura's connection with the surrounding plains.[38] Thomas Oldham, the head of the Geological Survey of British India, stated in his memoirs that furniture in Tura shifted like "grains of rice in a winnowing basket." Along Mymensingh's foothill borders with the Garo Hills, Superintendent of Telegraphs F. Mercer reported a series of cascading earth waves, "like rollers on the sea coast." When the waves subsided, the ground at his feet had cracked in two. The earthquake caused the Jinjiram River waters, that flowed through Rowmari, to rise by 20 feet.[39] Mercer noted a large fissure in Rowmari running southeast at right angles to the river bank for at least 500 yards until it was lost in a water tank.[40] Just across from Rowmari, he reported that in a similar riparian landscape the earthquake had caused the narrow river channels to be filled with sand and cause flooding.[41] British administrators were relieved that the flooding rivers did not damage the newly laid foundations of the Assam-Bengal railway, but an entire train—engine and wagons—sank into the ground along the riverbank.[42] Geologists planted a seismograph in Tura and noted everyday mild tremors.[43]

The earthquake's massive impact relocated Tura from a frontier outpost, now placing it within the larger domain of tectonic fault lines that extended beyond the boundaries of the British Empire. The vast scale of the disaster extended to Tibet, Nepal, and Bhutan, posing problems when it came to assigning a name to the disaster. Oldham desired to call it the "Indian" earthquake, as several provinces in British India were affected by it. But he also noted that more than a fourth of the disaster-affected areas were outside the boundaries of British India. From Tibet, for example, reports of damage to monasteries, relief measures, and customs control preventing people from entering Tibet, as

Figure 7. Earthquake fissures at Rowmari. From "India Geological Survey, Mem. #29," Figure 10 (Rowmari, India). 12 June 1897. Reproduced by permission of the University of California, Berkeley.

well as news about official and monastic prayers for averting future earth-quakes, reached Oldham. Given the impossibility of a geographical name, Oldham chose to record the 1897 earthquake as the "Great Earthquake," using the word "great" to distinguish it from previous earthquakes of lesser impact.[44]

In terms of military surveillance, the earthquake accomplished what Brit-ish mastery over the heliotrope could not achieve: it submerged the two hills that had obstructed the view between Tura and Rowmari. This visibility has stood the test of time, it has ensured that the Tura mountain range, even today, hovers over the foothills and *chars* of Bangladesh.

Meanwhile, scientific reporting on the earthquake mobilized the disaster to reinforce territory's relationship to race. British geological memoirs, disaster reports, and ethnohistorical texts armored the racial specificities of Tura's inhabitants. This disaster's ramifications lingered in the form of British documentation of Garo cosmologies in ways that were central to the production of the Garos as a tribe. As an event, the 1897 earthquake had enormous political repercussions in the form of its scribes, who came to irrevocably reorder the racial diversity and interdependence of the Garo Hills as a borderland. Captain Howell and Major Playfair reported that the Garos apparently believed that the world was flat and suspended from four ropes, and rodents—squirrels and rats—disrupted earth's fragile by chewing on the ropes. The earth's custodians were either demons who were struck blind for negligence of their duties or blind men attributed with special powers of vision.[45] Once the earth's balance was disrupted, earthquake tremors occurred.[46] In their disaster reports, British officials even stated that the Garos believed Queen Victoria—Britain's ruling monarch who was soon to visit British India—was unhappy with the consequences of the last earthquake, which did not cause enough damage, and had ordered this one as a more forceful disaster. British administrators wryly noted that if the earthquake had not devastated the administrators' houses as well, the Garos might have even suspected that they had a hand in the seismic event.[47]

The essentialist projection of the Garos by British officials and the repetitive invocation of Garos' beliefs in the Earth's flatness infantilized their geo-sensibilities. In the absence of Garo records on their own beliefs, we are left with colonial scripts that *made* earthquakes a critical racial register: its political and ethnological imprints unbound natural disasters from timescales that were limited to devastated landscapes and lives. By recording Garo geo-sensibilities with a combination of scientific rigor, humor, and concern, such scripts ensured that the "Great Earthquake" became intrinsically tied to the production of the Garos as a tribe and the imagined territorial unification of the Garo Hills. British official records inserted Queen Victoria's sovereign anger into the narrative not only to reestablish the region's inhabitants as British subjects but also to emphasize their role as emblems of local authority that the sovereign queen had vested in them. The upscaling of localized administrative authority to one of cosmic significance that accompanied the trimming down of Garo reinforced the specific nature of militarized labor, which combined disaster and ethnological scripts.[48]

The earthquake's aftershocks led to territorial dispossession and even more aggressive demands for conscripted labor. The writing of Playfair's magisterial text on the Garos progressed alongside his angry letters to Garo village headmen. His letters to Banuram Nokma, for example, contain his demands for Garo labor for the clearing of forests and making of pathways to facilitate official travel. When Banuram did not respond to Playfair's order for ten unpaid laborers who would construct a fort for the residence of military soldiers, he threatened that Banuram would be forced to do the unpaid labor himself.[49] By 1903–1904, the British records note that a total of 73 miles of cart roads and 126 miles of bridle paths were maintained in the Garo Hills.[50]

Playfair had even taken to court, imprisoned, and forbidden Sonaram R. Sangma to enter the Garo territory. A prominent Christian convert and the first political leader of the Garos, Sangma was a skillful and pugnacious activist who led mass protests against land loss, reserved forest incursions, and bonded labor. He had studied in the American Baptist School in Tura, knew English, and had secured a job in the Public Works Department as a road supervisor for ten years. He adopted the colonial language of property rights and contested the British "rule of law" on its own terms. His actions and struggles attested to the changing political consciousness of the Garos that Playfair dealt with a heavy hand.[51] In response to a petition submitted by Sangma and others, the Arbuthnot Commission that the government set up to investigate disputed land claims, reserved forests, and the establishment and the practice of bonded labor held that the system of forced unpaid labor should be abolished and replaced immediately with a contract system.[52]

Meanwhile, Tura's proximity to Bengal—where a growing nationalist agitation was gathering momentum—was also disconcerting to the British administrators. Knowledge of the Bengali language in the Garo Hills, which was taught in schools there, deepened their suspicions that Garos would be influenced by Bengali nationalists and revolutionaries who were prominent in the national struggle for independence. This suspicion led British administrators to disinvest in roads connecting Tura with Bengal, intentionally allowing the region's newly constructed roadways to lie in disrepair.[53] Soon after, the Partition of Bengal in 1905 resulted in Assam's merger with the newly created province of Eastern Bengal. Assam's incorporation into Eastern Bengal implied that it would no longer receive the resources that it had received under the chief commissioner. The 1905 partition further fractured the political field in which nationalist assertions came to be splintered along ethnic and linguistic (Bengali and Assamese), and religious (Hindu and Muslim) lines. Although the Partition of Bengal was revoked in 1912 due to large-scale protests, these fissures continued to shape territorial politics and everyday life. Even in its unrepaired form, and the imposition of borders, the ox-caravan route persisted as a passage. It paved the way for Ali's journeys in subsequent decades.

Jagged Histories

Ali and Mahfuz's descriptions of the erstwhile Rowmari *ghat* as the road's beginning, in contrast to British records that demonstrate that the road began in Tura, foreground time's unevenness. Rowmari's residents fail to register the segregation of the plains where they reside from Tura's hills, and yet in their romantic narrations of the "friendly Garos," they invoke racial registers of neighborliness. This separation, initially through legislative acts and mapping, and later through demands for slave labor, gradually transformed the Garos from a cluster of powerful "mountaineers" who both protested against and made possible British territorial intrusion. The borders that made maps and roads into infrastructures delegitimized prior territorial relationships and criminalized rural lives.

It is the power that infrastructures gather that makes old roads familiar even in their material remnants and fragmented afterlife between Bangladesh and India. The Rowmari-Tura road's current sandbag-lined barricades and cracked tarmac and the journeys of undocumented migrants foster what Oscar Martinez has evocatively called a "borderland milieu"—shaped by a sense of both proximity and distance. Writing in the context of the U.S.-Mexico border, Martinez has lucidly illuminated borders as entities that simultaneously divide and unite, entice and impede.[54] In the Northeast India–Bangladesh border, this sense of bifurcation and unity is irregularly distributed. Ali the cartman's expansive geographical sensibilities foreground a sense of time and place that contrasts with his neighbor Mahfuz's alternating pride and anxiety as a Bangladeshi as we walked from Rowmari in the direction of Tura. Roads—in their memories, as well as their contemporary uses for undocumented travel and labor—radically transformed the history of a borderland.

As I propose to show in the following chapter, even as a vibrant trade connector, the road came to split Tura and Rowmari's past and present in distinct and competing ways.

CHAPTER 2

Rice Wars and Nation Building

One winter evening in Rowmari, Bangladesh, not far away from the Rowmari-Tura road, Mahfuz's throaty cough interrupted our lively conversation over *peetha* (rice pancakes). We had gathered in the home of Manna, Khairun's neighbor and a schoolteacher by profession. Manna was telling us about his travels on the Rowmari-Tura road in the early 1970s. At that time, Bangladesh and India were friendly neighbors. The border was relatively open, and villagers regularly traveled without passports. "Even before looking at our faces, the Garos in Tura recognized us as Bengalis by the cut of our trousers!" Manna remarked. Despite Rowmari's geographical proximity to Tura, the India-Bangladesh border had divided the road. Since 1971, Rowmari had been part of Bangladesh, and Mahfuz and others became Bangladeshi citizens. A year later, Tura became a part of the new state of Meghalaya, Northeast India. The Garos, whom India had classified as "scheduled tribes," now comprised the largest ethnic group in the Garo Hills region of Meghalaya.

Seeing the elderly Mahfuz arrive, Manna hurriedly placed a chair on the narrow veranda that adjoined the courtyard where Nasima, his wife, was steaming the pancakes. The retired Imam came by twice a day to enquire about Khairun's and, by extension, my well-being. Khairun's husband, Kamal, a supervisor at a garment factory, resided in Dhaka. That evening, Mahfuz was concerned that our walk on the Rowmari-Tura road had been inconclusive. "There should be a map of the Tura road in Dhaka. But the city is nine hours by bus. There is no need to go there. Our *Amin* (land surveyor) may have a map for you." He turned toward his grandson-in-law Rezaul, who was a college lecturer, and asked him to take me to the Amin's house in Rowmari.

Figure 8. The Amin displaying an old map of Rangpur, Bangladesh showing dotted margins that comprise *chars*. (Photograph: author)

The following afternoon, we all arrived at the Amin's doorstep. After patiently hearing us, the Amin excitedly affirmed, "Yes, yes, my map mentions the old Tura road!" He rushed to his room, opened an old tin trunk, and hurried back. He carefully unfolded the map onto a chair and we eagerly pored over it. The map, dated 1937 to 1938, displayed Frank Owen Bell's signature endorsing the cadastral survey of the Rangpur district of British Bengal, within which Rowmari was then situated. The map's cadastral plots contrasted with the dotted margins. The dots represented the *chars*: land parcels in rivers that floods periodically destroyed and remade, displacing and attracting cultivators in turn.

Although—disappointingly for me—the Amin's map did not mention the Rowmari-Tura road, its legal use in Rowmari conferred it with a life extending far beyond the dusty archives. The photocopied map, torn and frayed at its edges, reinforced the original's authenticity. Along with Kurigram

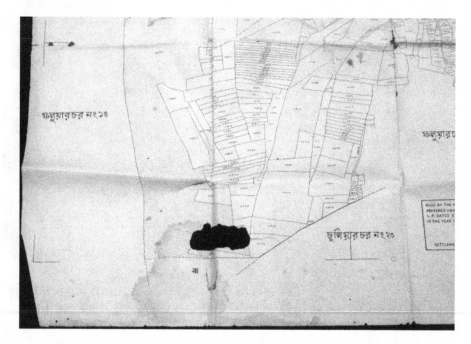

Figure 9. The Amin displaying a recent map of Kurigram District, Bangladesh. (Photograph: author)

district's cadastral map of 2005, this map vested the power to the Amin to arbitrate land disputes and transactions in Bangladesh. Its dotted margins persisted as anxious borderlands. As British provincial and agricultural territories transformed into the new nation-states of India and Pakistan, landless peasants reclaimed the unstable *chars*, making them cultivable. While ephemeral landscapes and agrarian extraction escalated the demands for land and rice as food, late colonial and early postcolonial territorial consolidations alternatingly prevented and facilitated hurried journeys across national margins. When rivers wiped out villages, migrant peasants acquired land in forests and grazing reserves in defiance of state regulations. Agrarian migration radically altered the terms on which identity and legitimacy were negotiated in this region.

From the printing of the Amin's map in the late 1930s to a few years before Manna and his friends traveled to Tura in the early 1970s—the time period that informs the following pages—the tense tug of war between land and rivers left lasting imprints on rice as a provincial, national, and border resource. While I will explore their contemporary ramifications in the remaining chapters of this book, in this chapter, I explore the varied ways in which rice functioned as a border apparatus to mark places and people. Rice—essential as food but controversial as claims to land—came to uneasily link the shifting *chars*, grazing territories, forests, and the fields. The unstable nature of the land clashed with its new status as an immovable, economic commodity. This applied to land as agrarian property and as provincial and postcolonial territories along the Assam-Bengal and later Northeast India–East Pakistan border. The relationship between the British provinces and emergent nation-states, as well as the creation and militarization of the region's borders, was deeply tied to rice. Yet, the reclaimed land parcels on which cultivators grew, raided, and consumed rice as a coveted grain and a tradable good constantly defied national boundaries. Rice brought together territories and raids, espionage and food, rural displacements and state violence. During these four decades, peasants came to acquire land and raid each other's rice harvests to survive and to gain control over and mark new borders.

Floods and political events led eastern Bengal's frontier peasants to relocate and claim land in Assam; in turn, their subsequent deportation from postcolonial India and resettlement in East Pakistan ended up displacing the mostly Christian Garos who resided along the plains of the East Pakistan–Northeast India border. I should emphasize that they are not the hill Garos of Tura in Northeast India whom I wrote about in the previous chapter. The entangled narratives of loss and gains surrounding rice, exemplified by their *hurmuri jatras*, invite us to rethink the conventional distinction between sedentary peasants and mobile indigenous cultivators. Their imprecisions are productively addressed from borders where territorial intrusions and the forging of national subjects coalesced around wet rice cultivation, smuggling, and consumption.[1] Late colonial and early postcolonial national and subnational histories of India and East Pakistan have either criminalized agrarian politics that surrounded rice cultivation as subterfuge or valorized dispossession by imposing morally compelling discourses of refuge and recovery. Political debates and discourses cast Muslim peasants of Bengali origin as either infiltrators or food producers in Assam. Similarly, official histories are quick to situate Assam and Bengal within religious categories and Assamese and Bengalis within well-defined ethnic and linguistic boundaries.[2] In the early postcolonial period, East Pakistan's official records affirmed that rice cultivators deported from Assam were Muslim victims of Indian Hindu oppression. Indian officials, on the other hand, alleged that East Pakistan persecuted the mostly Christian Garos as pro-Indian spies and Christian infidels. East Pakistan's Garo border residents were seen as helpless animists and tribal Christians who needed India's protection.

The changing predicament of rice cultivators as land reclaimers, food producers, and political actors disrupted the neat historical ordering that splintered peasants along ethnic (Assamese, Bengali, Garo), religious (Muslim, Christian, Hindu), and national lines (Indian, Pakistani). Rice wars demonstrated how historical contingencies and political forces impinged upon shifting landscapes and everyday rural lives in ways that realigned temporal conjunctures, transcending neat beginnings and ends. Rice cultivators forged alliances with political authorities to guard the borders as agrarian territories but also operated as independent actors. Sometimes rice wars coalesced around old and stolen maps, cultivation, and trade; at other times, rice wars were waged in the name of one nation-state or another. The quest for land and food was not a means to gain national recognition and material prosperity: peasants risked their lives to move across dangerous borders and reclaim land in the face of agrarian distress, as well as to petition the new states to redress their grievances. In the pages that follow, I show how rice as food and a commodity was situated at the nexus of the intimate and the political, as well as how the mobility and displacement of rice cultivators undergirded the tensions that surrounded this borderland as it came to be located at the crossroads of agrarian and national territories.

Shifting Chars

In Bangladesh's border villages where the old triangular boundary markers are hidden between rice paddy fields, gun-toting Bangladeshi border troops suddenly appear. One winter morning in 2008, I met Fazlur Rahman and Karim Nasir, rice cultivators who were deported from India in 1964, sitting close to one such field. While Rahman had reconciled his Bangladeshi citizenship since his deportation from India, Nasir had not. Every morning, he walked to the border and gazed toward India, at what he imagined to be the hills of Assam, his homeland.

Rahman and Nasir's narrations of the past illuminate the compulsions and anticipations that came to reshape the lives of frontier peasants from the late 1930s to 1947—the year the Indian subcontinent was partitioned. During this period, land shifts and agricultural production intersected with mass anticolonial agitations and the demand for an independent India and Pakistan. Hunger and agrarian dispossession blurred the boundaries between collective protests and familial distress. Rahman and Nasir's predicaments and actions counter-narrate the official classifications of frontier peasants as either criminals or victims—two classifications that are evident in the colonial revenue and administrative surveys, police and intelligence files, and bureaucratic correspondence.

In early 1940, Fazlur Rahman traveled by the Assam Bengal Railway from the flooded Mymensingh district of British Bengal to Assam. Floods had destroyed his homestead, which had been located on a *char*. While narrating his journey to Assam, he emphasized that he had paid a few *annas* (cents) for a train ticket and subsisted for two days on the *moa* (flattened rice sweets) that his widowed mother packed. He described how it was widely known in Mymensingh (now in Bangladesh) that Assamese society was more egalitarian than Bengal's oppressive, tax-ridden, and Hindu landlord-dominated society.

Rahman's anxious journey amid the floods takes us to the British records that document the creation of the map carefully stored by Rowmari's Amin. Even today, river waters and floods constantly challenge the inherent immobility of land, displacing people—including the Amin Mahfuz, and others—from one *char* to another. Like the Garo Hills, whose dense interiors and forest fires impeded militarized surveys, mapping Rangpur's marshes with their maze of intersecting waterways was a daunting prospect. British surveyors who sought to transform the land into measurable and taxable property were confused upon encountering the shifting lands. In desperation, Rangpur's land settlement officers sought legitimacy for their failure to map the land and trace the rivers by invoking historical precedents.[3]

British surveyors classified the migrant peasants, distinct from this region's Muslim residents, who arrived in Rangpur from other riverine districts in Bengal, such as Mymensingh, as "downstream peasants." Further, the British land survey records noted the *chars* as unruly zones of criminality where landownership was contested and where peasants apparently relied on muscle flexing instead of the rule of law.[4] These reinforced the anxieties surrounding agrarian resettlements in Assam, anxieties that cultivators such as Rahman and Nasir had to constantly contend with.

Fazlur Rahman's predicament as a youth, displaced by floods and relocated to a forest in Assam, illuminates how economic and political forces intersected in the 1940s. He emphasized that in many districts, including

Mymensingh, a popular slogan was "*Assam Cholo*"—Bengali for "Let's go to Assam." Although Rahman recalled the tedious journeys of the landless peasants who arrived in Assam, he also mentioned that others hoped to gain the rich, arable land in Assam that the Muslim League, a political party in power in Assam, had made available for cultivation in the early 1940s. Rahman stated, "They even traveled by boats that carried all their belongings and cattle." Rumors in his village about the possibility of making a living from the land in Assam, combined with his distressing personal circumstances, forced him to migrate. Upon his arrival, however, Rahman joined other landless peasants to look for land—an activity that was by then politicized as a means of realizing the Muslim League's territorial goal of incorporating Assam within an independent Pakistan. Soon, he brought a small patch in a forest under the plow—in a location where the British state had prohibited human habitation and cultivation.[5]

Starting in the late 1930s, anti-British political leaders mobilized and exploited ethnicity and language, as well as religion. Bengali versus Assamese, and Hindu versus Muslims to gather support for an independent India and Pakistan. Some hoped, and others feared, that Assam would become part of Pakistan. In Assam, legislative debates cast frontier peasants from Bengal either as encroachers who were displacing Assamese interests or as food producers and victims of landlessness.[6] When the Assam Provincial Congress Party controlled the provincial legislature, migrants from eastern Bengal who had arrived in Assam after 1 April 1937 were declared "illegal" immigrants. In 1939, the Assam Congress passed a resolution that barred peasants from settling in villages or grazing reserves. However, as soon as the Muslim League came to power in the provincial elections of 1940, they reversed this policy and opened more land for cultivation.[7] The Assam Congress Party protested that the League's "Grow More Food" campaign was a form of territorial takeover and the groundwork for the creation of a Muslim Pakistan. Rahman's displacement from Mymensingh and his desire to gain a permanent plot of land coincided with these political events, turning him into a pawn for the Muslim League.

In *Empire's Garden*, Jayeeta Sharma recalls the importance of agricultural improvement for expanding the tea plantation economy of twentieth-century Assam. This was accompanied by new demands for rice that subsistence-oriented single-crop agrarian regimes could not fulfill. Aided by their skills in land reclamation and cultivation, migrating peasants from eastern Bengal improved the techniques of rice cultivation in Assam. Those who were better cultivators and had access to capital—borrowed mostly from moneylenders—bought land from Assamese peasants to cultivate rice and pulses and to start small-scale poultry farming.[8] Despite these economic interdependencies between the Assamese and the immigrant peasants, cultural distance, crop failures in 1942 and 1943, and the 1943 famine in Bengal compounded the land conflicts. Legislative debates also reflected widespread moral panic about migrant peasants, who were criminalized as trespassers and thieves who had intruded into the land owned by Assamese peasants, raided their granaries and cattle, and forced forest dwellers to relinquish the titles to their lands.[9] The ease of transportation via the Bengal Assam Railway ensured that new migrants continued to arrive from eastern Bengal. Further, immigrant cultivators continued to purchase land in Assam despite ongoing public opposition from the Assamese elite.[10] In the years that followed, the assimilation of Muslim migrants would lead to the creation of a new category of exclusion in Assam: *natun asomiya musalmans* (new Assamese Muslims).[11]

Karim Nasir's family, on the other hand, had been cultivating land in Assam since early twentieth century. His father left the riverine zone to claim more stable land in a reserve forest. Nasir's assertion that he was Assamese was related to the fact that he was born in British Assam and was grounded in a strong sense of identification with land cultivation in an era prior to the contentious 1940s. Although fifty years or more separated Nasir and Rahman's resettlements in Assam, both acquired tax-free land in forest zones where cultivation was officially prohibited in early 1947.

Land Struggles

In early 1947—the year the British would partition the Indian subcontinent—colonial intelligence agents surveilling Assam's borders with eastern Bengal conflated such dissimilarities. Intelligence reports noted that the Muslim League in Assam had marked out settlement locations that were normally used for trade and bartering activities. Intelligence agents noted that Hamid Khan "Maulana" Bhashani, a charismatic peasant leader and suspected claimant of Assam's land for Pakistan, encouraged his peasant followers to plant the Muslim League flag in every government building as a mark of territoriality and mobilized them to reoccupy land.[12] Intelligence agents reported that leaders were mobilizing both evicted and newly arrived peasants to resettle land in prohibited areas. When state oppression escalated, police officers

emphasized that the peasants were resorting to passive resistance.[13] Through
official reports, all peasants of Bengali origin came to be understood as a unified community of Muslim land encroachers.

The Rowmari-Tura road's changing contours attested to the emergent
conversion of agrarian land and the *haats* (biweekly rural markets) from hubs
of regional commerce and sociality into warring national territories. At one
end of the road, British intelligence agents marked Rowmari as a Pakistani
quila (camp), identifying it as a Bengal Muslim League military base. The
agents speculated that the League would attack Assam from Rowmari; the
border police reported that Muslim leaders were delivering inflammatory
speeches inciting peasants to invade Assam from Rowmari. On 22 April 1947,
when the soldiers of the Assam Regiment—a British military force—marched
to the provincial border to view the Pakistan camp in Rowmari, a crowd of
1,000 people was reported to have assembled within minutes with the pur-
ported aim of conquering Assam. Intelligence reports noted that Muslim
leaders were mobilizing peasants to march with black flags through markets
and villages and to pull down the British flag as a gesture of territorial control.
While the intelligence officers stated that the Muslim League made inflammatory speeches in Bengali in Assam, senior householders in Rowmari, such
as Mahfuz and Ali, who were young adults during those troubled years, told
me that it was the Urdu slogan *"lar ke lenge Pakistan"* ("we shall fight and get
Pakistan") that resonated across Rowmari's *chars*. In April 1947, the colonial
police reported that Hindu families residing near Rowmari had fled to the
Garo Hills out of fear of Muslim League agitations. Since trade was hampered
in the frontier markets that adjoined the road, British administrators shifted
the markets away from what were now considered "enemy" locations in
Pakistan—such as Rowmari—to sites farther from the border.[14]

At the other end of the road, Tura hovered between British anxieties surrounding the fate of hill societies in an independent India and its uneasy geographical proximity to a Muslim League–dominated Bengal. The first anxiety
crystallized in secret British proposals on the political future of "Mongoloid"
regions, and administrators debated if Britain should govern this zone as a
Crown colony.[15] British administrators had excluded northern Mymensingh—
a zone inhabited by wet rice cultivators classified as Garo, Hajong, Dalu, and
low-caste Hindu and Muslim peasants—from Bengal's ordinary jurisdiction.[16]
This exclusion had encouraged the Garos, among others, to hope for an
adibasisthan—an indigenous homeland—that could be appended to Assam,
with Tura as an important center. An elite Garo Christian delegation petitioned

the Bengal Boundary Commission in Calcutta to include the Garo villages within Assam after the partition of the Indian subcontinent.[17] For British intelligence agents, Tura's proximity to a Muslim-majority eastern Bengal made them suspect that Garo leaders were aiding the Bengal Muslim League.

Rice Wars

On the eve of the partition, intelligence reports reinforced fears about an invasion of Muslim peasants from Bengal into Assam to harvest rice. In addition, the deputy inspector general of police, John Reid, speculated that the new Muslim migrants would not leave Assam but would instead wait until the rains, when the banks of the Brahmaputra River would flood and the state would be compelled to relocate them in the grazing reserves.[18]

Due to price differentials between the two provinces, rice smuggling was rampant and there were clashes between rice inspectors and smugglers. Just twenty days before the British state partitioned the Indian subcontinent, however, an intelligence report warned that rice smuggling between Assam and eastern Bengal was a "security threat."[19] Rice became a part of the security lexicon in Assam. Until mid-1947, security issues in Assam were related to the opening of roads for military passage, stolen military, and arms supplies. The suspicion that transborder rice cultivators from eastern Bengal were still arriving in Assam added to concerns that not only was Assam's rice leaving the territory but also Bengal's Muslim cultivators would take over Assam's territory for Pakistan. The neat classification under which British agents filed reports—"communal," "Hindu affairs," "Muslim League," "communist," and "labor"—makes it obvious that people were identified as troublemakers on the basis of their religion, political orientation, and migratory status in ways that linked their relationships with land, labor, and rice to larger territorial aims.

Along Assam's uncertain borders, the British police differentiated between migrant and evicted peasants. They classified the migrant peasants under the categories "political" and "communal." This reinforced the moral panic surrounding Muslim immigration as well as the image that Bengal's rice-growing frontier peasants were land encroachers in Assam. In contrast, the reports classified Muslim peasants leaving Assam for eastern Bengal as refugees under the "miscellaneous" category.[20] By leaving the word "refugee" ambiguous, colonial intelligence records underplayed what could be seen as a major exodus of rice-cultivating peasants from Assam. Police records

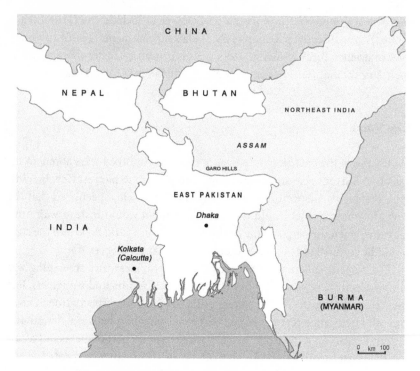

Figure 10. Map of Northeast India and East Pakistan, 1947.

portrayed border crossings as part of a larger political plot to reclaim Assam's land for Pakistan. Anticipating territorial skirmishes, the police deployed additional troops to protect Assam's territory and prevent its incorporation into Pakistan.

On 15 August 1947, the partition of the Indian subcontinent created a violent and chaotic border. The new border bifurcated Pakistan into East and West Pakistan, with the newly independent Indian territory in between. The Rowmari-Tura road came to be divided between East Pakistan and India. Mymensingh, provincial Bengal's largest district, was also placed within East Pakistan, and the Garos became Pakistani. Tura became part of Assam, which was included in India. The Garos in Tura, along with Muslims of Bengali origin in Assam such as Nasir and Rahman, became Indians. On the other hand, the Muslim-dominated district of Sylhet, earlier a part of Assam, was included in East Pakistan.[21] Assam was the largest state in Northeast India, a region only tenuously connected to the rest of India. Since 1947,

India has marked and patrolled this region as an internal and external zone of dissidence and territorial threats.[22] Meanwhile, the dotted zones on the Rowmari Amin's map acquired new political implications as the site of shifting national territories.

The changing course of the rivers made the international boundary fluid. After August 1947, when the rivers silted and created new border *chars*, these new lands became sites of contention between India and East Pakistan.[23] The ad hoc border truncated rural landholding patterns and disrupted trade routes.[24] Although India's official policies permitted the harvesting of produce located in East Pakistan, transporting that harvest back to India was illegal.[25]

Postcolonial Harvests

Despite the division of the Rowmari-Tura road, it remained a trade connector between East Pakistan and India. From Rowmari's marshes, Ali, the now-retired cartman, transported traders and goods to Tura in his oxcart, continuing to function as if the new international border did not exist. The road's bifurcation, which his memories gloss over, affirms the uneven relationships between land, produce, and identities that surrounded rice cultivation and trade that was evident in the late 1940s and early 1950s. East Pakistan and India controlled rice smuggling and imposed rice taxes to feed border patrols and deportees, as well as to discipline cultivators who belonged to religious minorities. For villagers and state agents, rice control, protection, and raids were crucial to surviving the newly imposed border. The border police exerted control over rice cultivation and transportation as a means of nation building. Peasants living along the new borderland also raided each other's harvests to cope with state violence and starvation.

In Assam's hill regions, India's restrictions on trading rice with East Pakistan resulted in food scarcities. Among others, the Garos in Assam had depended on food from adjoining regions that were now in East Pakistan. Despite the Assam state government's efforts to source food, the tedious process of transporting rice to remote border villages made rice sourcing and purchasing very expensive. Procuring a bag of rice from across the border was illegal, but it was also easier and cheaper.[26]

Rice came to be militarized, controlled, and policed in the interests of early postcolonial territory making. Indian police and intelligence agents would reproduce and amplify rice smuggling as actions that demonstrated

East Pakistan's territorial takeover of India. Unlike earlier reports, which did not note the religious identities of the smugglers, by December 1947, the category "Muslim" had become an important marker that conflated rice smuggling with national security issues in India. One police report noted that, after officials had arrested rice smugglers and seized their goods, "200 Muslims" had "rescued" the smugglers and rice.[27] The Indian state considered rice smuggling to be far more than a criminal offense. In using terms such as "rescued," reports labeled the actions of Muslim cultivators as seditious and deliberately anti-Indian. Even ordinary agrarian activities of Muslim rice cultivators were classified as "communal" in intelligence reports. For example, the arrival of 7,037 rice harvesters from East Pakistan to Assam was reported under the "communal activities" category, despite the fact that no "communal incident" had occurred.[28] From its prior use to record incidents of clashes, mass mobilization, and collective protests, the term "communal" now applied to Muslim rice cultivators and traders.

At this juncture, the entire territory of the Garo Hills, including Tura, which was part of postcolonial Assam, came to be slotted in intelligence reports under "Muslim Affairs." Indian intelligence agents regarded the arrival of visitors from eastern Bengal to Tura with suspicion, suspecting that Muslim League leaders such as Bhashani, who were now located in East Pakistan, were carrying out a "secret infiltration" with the intention of bringing large areas of the Garo Hills under his control. Agents noted that he had ordered his supporters to hoist white flags outside their houses on border *chars* to offer asylum to the "infiltrators." They suspected that the Muslim League leaders were circulating secret maps in which Assam's territory was redrawn, with a view to incorporating it within East Pakistani territory in the future.[29]

Deportations and Resettlements

In March 1950, an important legislation left lasting imprints on Assam's rice field borders with Mymensingh, East Pakistan. The Immigrants (Expulsion from Assam) Act conferred the police the power to conduct deportations from Assam through the government of India.[30] This act made Muslim peasants into "illegal Pakistanis," and legitimized the actions of the crowds who burned their houses, stole their cattle, drove them out of Assam, and even robbed them as they fled to East Pakistan.[31] Newspapers in East Pakistan reported that the police had detained and charged Muslims residing in India's border villages as Pakistani spies. Some reports alleged that they were arrested to prevent them from exposing the illegal activities of Indian troops.[32]

The 1950 act contained a significant exemption clause: it did not apply to those who feared for their lives or would be persecuted in East Pakistan. This meant that Hindu Bengalis from East Pakistan could easily seek shelter in Assam on the grounds of religious persecution.[33] To save what were officially listed as "abandoned" lands and rice harvests since Muslim cultivators had been driven out, Assam granted Hindu Bengalis temporary leases of the cultivated land. The listing of land as "abandoned" concealed India's persecution of Muslims and rendered their agrarian labor invisible. The act of harvesting rice was a disciplining measure for recruiting newly arriving Bengali Hindu refugees into productive activities and making them work for their food. Temporary land transfers were made on the condition that the land would be relinquished after the harvest, but Hindu Bengalis violated this clause.[34] Although their resettlement in Assam was politically explosive for reasons of language and ethnicity, their right to harvest rice translated into land acquisitions. This legitimized their identity as Hindu Indian citizens. In the context of early refugee rehabilitation, rice harvesting was seen as an urgent, productive, and strategic act. Though Indian official records make evident that state agents were concerned about saving abandoned rice harvests, they gloss over how the rice harvests came to be deserted in the first place.

By mid-1951, East Pakistan estimated that India had deported seven million Muslims from Assam and other states.[35] In Assam, the police often handed out deportation orders to Muslim peasants based on undefined charges. For instance, one morning the border police suddenly detained Abdul Kader, a Muslim cultivator in Assam, as a "threat to public order." Much to his surprise, he was served a deportation notice and ordered to leave for East Pakistan immediately by train. In his petition to the Relief Commissioner of East Pakistan, Kader emphasized that he had hurriedly returned to Assam after his deportation to reclaim his rice harvest but found that newly arriving Hindus from East Pakistan had already taken possession of his land, livestock, and house. The petition also noted that when resettled Hindu Bengalis clashed with Muslim cultivators in Assam, the police supported the Hindus since they were the religious majority in India.[36] Since Assam's district officials had rejected his desperate petitions to reclaim his land, he was compelled to seek rehabilitation from the Relief Commissioner of East Pakistan.[37]

While East Pakistan condemned India's unjust deportation of Muslims, its policies viewed the Garos, Hajongs, and other rice cultivators as an ambiguous and suspicious group of "mongoloid aboriginals." Due to anxieties over losing border territory to India, as well as the long history of peasant insurgencies along the foothills of Mymensingh in which Garo and Hajong peasants had collectively participated, East Pakistan viewed these border residents as revolutionary communists and the border zone as a conduit for pro-India activities.[38] In response, the state opened the partially protected foothill regions for land settlement.

Contrary to this image of communist unity in the foothill borders of India and East Pakistan, the boundaries between the Garos and the Hajongs had sharpened since the peasant rebellions a century before.[39] The mass revolution–oriented political solidarity that once existed had given way to a clear division between Garo Christian reformists and Hajong revolutionaries who were inspired by Bengal's communists. Unlike the Hajongs, who fled to Assam in large numbers, the Garos were reluctant to leave their land, harvests, and religious congregations. For the East Pakistani state, spatial and ethnic proximities erroneously implied political solidarities. When East Pakistan persecuted the Hajongs, they took shelter in Garo villages, leading the border police to doubt Garo loyalties as well, raiding their houses and interrogating them. Since the Garos now needed to cross the border into India to maintain family and kinship ties and to trade in the markets, East Pakistani authorities suspected them of sympathizing with Indian communist revolutionaries.[40]

An East Pakistani official circular in 1948 noted that the political activities of the Garo villages were to be closely watched for the circulation of unlicensed arms. Yet, East Pakistan soon disarmed its aboriginal border inhabitants.[41] Memoranda and intelligence reports contained racially pejorative descriptions of the foothills as infested with "armed tribals" and "disloyal elements" who hurled "primitive weapons" and "arrows and stones" at the border police. East Pakistan initially deployed additional police for six months but later extended their border duties.[42] The state instructed them to shoot suspected communists and rewarded those who did so. For instance, in 1949, cultivators plowing their land near the border were frightened to see the East Pakistani police approaching them. The police report states that, upon seeing the nine armed constables who were performing their usual border patrol duty, the armed cultivators raised an alarm, at which three hundred men, suspected to be communists sheltered in Assam, attacked the patrol. The judicial enquiry that followed underscored that the border police wanted the cultivators to go with them to their station, but, unsure of the constables' intentions, they had refused. In the end, the official summary created

after a long sequence of internal correspondence justified the police shoot-
ing and restated that the "lethal" rice cultivators were communists.[43]

Rice Raiders

During the 1950s, rice raids evolved from dispossessed, desperate peasants
raiding each other's harvests in a remote border region into established national rivalries. East Pakistan sought to contain communism by imposing punitive taxation that would finance additional reserves of border police along
the foothills. Taxes were both monetary and in kind, with the latter including rice, cattle, and corrugated iron sheets—all important resources in the
region. By November 1950, rice taxes amounting to 2,677 *maunds* of paddy
(equal to 99,916 kilos) and PKR 3,012 in cash had been collected.[44]

Punitive taxation made rice still more precious as a food and as a border
resource. When the East Pakistani border police destroyed Hajong rice harvests in the attempt to starve them to death, the Hajong in turn raided the
granaries of Garos residing in India.[45] The Garos living in East Pakistan's
foothills struggled to guard their harvests from the Hajongs who had found
shelter across the border in Assam, other transborder raiders, and even the
Indian police. To further complicate matters, Hajong rebels sheltered across
the border in India now regarded the rice fields in East Pakistan as enemy
territory and frequently staged raids into the foothills there. In September 1950, East Pakistan relaxed its arms restrictions and issued guns to
peasants who volunteered as border guards.[46]

The recruitment of border villagers for espionage by both India and East
Pakistan compounded the territorial issues. State recruitment drives encouraged peasants to act in national interests through direct employment or by
assisting the border police, with whom they shared ethnic and religious affinities. Sometimes peasants helped state agents conduct rice raids; at other
times, they sought police protection to raid granaries across the border. As
cultivation and harvesting shaded into spying, East Pakistan's policies toward
villagers classified as "aboriginals" became more unclear. In some situations,
they treated the Garos as able-bodied agents who could be entrusted with the
duty of guarding national territories; in other instances they were seen as
untrustworthy, revolutionary peasants.

The angry official correspondence between India and East Pakistan exposes
the links between territorial intrusions and the induction of Garo villagers into

border police and espionage. In 1951, India reported the disappearance of a Garo border constable named Elliram Marak and alleged that the East Pakistani border police had trespassed into Indian territory and abducted him. East Pakistan responded that the police had found Marak in East Pakistani territory carrying five border area maps and petitions from Garos living in northern Mymensingh. They charged him with spying on the number, strength, and military mobility of their border outposts and imprisoned him.[47]

Transborder raids intensified when the rice was ready for harvesting. East Pakistan accused India of conducting 263 rice raids between January 1951 and 1952. Most raids were carried out when the crops were ready for harvest. Raids on both sides of the border were intended to gain control over food grains and starve the enemy nation's border citizens. The introduction of passports in 1952 only heightened suspicions. Records of arrests that year expose the everyday anxieties of living along Assam's borders with Mymensingh. Between January and June 1952, Indian border guards arrested ninety-four East Pakistani nationals. Only seventeen were government employees, and the rest were villagers; forty-nine were released after being detained on suspicion without trial.[48] Disputes over rice harvests and trade accentuated the border's geographical imprecisions. During official enquiries, officials and witnesses pored over local maps in inconclusive attempts to determine the exact border locations.[49]

Peasants and the police formed complex alliances in attempts to gain control over the border, and rice raids gave way to warlike situations when peasants and policemen faced their counterparts as soldiers in preemptive combat. In August 1953, East Pakistan accused Indian Garo peasants and policemen of plundering agricultural land and rice harvests on its side of the border. East Pakistan alleged that when its border police arrived to arrest the raiders, the Indian police and Garo peasants had left East Pakistani territory. The respective forces maintained combat-ready positions on the international boundary for several hours before retreating.[50] In none of these confrontations did the prospect of the destruction of crops arise. Rice was too precious a food grain.

Though East Pakistan used the Garo as spies and inducted them into guarding the border, state oppression continued unabated. Once again, state-led land grabs were used as a means to dispossess the Garos. East Pakistan selected Garo-inhabited areas formerly and partially protected from land acquisition as the site for resettling the large numbers of Muslim deportees arriving from India. In 1953, an official memorandum asserted, "These tribals cannot be trusted to settle along the borders. Besides, their possessions are now in the hands of Assamese refugees who went back and got nothing in return, neither their houses nor their lands. We cannot make room for these tribals at the cost of throwing out Assam refugees who have nowhere to go. The Hajongs and other tribes have come back leaving their families in the Garo Hills to claim their lands, with the intention of carrying out subversive activities on Pakistan soil."[51]

Intimidated by state repression, the Garos abandoned their rice harvests and fled to India. While East Pakistan's official internal memoranda described the Garos and others as pro-India traitors who abandoned their lands, its official correspondence with India portrayed them as East Pakistani citizens. East Pakistan sent official letters describing them as helpless "East Pakistani peasants" struggling to protect their rice harvests against Indian rice raiders. Administrators emphasized that Indian peasants were assaulting East Pakistanis along the border, preventing them from reaping their harvests, stealing their paddy, and torching their houses.[52] Such official accusations against India ignored East Pakistan's own attacks on the Garos.

Indian newspapers, on the other hand, described the Garos in East Pakistan as infantile minorities, "helpless aboriginals" who needed India's protection. India alleged that Muslim refugees had been settled on land from which the Garos were forcibly displaced in a bid to build "natural frontiers" of loyal Muslim citizens. India further accused Muslim refugees with helping the East Pakistani border police intrude into Indian territory.[53] India alleged that East Pakistan was forcibly converting Garos to Islam by withholding agricultural loans on religious grounds and compelling Garo women to marry Muslim border policemen.[54] India's print media reported that East Pakistan was persecuting "semi-tribal people" of "simple . . . Mongolian extract[ion]" who were "hardy, persevering, stocky-built and simple minded."[55] India's official correspondence with East Pakistan depicted the rice-cultivating border peasants as a mass of persecuted tribes.[56] India's attempts to recover the Garos residing in East Pakistan reinforced the racial stereotypes that tribes were physically strong but easily manipulated and disempowered subjects. East Pakistan responded that some Garo families had embraced Islam but only by choice.

Meanwhile, Christian proselytization in Garo border villages added to East Pakistan's worries.[57] By the mid-1950s, there were sixty Catholic-majority villages, and Catholics under the jurisdiction of one church also inhabited an additional 126 villages.[58] State officials filed charges against missionaries along the border zone, stating that they had assaulted those who—according to the officials—had voluntarily embraced Islam. They accused churches of coercing converted Muslims to Christianity "by threat, intimidation, and use of force." The priests were warned that they should forget about creating a "Mission Raj" or Christian colonies in these areas.[59]

India continued persecuting Muslim peasants. When Jaharullah Munshi, a rice cultivator in Assam, refused to hand his newly harvested rice paddy over to his Hindu neighbors in Assam, the police assaulted him. In his petition to East Pakistani state officials, he claimed that the police had forcibly entered his house, intimidated him, and demanded that he leave for East Pakistan. India's persecution of Muslim minorities pushed them across its foothill borders, leading Munshi and other arrivals to resettle in East Pakistan's northern Mymensingh's Garo inhabited areas.[60]

Religious persecution and the loss of rice paddies continued alongside large-scale rice scarcity and smuggling. In 1957, the situation was so dangerous that the Pakistani army and air force guarded the border to prevent rice smuggling. In 1958, a quasi-military police force called the East Pakistan Rifles took charge of border duties.[61] From its previous status as a grain widely consumed on both sides of the border, rice quickly took on the connotation of a national commodity that made the smuggling of rice from India into East Pakistan an unpatriotic activity. For the newly posted border troops who were mainly from West Pakistan and who consumed wheat as their staple cereal, rice did not have the same affective connotations as it did for the villagers. The arrival of these unfamiliar border forces made rice fields into even more unstable locations.

Competing Loyalties

Every morning since his deportation from India and resettlement in East Pakistan, Karim Nasir had walked toward the border. Sitting with his back to a newly harvested rice field of golden stubble, Nasir reminisced about the 1964 crisis during which harvesting rice in East Pakistan was essential for his survival. He sat on a bamboo bench, gazing at what he imagined to be Assam's hills.[62] Speaking to me in Assamese instead of Bengali, our shared language, Nasir thumped his fist on the bench to emphasize, "I am Assamese, not Indian or Pakistani." He conveyed that he was born of "Assam's soil," soil that he had cultivated for years.[63] His misty eyes expressed a longing for both his homeland and his tax-free cultivable plots. Nasir had lost it all when, one day in 1964, the police had suddenly charged him of being a Pakistani spy.

In the early 1960s, both local and faraway events cast turbulent shadows that altered Nasir's life in the reserve forest in Assam. In 1961, the Registrar General of the Census in Assam stated that over two hundred thousand Pakistanis had "infiltrated" India.[64] From the next year, India intensified its border patrolling. In response to rumors that East Pakistani immigrants were assimilating with older settlers in Assam, the police extended their patrolling and surveillance to forests and grazing reserves.[65] Then, in December 1963, a holy relic disappeared from a mosque in the state of Kashmir, which lay on India's northern border with West Pakistan. In response to what was suspected to be a deliberate Hindu misdeed, large-scale Hindu-Muslim rioting ensued in both India and Pakistan.[66] In 1964, a new legislation—the Prevention of Infiltration of Foreigners Scheme for Assam Act—set up a special border police force and "Foreigners Tribunals" to deport illegal immigrants from Assam.[67] While I will explore the contemporary ramifications of judicial trials in Assam's Foreigners Tribunals in Chapter 6, then this legislation stressed the importance of religion and ethnicity, which political events and material uncertainties since the 1930s had solidified and had devastated many lives in 1947 and since. Assam's newly constituted border police force intensified their search for "Pakistani spies."

Recalling the political confusions of 1964, Nasir stated that "one day, some riots somewhere else, far away" made him "illegal" and a "Pakistani." Although he was born in Assam during "British times," the police randomly dubbed him a Pakistani spy and, much to his grief, deported him. Like Nasir, who considered himself Assamese since his forefathers had arrived there long ago from eastern Bengal, Ayesha Khatun, another 1964 deportee from Assam, perceived herself as Assamese. In 1964, her family had been living in Assam for two generations. However, the deportation notice imposed gendered hierarchies by equating Khatun's identity with that of her husband, who had migrated to Assam in early 1940. On the other hand, Fazlur Rahman, the youth who had come to Assam by train and claimed land in a reserved forest, was conscious that he had migrated from eastern Bengal in the 1940s, at the peak of provincial animosities. Although he emphasized that his deportation order had been long overdue, he did not leave of his own accord and waited for the police to serve him a deportation notice.

Nasir and Khatun recalled how the police set up "mobile courts" in 1964 hastily assembling tables and benches near police stations. The court procedures were rushed. When the police summoned suspects to appear before the tribunals, it was only to hand them deportation orders. There was no scope to contest the verdict and petition the higher authorities. After serving notices and deporting Muslim families from one locality, the police would survey a new area and quickly set up mobile courts there. Khatun recollected that "since the 'Quit India' [deportation] notice had been served, there was nothing we could do. Suddenly we were left with nothing. We were given twenty-four hours to pack our bags. Imagine! My father and my brothers argued that our forefathers were from this soil. They pleaded that my husband and I should not be expelled. Our pleading fell on deaf ears." The police taunted her, saying, "You have eaten off of our lands for too long. Ayub Khan [the president of Pakistan] is calling you back to Pakistan."

The metaphor of eating anguished Khatun and Nasir, because it dismissed their labor as food producers. With a day's notice and an allowance of one bag per person, the police herded them into military trucks and physically pushed them across Assam's borders into Mymensingh. Ironically, the phrase "Quit India," which had been an important slogan and movement during the anticolonial struggle, was now applied to accelerate *hurmuri jatras* of erstwhile colonial subjects.

East Pakistan's print media condemned India's deportation drives as unlawful campaigns to evict Indian Muslims. In May 1964, the *Pakistan Observer* newspaper reported that 150,000 Muslim refugees had officially registered with the authorities in East Pakistan.[68] India's anti-Muslim policies reinforced East Pakistan's pro-Muslim ones. In February 1964, Catholic priests in East Pakistan reported that large numbers of Garos were fleeing across the border into India because the government was persecuting them as infidel Christians.[69] Border villagers heard conflicting news about riots because the radio signals of both states converged at the border: they listened to Indian radio broadcasts about East Pakistan's persecution of Hindus and Christians as well as Pakistani ones about India's persecution of Muslims. In the early months of 1964, All India Radio reported that Muslim refugees along with *goondas* (thugs) had forcibly grabbed land that belonged to the Garos. On the other side, East Pakistani radio broadcasts asserted that India had not only used rice rations and medical care to lure Garos into migrating there but had also violently prevented them from returning to East Pakistan.[70] East Pakistani officials made formal gestures to prevent the Garos from abandoning their land in Mymensingh. District officials, along with border guards, visited Christian missions to ask priests to distribute notices urging Garos in East Pakistan not to leave and also asked those who had fled to India to return. The archbishop of Dhaka, concerned with the dispersion of the Catholic congregation to Assam, persuaded the priests to prevent Garos from leaving and posted additional priests along East Pakistan's foothill borders.[71] The missions wanted to retain their congregations; the Garo laity were abandoning their land as a consequence of the 1964 riots.[72] By August 1964, out of the 17,000 Christian villagers under the jurisdiction of one Catholic church in northern Mymensingh, only 6,599 remained in their villages.[73]

The displacement of the Garo cultivators made precious rice harvests available to deportees such as Karim Nasir and Ayesha Khatun. When they arrived destitute in East Pakistan, they were greeted by vast fields of rice ready for harvest. Having lost their land in Assam, Khatun and Nasir gratefully turned their attentions to these abandoned harvests. Sitting in her courtyard, Khadija, another deportee from Assam, recalled, "Despite our rushed deportations and journeys, there was some comfort when we arrived in East Pakistan. Rice was abundant—there was food." At the mention of rice, her until-then gloomy tone changed. Smiling at me, she emphasized, "The fields were golden with ripe paddy . . . when we were allotted lands . . . you should have seen the harvest! The fields were all golden. We did not have to go hungry . . . after leaving everything behind, and carrying nothing. . . . All at once we divided ourselves. We ordered those who were peasants, the Mymensinghas, the ones known for being sturdy and hardworking, to get into action; the rest of us worked less . . . we set about reaping the harvests and eating rice."

For the dispossessed Khadija, the sight of unattended rice harvests provided a sense of compensation for her humiliating deportation. However, she was silent about the details of land allotment along East Pakistan's foothill borders. With the future uncertain after the 1965 India-Pakistan war, Nasir and Khadija were distressed by the lack of any prospect of returning to Assam. In 1965, after the war ended, India set up the Border Security Force, a state-led paramilitary force, along its western borders with Pakistan. It sent its officers to distant villages in other states to recruit "sturdy types" to enlist in the border force.[74] The deployment of border patrols from other parts of India along Assam's rice field borders gradually distanced policing from cultivation. As with East Pakistan's border forces, rice was not an important food item for the newly posted wheat-eating border guards. Routine agrarian actions such as reaping rice harvests complicated the moral neutrality of rice as food; rice harvesting now became implicated in the act of land acquisition.

Among the Garos who fled to Assam from Mymensingh was Theophil Marak, who, along with his family and neighbors, had taken temporary shelter in Assam. Here they lived with the meager rehabilitation facilities in Assam's overcrowded refugee camps.[75] Seen as refugees and with a distinct ethnicity from the hill Garos, in popular discourse they were pejoratively identified as "delinquent" East Pakistani refugees.[76] Out of concern for their abandoned harvests and unattended land, many left the relief camps and returned to East Pakistan—only to realize that they had already lost their harvests and lands. East Pakistan trumpeted their return as evidence of their disillusionment with India.[77]

Many dispossessed Garo families scattered throughout Assam's foothills and reserve forests, while others became town dwellers in Tura. Village councils had informally allotted Garo refugees land in forest reserves in the Garo Hills in Assam where human habitation was regulated. Theophil Marak came to live alongside the Hajong exiles who had resettled in Assam in the early 1950s. It is worth noting that, decades before this happened, Nasir and Fazlur Rahman had reclaimed land and cultivated rice in similar locations. Though some people managed to claim land that was formerly sowed by Muslim peasants, their hold on it was sometimes temporary due to their "protected" status as reserved forests. Marak and other displaced Garos sought legitimacy through India's affirmative action policies, especially by attempting to join the civilian police. His multiple displacements from Mymensingh until finally resettling in Assam as an Indian citizen reinforced his identity as a Garo Christian while losing his role as a rice cultivator.

The Garos who remained in East Pakistan became Bangladeshis in 1971. Muslim deportees from Assam who had arrived in East Pakistan as refugees during the 1950s and 1960s, such as Karim Nasir, also became citizens of Bangladesh. By this time, Garos landholdings had diminished even further and, despite their participation in the Bangladesh's Liberation War, they were disillusioned.[78] Garo landholders recalled the presence of resettled cultivators from Assam and others whom Bangladesh had rehabilitated from other devastated zones. Some convinced Garo landowners to sell their land at very low prices, while others secured deeds through deceitful friendships. Lily, a Garo landowner and politician who was coerced to give up several plots of agricultural land in northern Mymensingh, recollected, "We were confused, also, with all the events that were taking place.... When things calmed down, we fell for such friendships.... We felt that if we made friends with the settlers, peace would return.... We often lost much more than we had bargained for."[79]

A few miles from Lily's house, Nasir continues to live with old maps like the one that Rowmari's Amin produced for us; their frayed margins still shape his sense of belonging. His unflinching gaze toward what he still imagines to be Assam's hills as he sits by the rice fields reinforces his sense of abandonment and loss. Nasir's regular arrival at the border demonstrates how displaced rice cultivators did not identify with either India or East Pakistan. His deep sense of longing for his homeland in Assam, as well as his actions of cultivating revenue-free land, have come to shape both the hidden boundary pillars and India's new border fence that today barricades the Rowmari-Tura road.

Beyond Zomia

The borderland that Nasir and Marak cultivated, moved across, were displaced from, and rebuilt their lives again, invite us to rethink how rice—as a grain that was consumed, raided, sold, and policed—functioned as a frontier. In these overlapping zones of authority and power, nation-states floundered to find their margins, and border troops and villagers battled but also forged productive alliances. At borders, politics and everyday life transcend what Liisa Malkki once famously critiqued as a "sedentary metaphysics" that limits the possibilities of anthropological engagement by territorializing the study of nations and cultures.[80] As locations of strife and struggle, shifting borders that came to be laboriously made agrarian illuminate the relationship between violence and displacement that Malkki so powerfully foregrounds.

James C. Scott's critique of the scholarly reliance on the sedentary to define the political further inspires us to ethnographically rethink Asia's border societies under the rubric of Zomia. Scott's *The Art of Not Being Governed* draws on Willem van Schendel's proposition that Zomia is a geographically expansive political highland zone that enables a departure from methodological nationalism and the dominance of political histories. For Scott, however, the spatial isolation and political terrain of Asia's highlands and its inhabitants' mobile dispensations inspired an anarchist reading of politics embedded in mobility, flight, and escape. The highlanders' proclivity for abandoning land and the "utter plasticity of social structures" that defined their politics led him to consider shifting cultivation as an "agro-political strategy" against "raiding, state making, and state appropriation." Yet, for the tax-paying, lowland wet rice-growing peasantry who submitted to the fiscal regimes of empires and states, such strategies of escape were impossible.[81]

However, in the East Pakistan–Northeast India borderland, rice wars marked borders and built nations. Floods, agrarian distress, and political events that shaped displacement and mobility, as well as the labor required to make *chars* cultivable, enabled rice cultivators to forge new identities. Rather than inhabiting the gaps of nationalist histories and state paternalism, rice cultivators were territorial actors, food producers, attenders of abandoned harvest, and raiders who marked borders when the political entities were unsure about their exact geopolitical configurations. Wet rice—a grain that was precious—held emotional connotations for its cultivators: their registers of loss and gain were fundamental to histories that transcend nations.[82]

Rice wars are crucial to scholarship that delinks Asian borderlands and their inhabitants from studies of either national histories or of locally bounded communities. An extension of anthropological sensibilities to Assam's surrounding regions, as well as the peasants who made late colonial and early postcolonial Assam, reveals the possibilities of a complex political field and its improbabilities in motion. These registers made peasants, tribes, and ethnic minorities national subjects and suspects in the decades that followed. Soldiering for coveted grains and scarce land make 1964 as poignant and as forceful a historical turning point as 1947 was.[83]

In her insightful analysis of the political complexities surrounding rice, Emiko Ohnuki-Tierney argues that, as a dominant metaphor for Japanese identity, rice has connotations far beyond its use as a grain of sustenance. Rice paddies linked notions of the self to land, village, region, and nation, and at different historical junctures, golden and ripened rice implied wealth and money as well as the entrenchment of the landless as transgressive subjects. On an island such as Japan, rice's powerful symbolism did not lead to demarcations of physical borders but instead reinforced the importance of symbolic boundaries.[84] In East Pakistan and India, by contrast, battles over rice have entrenched rootedness and displacement in ways that entwined religious and ethnic identities and came to shape imprecise national borders.

Even today, muscle flexing over *chars* and the redrawing of identities by force and violence realign sovereignties. Rice reminds people of their deep sense of displacement and alienation, even as it nourishes them to struggle another day against the same borders that the grain and their own actions have helped make.

CHAPTER 3

Cow Smuggling and *Fang-Fung*

I woke up after midnight in Rowmari, Bangladesh, to the sound of loud voices, motorcycles, and trucks. The noise filtered through the corrugated tin walls of Khairun's house. Convinced that the Indian border bandits frequently mentioned by Rowmari's residents were attempting to enter the house, I quickly woke up Khairun's nineteen-year-old daughter, Ameena. Ameena responded to my concerns with a nonchalant murmur: "It is nothing, the cows have arrived. Go to sleep." Unlike me, she slept through the commotion. I continued waking up to a rattling sound inside our room. The two baby goats with whom we shared our room rubbed their tails against the walls in anxiety.

Just three miles away from Khairun's house, in a border *char* in Assam where I had earlier resided, in a similar landscape interspersed by the Brahmaputra River, muffled voices and the sound of hooves had woken me up at night. Traders and intermediaries from the states of Rajasthan, Haryana, Uttar Pradesh, and Bihar, where cattle slaughter is prohibited, struck deals with traders in Assam's *chars*—leading Zebu cows and bulls to arrive at such a remote border village. In this borderland, these animals are referred to by the English word "boulder" and "Zebu" for their massive size and humps; they were far bigger than the "home *goru*," the smaller locally bred cows that were traded in cattle markets. Trading in Zebu is distinguished from trading in local cattle by scale of investment, skill, and risk involved. The Zebu cattle are highly valued for greater volumes of meat and leather that they produce as compared to "home goru," which small-scale traders smuggle. The Zebu cattle route stood apart from the biweekly cattle markets that operated on alternate days along either side of the border and dealt in only locally bred cattle. As "foreign" animals in Assam's *chars*, Zebu bulls are not found in the cattle markets; the affluent traders hid their consignments from public visibility.[1]

The export of live cows and bulls and beef consumption in India is a politically volatile issue. Hindu nationalists consider cows to be sacred. Cow slaughter is prohibited in many states of India, excluding states such as Assam and Meghalaya, where it is legal.[2] Despite having one of the largest cattle populations in the world, India restricts cattle transportation within the country and prevents livestock exports.[3] Exporting cows to Bangladesh, a Muslim-majority country where they are likely to be slaughtered and eaten, is unthinkable in India. Since 2014, under India's Bharatiya Janata Party (BJP) led Hindu nationalist government, cow protection policies that prevent trade and transport have amplified the anxious orchestration of cattle movement across the borderland *chars* but not foreclosed it. In fact, India continues to be a leading exporter of carabeef (buffalo meat) even with the BJP's ascendance in national politics.[4]

The large deployment of mostly Hindu soldiers in the Indian Border Security Forces (BSF)—who sometimes refuse to allow cows and bulls to cross India's newly built fence for religious reasons—complicates cattle smuggling, but ways including bribes are found to facilitate this highly lucrative trade. Once the troops give clearance, transporters with huge sticks and flashlights guide the animals across the rivers. At the international boundary, traders, skilled handlers, and boatmen wait in silence for the final signal. Upon receiving it, they transport the cattle to Bangladesh, where Bangladeshi traders receive the consignments and escort the herds to "animal corridors." Here, Bangladesh's border forces and locally recruited staff impose fines on traders for smuggled cows that arrive through the night and early morning from Assam's *chars* and the Garo Hills. They hand out penalty receipts that legalize the smuggled animals as seized goods. The traders would then transport the animals to markets all over Bangladesh. Eventually, slaughterhouses would produce beef and sell hides to the leather industry.[5]

Fang-Fung Economies

This chapter shows how borders and fences create sophisticated capitalist relationships and influence local and transborder politics of territoriality. In looking at state boundaries as distinct commodity enclaves, I argue that forms of value conversion prompted by Zebu smuggling reshape the relationship between notions of the sacred and ideas of economic exchange.[6] An expanded understanding of the sacred and its interplay with market forces complements the well-investigated religious, symbolic, and sacred connotations of the cow. Notions of the sacred intersect with capital in innovative ways at borders, demonstrating how asymmetrical risks are brought into play. In evaluating what the implications of moving from a smuggled economy to a formal economy are for the commodity, I show how the mobility of cattle confers the animals' value. The unstable alliances among border brokers—Zebu traders, politicians, bureaucrats, and border troops—that facilitate the transformation of cows and bulls from legally immobile commodities in India to highly mobile ones in Bangladesh render the borders of the sacred and the market porous. In addition, as infrastructures such as border fences and floodlighting take shape on the Indian side, regulations, markets, brokerage, and local electoral dynamics support a culture of all-powerful men to produce commodity value. Complex local and transborder logistics generate profits. Cattle seizures and penalties in Bangladesh's cattle corridors legitimize the profits from smuggling and animal transport for slaughter, accumulating prestige.

The uncertainties and risks that define Zebu smuggling find expression in the frequent invocation of *fang-fung*, a common word in the *char* borderland. It denotes at once both duplicity and dependency. Though *fang* and *fung* have no meaning as separate words, their semantic union is ascribed to muscle-flexing men and their seemingly devious actions and dispositions at the border. The expression *fang-fung* is rooted in masculine and moral debates about profits, sustenance, and patronage in riverine regions where land and male employment cannot be taken for granted.[7] *Fang-fung* people, mostly men, manage the business of border brokerage and passage. Integral to *fang-fung* actions are carefully calculated cattle seizures and releases on both sides of the borderland, which constitute one of the important strategies of the Zebu trade. These actions, in turn, confer value to the animals and legitimacy to the actions of landed elite, service holders, politicians, and traders who operate across contrasting legal regimes. The masculinity and machoism that drives such practices mines value out of both legally prohibited, extremely risky, seemingly immovable bulls in India and those that are rapidly incorporated into Bangladesh's formal economy. In the borderland *chars*, politicians, traders, and brokers alternated between being dangerous cattle raiders and benevolent social reformers. Zebu cattle traders and brokers are masters in deceitful transactions, and therefore villagers cannot entirely trust them. But as they are employers, moneylenders, distributors of largess, and benefactors, villagers also cannot dismiss them. As Thomas Blom Hansen foregrounds, the culture of big men who control electoral politics, distribute services, adjudicate disputes, and incite collective violence establishes the diffused structure of governance and sovereignty. Notions of masculinity and the violent acts that accompany it shape public authority in India.[8]

The simultaneity of India's border building and BJP's cow protection policies, as well as Bangladesh's animal corridor projects, have reordered the smuggling landscape by escalating the stakes involved in Zebu smuggling. Operating in an environment of external risks—floods, local electoral dynamics, trading jealousies, competition, and national security—that is beyond people's control, *fang-fung* actions seek to negotiate and mitigate these dangers to life and livelihood. In fact, *fang-fung* people and actions further confer value to Zebu cattle by blurring the boundaries of illegality and the legality.[9]

Janet Roitman foregrounds how cross-border commerce are claims of economic citizenship from the margins of states, where people innovatively reorder geographic and economic boundaries. These are not regarded as corrupt activities that arise from weak and predatory states. The existence of plural authorities in border zones regulates economic life, reflecting what she calls the "rationality of illegality" as a disposition that is both economically calculated and socially industrious.[10] If notions of Hindu sacredness make the movement of cows and bulls within and across India's borders illegal, for border residents, the larger social implications of smuggling, especially livelihoods, employment generation and money lending, are used as arguments to justify such trading. Despite the money and the high profits, some traders— especially on the Indian side—did not gain in social status. This was especially for those who did not lend money or feed the poor during difficult times. Villagers still referred to them as the "cattle thieves" who made money through illegal means. On the Bangladeshi side, because of the legitimacy of the penalty receipts, cattle trading was seen as a respectable state-supported profession, one in which even middle-class urban women were involved.

The shifting alliances among Zebu traders, politicians, and border troops that facilitate the conversion of sacred commodities into beef and leather sustain a violent border where cattle rustling becomes an ambiguous expression for nation-states to justify the militarization of a "crime-infested" landscape. Killings and torture by Indian border troops aimed at Muslim cattle workers who deal with low-value "home *goru*" or local cattle reinforce the imagined location of the border *chars* as violent and disordered regions that nation-states struggle to control and reform, while actually profiting from high-value Zebu smuggling. Cattle transport and transactions challenge the long history of cattle quarrels that is recalled in scholarship as primarily dividing people and places in the Indian subcontinent along narrow religious lines. In the final pages of this chapter, I show how contrasting narrations of cattle's legality and illegality join the boasting and profitable *fang-fung* with the intimate world of loss and love in the nebulous *chars*. Let me begin in a border *char* in lower Assam where I resided and where the English words "line clear" and "line cuts" were in common circulation.

Line Clear and Line Cuts

The word "line," as the politician and border broker Aladdin explained to me, related to the network of interconnecting nodes that enabled the physical transportation of Zebu cows and bulls. In his early forties and the son of a reputed schoolteacher, Aladdin was a politician from a border *char* in lower Assam, adjoining the Garo Hills. When I first began fieldwork in the village in 2007, Aladdin was campaigning for his elder brother, who was seeking a seat in the provincial legislature. At a given time, Aladdin held that these lines stretched over 1,500 miles—the longest started in northern and western India—from the states where India prohibits cattle slaughter to the border. During their transit from other states into Assam, the Zebu cattle were the responsibility of the intermediaries who were in charge of their travel to Assam. Aladdin emphasized that once the animals arrived in Assam, line management was the local traders' responsibility. These lines included the checkpoints of entry into the *chars*, the locations including those in the Garo Hills where traders secretly sheltered the animals, and finally the routes from which they guided cattle out of Assam into Kurigram, Bangladesh. The irreversible and unidirectional flow of Zebu cattle means that right from the point of origin, there was high risk of seizure and loss, and line clearance had to be maintained through connections and bribes. From the perspective of the value transformation, the movement of the animals in their transport and transit to Bangladesh is fraught with risks to life and commercial ruin. Cattle routes not only were geographical but also greatly relied on traders in other states, migrant intermediaries who struck deals in Assam, and state agents who facilitated smuggling from Assam to Bangladesh. Upon landing in Assam, they became integral to local and transborder cultures of status and prestige, authority, and electoral aspirations.

Zebu cattle first arrived in Assam's riverine borders with Rowmari—ironically, due to the construction work on India's new border fence with Bangladesh. By 2005, the construction of the new infrastructure and installation of floodlights in the Indian state of West Bengal, which shares a border with Bangladesh, had disrupted several existing cattle routes between India and Bangladesh. As a result, traders and brokers from northern and western India covertly set up new routes through the low-lying plain areas of Assam. The border *chars*, with their interspersed rivers, ensure that passages could still be negotiated despite India's border fencing and escalated patrolling. For this reason, Bangladesh has initiated new animal corridors just across Assam's *chars* in Kurigram since 2006. Because of India's prohibitions on beef exports, Bangladesh's demand for beef was met with the orchestration of live animals across the riverine landscape rather than the export of meat. No one involved in this trade spoke about the final products i.e., meat and leather.

During our initial conversations, Aladdin boasted to me, "I am a *fang-fung* person, I do *fang-fung* for a living, I have no qualms about telling you where and how goods move—if you want, you may think I am the world's best-known smuggler." To make a living, Aladdin managed "border development." This involved negotiating local crime-related issues on behalf of the sub-divisional police and acquiring funds for the political party that his elder brother represented. In between handling domestic violence complaints and other disputes, he carefully calculated cattle seizures. In Assam's *chars*, *fang-fung* illuminates the location of Zebu cattle as "foreign" commodities that exceed local demand. Maintaining Zebu routes requires heavy investments in "line clearance." The practice of trading in large consignments of live animals without export licenses involves high risks, bribes, investments, and negotiations with Indian bureaucrats and border troops. When Indian bureaucrats and border commanders clear the lines, transporters move across the international boundary. Zebu traders were perennially anxious about guarding the business deals and geographic routes through which they transported bulls to Bangladesh and for which they relied on brokers such as Aladdin.

Aladdin was infamous for "line cutting": he frequently disrupted the passage of animals through cleverly orchestrated confiscations. He made arrangements with the local police to seize the animals while also negotiating their release, often for the same consignments that he had arranged to be seized. He used these gains for various purposes. He simultaneously positioned himself as a benefactor and social worker, provider of a new concrete house for his wife and children, and a supporter of his elder brother's electoral campaign. "Line cuts" were also rampant during cycles of high border security in Assam and last-minute commercial disagreements between traders, brokers, border commanders, and local bureaucrats. Another kind of "line cutting" happened when Indian traders reported each other to the police. Widespread disruptions in cattle passages made cattle invisible in the border *chars* of Assam: traders concealed them in secret enclosures in the Garo Hills and guarded their routes from competitors who could leak information. It would result in additional bribes to the police.

Even as Zebu and "boulder" bulls and line cuts inevitably filtered into every conversation in Assam's border *chars*, the animals were invisible. Small-scale Indian traders and transporters such as Alibaba, who traded in local cattle, told me with admiration, "The boulders have huge bumps on their back; you should see them . . . but only at night." I traveled with Aladdin's aide Mohsin to the Garo Hills to search for the animals arriving from northern and western India. Our nocturnal journeys in an auto-rickshaw fell into a predictable pattern. They began with Mohsin's excited phone calls to confirm the routes, upon which he guided our auto-rickshaw in the direction of hidden shelters. We left the village where I resided, traveling in the direction of Tura—on the Rowmari-Tura road—where cattle handlers waited silently with torches and long sticks. Although Mohsin quickly tracked route changes, our journeys invariably led us to vacant shelters near Tura. On our return journeys downhill, the cattle handlers along the highway had disappeared. Despite my attempts to travel between Assam's low-lying marshes and the Garo Hills, I failed to set my eyes on the massive animals.

Borders of the Sacred

In the Hindu household where Aladdin and Moshin had arranged my accommodation in Assam, I initially struggled to make sense of smuggling. I was residing with Ghosh, an elderly Hindu businessman and politician, along with his wife, their five sons, one daughter-in-law, and seven nephews. Several other villagers had declined to accommodate me on the grounds that sheltering a female Hindu scholar in crime-infested border *chars* would place extra responsibilities on the mostly Muslim householders. Ghosh devoted himself to full-time party politics while his sons and nephews managed his reasonably lucrative electrical goods business. Villagers who arrived at Ghosh's house at dawn often interrupted his routine questions about my fieldwork plans for the day. I sensed these were about border deals, but I did not know what the subject was.

Aladdin did not converse with Ghosh about cattle deals. In the evenings, between discussions about political canvassing, Aladdin and Ghosh romantically recollected the fertility of the vanished Sukhchar. Always pronouncing the name with a pause in between to emphasize *Sukh* (translated from Bengali as happiness and affluence), they narrated, "Traders from Rangpur and Dhaka from the province of British Bengal flocked here. . . . And then one morning, Sukhchar suddenly vanished. There was only water." Like other *char* dwellers—*nodi bhanga manush*—they broke into soulful conversations about losing land. Aladdin added that even their newly located *char*, which was relatively prosperous, could not match Sukhchar's bounty. Aladdin and Ghosh's political connections and income from electoral politics, state jobs that their family members had acquired, and their investments in local businesses, ensured good money. This was unlike the landless agrarian laborers such as Alibaba, who was also displaced from Sukhchar. Unable to either depend on daily wage work from disappearing agricultural land, or to gain employment for building India's border infrastructures (that required workers who were not from the immediate area), the latter increasingly relied on making a living from small-scale border deals and transporting goods. Youth left these remote regions to work in Tura and Guwahati as daily-wage construction workers.

Unlike Aladdin, whose affluence and political proximity to Ghosh ensured him entry to their living room despite him being a Muslim, other Muslim traders waited in Ghosh's outer courtyard. While they had the financial means to negotiate with Ghosh, the traders could not cross the well-established purity boundaries between Hindus and Muslims, even though the *chars* were primarily inhabited by Muslim householders. Respecting the sanctity of a pious Hindu household, Muslim traders anxiously paced up and down the courtyard while Ghosh's wife muttered her morning prayers to a constellation of Hindu deities in the corner temple. Since Muslim traders respected Ghosh as a religious Hindu, they did not mention the word *goru* ("cow" in Bengali). Neither did Ghosh. Even after a month of residing with the Ghosh family, I was unable to figure what the transactions involved, until his daughter-in-law Monju complained about the dust trails left behind for her to clean.

Figure 11. Cattle handlers and transporters herding Zebu "boulder" cattle from the hills of Meghalaya to the *chars* in Assam at dawn. (Photograph: author)

Ghosh feigned disinterest when traders arrived in his house. Yet, he regularly mobilized his position as a politician to make money from smuggling. He used his seniority as a Hindu Bengali politician in Assam's Muslim-populated *chars* to command respect from Hindu Bengali-speaking clerks. When deals went wrong, the clerks who managed senior bureaucrats were more open to discussions with him than with the Muslim traders. In his courtyard, the borders of the sacred were constantly subject to negotiations with market forces. While in northern and western India, market forces triumphed over the sacred nature of cows and bulls past their prime and enabled large consignments to arrive in Assam's border *chars*, their unstated recognition as sacred in the Ghosh household ensured that these animals could not even be named by family or traders. It reinforced the sacredness of cattle.

As the Ghosh family went about their everyday morning duties of taking turns to bathe and paying their respects to the deities in the courtyard, Monju grumbled that she had to brew tea for endless visitors in addition to attending to demands from the family members. Because I resided with them, I inadvertently acquired more cattle-related news than was intended. I quickly erased the details from my memory, never noting them down, frightened that this knowledge would harm me in ways that I did not know. Even when I followed bovine trails, I was so scared that I replaced the word "cow" with the word "almirah" in my fieldnotes.

Meanwhile, traders and their families invited me to celebrate "good" days when brokers and border troops granted line clearance, such as when the border passage of 48,000 head of cattle in two days was granted in the summer of 2007 and 56,000 in the winter of 2008. The traders threw a massive feast of fried rice and goat curry at a roadside eatery. During the general revelry, one occasionally thumped his fist on the table and claimed to be a *fang-fung* person.

Border Brokers

In other instances, Zebu negotiations were more open. Unlike Ghosh, who carefully concealed his pivotal role in cattle deals on account of his seniority and Hindu religion, the younger Aladdin was less discreet. He negotiated crime-related issues on behalf of the sub-divisional police. Both bureaucrats and the police relied on brokers such as Aladdin to take care of grievances and family disputes in the border villages. Aladdin elevated this brokerage to generosity, "social work," and a pro-poor orientation. Sometimes, for a token fee, he cared for his fellow villagers with whom he shared a nostalgic world of land loss. Patronizingly, he called them *dukhiyas*, or the downtrodden. At other times, when he led cattle raids on traders who supported rival political parties, the harshness of his tone conveyed the lethal edge of his character as a politician-cum-cattle rustler who had enormous resources at his disposal.

One summer morning in 2007, I was able to see this convergence. In a gesture of self-importance, Aladdin announced that he would enable my entry into a cattle "jail" located behind the police station. By this time, I had convinced Aladdin that cow smuggling was worthy of scholarly engagement. I had also nodded my head vigorously when he asked if my study on smuggling would enable me to secure a good job as a college lecturer. That morning, Mohsin quickly arrived to escort me to the house where Aladdin was holding an audience with his aides, breathlessly whispering that twenty Zebu bulls had been seized on Aladdin's instructions. I promptly arrived at Aladdin's residence with Mohsin, walking past the crowd of people outside his door who needed his intervention. They nervously waited for an audience with Aladdin, clutching letters and legal papers that ranged from divorce settlements to accusations of murder and rape.

Inside the room, Aladdin ignored the petition-clutching crowd. He exchanged pleasantries with me. Soon, an edgy Moi Ali, who had invested all his earnings in twelve heads of Zebu cattle, made a dramatic entry, almost falling at Aladdin's feet. Usually, traders such as Moi who were transporting Zebu for the first time were more nervous than the seasoned players. Scaling up from domestic cattle to Zebu trade was a big jump that required not only large investments but also strategic connections. Aladdin barely listened to Moi's laments; instead, he gestured to me and said, "Data for you, this one is among those who make a living by cutting fences." Moi, who had started by small-scale peddling, had brokered a few profitable border deals and moved to trading in local cattle. However, his reputation rested on his skills in cutting border fences to smuggle goods—a *tar kata manush*—a man who the villagers both feared and revered. Within minutes of our conversation, though, Moi broke into a sweat under the slowly circling ceiling fan. He screamed in desperation, "Fix the line, elder brother, instead of fixing me." Aladdin laughed at his discomfort and asked his aides to show him the way, promising that the "line" would be cleared in due course. Glancing at me, Aladdin remarked that Moi was still "one of the *dukhiyas*, grassroots you may call him, who fall under my jurisdiction." So he would not charge him fees.

Moi and Alibaba the cattle transporter, whom Aladdin called "grassroots," were important players in village-level electoral campaigns. They mobilized crowds to attend rallies for Aladdin's brother. Aladdin's pro-poor orientation, however, did not extend to offering employment to Alibaba to transport "boulder" cattle to Bangladesh. By this time, I had spent several months with Alibaba and his family, seeing them struggle to make ends meet. Unlike rich "boulder" traders, small-scale traders had modest means and could not offer big bribes to the border forces. Despite Aladdin relying on the labor and political support impoverished villagers, Alibaba was too "grassroot" for Aladdin to be bothered about his unemployment and hunger.

After Moi's exit, we rushed to the cattle enclosure behind the local police station. It was vacant except for cow dung and a few khaki-clad young police constables who stood around it. Aladdin, surprised but nonplussed, murmured that the "line must have been resolved simply." Clearly, before Aladdin or other politicians could arrive at the scene, the newly appointed police chief Sangma had settled the matter by releasing the consignment for a bribe. Zebu traders routinely hounded Sangma, interrupting his evening sessions with Aladdin. Insisting that cattle thieves, smugglers, arms dealers, and people who could not be trusted infested border villages, he cautioned me against the border villagers. Sangma also bragged about the rapidly declining crime rate under his leadership. Like other English-speaking bureaucrats in Assam, he explained his presence in a crime-infested border zone by waxing eloquent about the scenic Brahmaputra River and making explicit his preference for requesting official postings in idyllic locations. Bureaucrats monetarily benefited from the official restrictions that the Indian state imposed on cattle that had to move across "crime-infested" areas. The illegal transportation, entry, and transit of Zebu cattle ensured that both traders and intermediaries depended on state agents to facilitate illegal flows. State agents made "sacred" cattle prices escalate in the *chars* by officially pretending to impede supply while secretly facilitating it.

Aladdin routinely kept Sangma, who resided in this remote village without his family, jovial company in the evenings, but he did not discuss border transactions with him. Instead, pretending to be a friend, he secretly ridiculed him for being "an insect-eating Garo," a pejorative term that demeaned Sangma's identity as a "tribal" Garo.[11] During their evening sessions, he ignored the fried insect snacks and pushed a big plate of fried potato chips toward himself along with a glass of beer. In between rushing to zonal crime conferences and managing border villages, Sangma miscalculated cattle deals. Partly unaware and often ignoring the bidding of politicians, he seized cows that local politicians had cleared for passage and released consignments that they had ordered to be seized. His tenure as a controller of crime was short-lived. At the onset of the heavy monsoon rains that same year, he was transferred from this border district.

Despite the flooding and river waters that gushed from the courtyard into the long L-shaped room that I shared with Ghosh and his wife, as well as the difficulties of traveling between *chars*, I finally saw a cattle pen during the monsoon. One afternoon, the waters had miraculously receded when Mohsin arrived to get me in the district library. I was chatting with the village volunteer in charge of English novels, who was bemoaning the lack of readership.

We rushed to the cattle enclosure. Seeing us, Aladdin joked with Mohsin and his other aides about whether the animals in the slushy enclosure were camels or bulls given their massive size. Before us, sixteen bulls were huddled

Figure 12. A Zebu cattle enclosure adjoining a police station in Assam, Northeast India. (Photograph: author)

together. Round red circles stamped on their backs ambiguously marked them as belonging to a specific consignment. Instead of the imposing snow-white bulls that the villagers compared to moving mountains, I was confronted with emaciated animals. These animals were seen as cheap commodities and often dispensed after extensive milch and agrarian use. However, as Radhika Govindrajan shows, cow vigilantism in India coexists with and does not override the ritual and agrarian economies of care that shape people's relationship with cattle as domesticated animals, including when they are sold for slaughter. Govindrajan powerfully establishes the connections between the seemingly incommensurate worlds of political mobilization that uses cows as a rallying point for violence against non-Hindus and the everyday care of animals that is spiritually grounded in Hindu rituals.[12] In the India-Bangladesh borderland *chars,* such complexities bear on our understanding of borders as generating new economies of risk.

The extraordinary regulations on cow slaughter, transport, and beef consumption in India escalated the animals' value in Bangladesh, making cattle smuggling a risky business in Assam's border *chars.* Rather than protecting animals from the cruelty of killing, India's cow protection policies push cattle toward slow deaths. In the context of killing animals, Bhrigupati Singh and Naisargi Dave have recalled the interconnected spaces of ritualized sacrifice with industrialized slaughter.[13] This interplay of the sacred and the capital was evident during the long journeys that Zebu cattle travel in order to reach the Northeast India–Bangladesh border, cramped in trucks without pasture and rest and experiencing hunger and stress. Illegality and secrecy in Assam's riverine regions further withered them to the extent of making their ribcages protrude. The day I was able to see the bulls in the enclosure, the rain had soiled their bodies. Some were too weak to even stand. The coir rope between their nostrils and necks was not removed. This indicated that they would be quickly released. The laughter that Aladdin's boastful statements elicited in the presence of bare-chested young police constable trainees contrasted with the frailty of the seized animals.

The resurgence in cow protection in India as well as Assam's BJP-led state government policies that seek to curb cattle smuggling have stalled the transport of animals disrupting even legal trade within Assam. By ensuring the widespread feminization of cattle as the "cow mother," it has helped sustain a masculine and aggressive border culture of *fang-fung*. These policies have made cattle passages even more difficult for the animals and led to an escalation in cattle seizures at the India-Bangladesh border.[14] While checkpoints and demands for high bribes make the journey of the locally bred "home *goru*" more tedious and riskier, the high-value business in Zebu bulls continues to flourish.

Affluent traders forge alliances with local politicians and offer higher bribes to Indian border commanders. The manipulation of morality and reform that accompanies the oscillation of cattle as sacred and coveted not only generates new economies and social arrangements but also perpetuates state violence. The recurring motif of the border materializes through the fear of torture and shootings of small-scale Muslim cattle workers such as Alibaba. The low-stakes smuggling of locally bred cattle as contrasted with Zebu ensures that Indian border troops shoot at sight impoverished Muslim cattle workers. Border guards harass villagers who prevent cattle traffic over their agricultural lands and arrest them on false charges.[15] In shifting landscapes, the material fluidity of borders and their flexibility to capital and market forces entrench the permanence of state violence in the lives of *char* dwellers.

The overlapping profits of smuggling and violence through *fang-fung* ensure that duplicity and danger, political gains and facilitation of illegal flows, macho boisterousness, and fears of death shade into one another. As sites of varied legitimacies, plural forms of regulation, and value conversions, borderlands reconfigure notions of governmentality. The violence that accompanies the production of economic extraction and regulation also constitutes acceptable and legitimate behavior.[16]

Exerting his authority as a member of the local elite, Aladdin self-importantly remarked that he had yet to decide whether to clear the line in exchange for a fee and political support or to hand the bulls over for auction to the customs department. Within an hour, Aladdin had made up his mind

Figure 13. Visible in the water near the front of the boat are Zebu bulls. The animals are being herded for border passage and are tied to the boat. In this case, the river Brahmaputra forms the international boundary. (Photograph: author)

and settled on a deal that ensured electoral funds. The trader to whom the consignment belonged paid Aladdin a hefty fee and committed to patronize his political party with additional electoral support.

In Assam's border *chars*, cattle seizures were an important source of income for state agents and a way for politicians to collect funds for election campaigns. The modus operandi of line cutting was more complicated in these instances, requiring the machinations of local politicians who mediated and meddled in the transport of high-value commodities across their constituencies. Electoral dynamics enabled the rapid confiscation and release of Zebu cattle. Politicians, irrespective of their religious affiliation, regularly negotiated in cattle seizures and releases, as well as cleverly orchestrated confiscations. The flamboyant broker Aladdin and the sober senior politician Ghosh, both wily profiteers, intervened in the transport of these high-value commodities that passed through their constituencies in lower Assam.

My visits to district offices in Assam coincided with those of traders, brokers, and politicians who had gathered anxiously to meet with senior officials who could mediate cattle flows. Indian bureaucrats posted in "crime-infested" areas benefited from the official restrictions that the Indian state imposed on cattle. By not legally permitting this trade, the Indian state makes its presence more pronounced and the traders and intermediaries dependent on state agents for illegal flows. Bureaucrats interceded when Indian border guards, mostly Hindus, would refuse the passage of cattle on religious grounds. When they did so, cattle easily trailed past district administrative offices and police stations long before the break of dawn; swishing their tails to ward off flies. Local elites combined positions of accumulation and power as they embedded themselves within flourishing transnational economies. Further, when state agents protected and regulated illegal flows, by participating in clandestine trade, they legitimized local leaders and smugglers. In fact, so intertwined were these roles and functions that it was difficult to discern the boundaries between smuggling and state power.[17]

Indian border commanders maintained an official silence on cattle smuggling. Conversations about cattle seizures were invariably about locally bred cattle, as if Zebu bulls did not arrive in these borderlands. Usually, commanders spoke at length about lone cows straying across the international boundary. They emphasized that unlike people, cows, bulls, and goats were unaware of the international boundary. When cattle crossed over from India to Bangladesh or vice versa, the border guards of both countries called for a joint meeting known as a "flag" meeting. They also stated how border patrolling occasionally extended to combing border villages to check whether householders were keeping anything other than homestead animals.[18]

When India's news-hungry media landed at the border with camera crews, they compelled Indian border guards to make staged gestures of cattle seizures. Some journalists amplified the plight of the patriotic Indian border troops who were battling Muslim criminals and smugglers.[19] Cattle auctions were big *fang-fung* events in remote villages. Even as traders furiously waved their tender sheets above their heads to get the clerks' attention, the clerks had already worked out releases for pre-negotiated deals. *Fang-fung* auctions ensured that clerks would release the bulls to the same traders who had procured them in the first place in exchange for hefty bribes. Even when the customs department auctioned and released cattle in the late afternoon, the animals were not transported back to the states from where they were procured. Instead, herders once again secretly hid them in the Garo Hills before transporting them across Assam's *chars* to Bangladesh. The cultures that *fang-fung* produced entailed a transit so brief that it left only the stench of cow dung in the air.

At every stage of the transit through Assam's *chars*, the massive "boulders" were valued as coveted goods. If the depreciating value of cows and bulls as sacred animals that had outlived their utility in Bihar, Rajasthan, and other states of India led the animals to the border, their transit through the riverine landscape ensured that they came to signify far more than tradable animals of demand and supply.

Late at night, when the often exhausted Zebu failed to keep pace, herders liberally goaded them with sticks, creating mini dust storms. Noise of thuds and voices filtered easily into the Ghosh household, at the far end of which was my bed. By the time Monju started complaining as she swept the courtyard, the cattle had already crossed the border and arrived in Rowmari in Bangladesh.

Legalizing Cows in Rowmari, Bangladesh

Although Rowmari's shifting *chars* were strikingly similar to the ones where I had resided in Assam, the cattle dynamics vastly differed. Unlike the disorder that was integral to cattle transport in Assam, Rowmari's nocturnal commotions led to well-ordered mornings that had an aura of official bilateral trade. In Bangladesh's animal corridors, vigilant customs officials and border troops neither chased smugglers nor confiscated their goods. Rather than absconding and fearing imprisonment for smuggling, Bangladeshi traders waited in anticipation along with the border forces. Everyone looked towards the border. Neither the winter fog nor the floods prevented the troops and volunteers from efficiently organizing cattle corridors early in the morning.

Rezaul, Khairun's lecturer son-in-law, accompanied me to one of the "animal corridors." As an Indian national, Bangladeshi customs officers had earlier declined to give me appointment for interviews. At the break of dawn, we arrived at the corridor and walked through the enclosure carefully avoiding the exhausted animals. The winter mist had enveloped India's border fence, rendering its neatly planted metal pillars invisible. We passed bright blue wooden counters that were labeled "animal corridors." Here, traders had lined up their consignments. State employees and staff excitedly pored over registers, collected money, and handed over penalty receipts to traders. Their newly minted status as a "seized" and "released" commodity ensured the transportation of the cows and bulls to other districts of Bangladesh. By late morning, animals blocked village roads, congested national highways, and found their way to the numerous cattle markets. In Bangladesh, the duplicity behind officially seizing smuggled Zebu cattle imposed an aura of legality

Figure 14. An auction penalty/tax counterfoil generated by an "animal corridor" checkpoint in Kurigram District, Bangladesh. (Photograph: author)

Figure 15. A cattle shelter in a border *char* in Kurigram District, Bangladesh, located next to an animal corridor checkpoint where cattle are taxed. (Photograph: author)

that formalized the cattle's illegal entry into the country. Unlike the aggressive verbal economy that guided Zebu cattle lines in India, documentary practices guided the seizures in Bangladesh. State agents and volunteers who levied the penalty of 500 BDT (around US$7) per head of cattle and handed out auction counterfoils to traders, made cattle a "legal" commodity.

Boldly titled "tax levied at cattle corridors," this important identity document made cattle mobile and legally tradable. Like official receipts, the penalty counterfoil was meticulous, mentioning the route by which each animal arrived, in accordance with legal customs guidelines that specified that imports could occur only along specific routes and through designated checkpoints. It stated the name of the owner, his father's name, and address. The identity of the animal was central to the receipt—size, color, and distinguishing marks such as a broken horn or short tail, which certified that the bull was produced for "auction." At the bottom of the receipt were endorsements of state employees and the company commander of the nearest border outpost under whose territorial jurisdiction the cattle consignments arrived. Often, while the endorsements were apparent in the portion of the receipt that was kept at the "animal corridor," the signatures on the counterfoil were missing. The *fang-fung*(ness) of the penalty receipt, transformed into an official document, distinguished it from other forms of local and informal taxes prevalent in many parts of Bangladesh and India.

Unlike traders in Assam who discreetly made phone calls, Rowmari's traders flashed mobile phones and openly discussed the cattle business at local markets as they awaited consignments. Monzur, a trader in his early thirties, escorted me to a series of cattle shelters regulated by local area committees and emphasized that their "tax" paid for these. The Bangladesh state conferred legitimacy to cattle traders as long as the cattle passed through designated "animal corridors." The cattle "tax," as traders in Rowmari reminded me, demarcated their honest actions from that of the corrupt Indian "smugglers." If Bangladesh's unilateral legalization and Bangladeshi border troops' facilitation of the cattle business reinforced the geographic separation between India and Bangladesh, the distinctions between Indians who managed "dubious deals" and Bangladeshis who were "tax" payers further divided the trading communities. Border solidarities were often complicated because even if cow smugglers valued the border as a resource, they also strongly guarded their national identities and invoked them in trade.

Shahjahan calmly discussed business with me in a border market. Like other Bangladeshi traders, he projected himself as an honest taxpayer. "I could actually sleep and still do these transactions; my counterparts in India do the entire running around! Only sometimes, I walk to the cattle market to sell the cattle, that too, only on days when buyers are not waiting at my residence," he remarked casually as he spoke about regular gains from trading in cattle. Shahjahan invested in the cattle trade once the "animal corridor" was set up in Charbhanga, a border *char* in Bangladesh. Shahjahan told me, "My business is very small scale—I am only doing *fang-fung*."

Fang-fung masked deceit with false modesty. Driven by high demand and profits and a state that quickly inserted cattle into the formal economy,

Rowmari's traders cheated their counterparts in Assam. Shahjahan and Monzur frequently switched alliances; sometimes, after placing an order with one trader in Assam, they moved on to another who could supply at cheaper prices. As suppliers who dealt with legally immovable commodities and the vagaries of a heavily patrolled border, Indian cattle traders were in no position to dictate the terms of trade. The massive bulls could not be hidden indefinitely. However, Bangladeshi traders were in a position to ignore the verbal contracts that guided cattle transactions, especially when consignments arrived late. Sometimes, money transfers simply failed, as Bangladeshi traders did not make them even after receiving the consignments.[20] Since Bangladeshi traders released money only after they received goods, they had the advantage of willful default.

In matters of default, they seldom handed them over to the police; money matters were resolved within the trading community. However, in retaliation, cattle traders in Assam often kidnapped visitors from Rowmari and its surrounding *chars*. Ironically, these abductions also inducted new members into cattle trading. Shanai, a Bangladeshi college student whom Indian traders had kidnapped in Assam against a ransom payment for a Bangladeshi cattle deal gone wrong, subsequently decided to trade in cattle. He quit studying in the local college and traveled to Assam's cattle markets, seeking to strike cattle deals, even as Indian traders warned Bangladeshis like him that their entry was "illegal" and demanded a ransom to recover losses. Cattle traders manipulated their nationalism for profits and recovered losses, while trade interests masqueraded as national ones.

Local and transborder arrangements that entail the movement of humped cattle signal a diffusion of *fang-fung* public authority in borderlands that include politicians such as Aladdin in India and traders such as Shahjahan in Bangladesh. In Bangladesh, local leaders assume the stature of all powerful *mastans* (gangsters) in ways that prolong and perpetuate their rule.[21] When local politicians control the movement of smuggled cattle over their territories and on the basis of political favors and profits, decide who can smuggle and who cannot, they further consolidate their power and prestige.[22] The well-regulated "animal corridors" in Bangladesh show how local musclemen and state agents intertwined to such an extent that it is impossible to discern their boundaries. Local power structures and transborder arrangements become even more relevant as the land itself is a shifting frontier. The sacred and material values ascribed to cows ensure that *fang-fung* materialize through local electoral politics in India and state mediation in Bangladesh.

Both entrench traders' dependence on state agents for border passage and legalization.

Cattle smuggling complicates the notion that India can prevent smuggling by building and patrolling a high-security border fence, along with exposing the fake legalization that Bangladesh has created by setting up animal corridors. The "efficacy of state power" that structures the material and social relationships in border zones, as Brenda Chalfin reminds us, coexists with high levels of state scrutiny in border regions.[23] The pronounced presence of Indian troops in Assam's Muslim inhabited border *char*s, the building of new infrastructures, radar, night cameras, and drone surveillance have added to *fang-fung* in trading by providing avenues through which national security can be selectively invoked for commercial gain. In Bangladesh, official statistics on cattle seizures further testified to *fang-fung*. These figures range from underreporting seized cattle to unilaterally shifting the goalposts through which cattle imports operate in Bangladesh.[24] Bangladesh officially states that smuggled Indian cattle harm Bangladeshi dairy framers and that they welcome India's attempts to control cattle smuggling. Yet, Bangladesh's border troops continue to operate the animal corridors.[25] In 2017, when cattle transport, slaughter, and beef consumption became controversial in India after lynching and violent mob attacks on Muslim cattle dealers, Bangladesh's border forces officially held that Indian cattle could only enter the country through designated animal corridors.[26] In 2019, the Border Guard Bangladesh officially registered the total number of cattle seized in the corridors to be 187,872 and tax collected to be U.S.$1,124,090.[27] These send mixed messages and push Bangladeshi cattle workers toward risky and unauthorized border crossings to meet the nation's demand for meat and leather.

In Bangladesh, state support for cattle smuggling transformed emaciated cows and bulls into sites of temporary care at the border. A spirit of pragmatism is afforded to weak animals who are valued for their meat. Here, local cattle committees fed the almost starving animals after their long haul from India. The committees had also allocated funds for making elevated structures along the main highways that would allow the smooth herding of cattle onto trucks for supplying to the rest of the country.

Fang-fung actions of state agents addressed questions of sustenance and wealth creation by differentially facilitating a constellation of transborder flows. Despite the deceit and treachery that accompany this trading, it is not regarded as a *du nombori bebsha*, implying smuggling and criminal activities or *haram* (sin). On the Indian side of the border, people who are not involved with smuggling refer to the constant flurry of Zebu cattle with mild annoyance. However, senior householders, teachers, and even priests, both Muslims and Hindus, also regarded the circulation of money, employment, and the attraction of laborers to the border as a critical crime control measure.

Bangladesh's demand for meat and leather ensures large numbers of unemployed village youth who have no recourse to a regular income get regular employment in the cattle sheds near the "animal corridors." On both sides of the border, people felt that cattle smuggling generated employment and prosperity; in fact, everyone that I spoke to believed that the business of cattle smuggling had reduced cattle rustling and theft. The prosperity that Zebu smuggling generates is obvious in new signs of affluence; interspersing the mostly mud-walled thatched houses are large concrete houses with glittering corrugated iron roofs. The constant purring of Enfield Bullet and Honda motorcycles on newly constructed border roads indicates that the border is "alive" and "running." The smooth running of the "animal corridors" in Bangladesh, Bangladeshi traders who presented themselves as tax-paying businessmen, and the well-functioning cattle sheds had convinced Rowmari's residents that Indian cattle arrived in Bangladesh as legal exports.

Riverine Losses

Let me return to Khairun's house in Rowmari, where I was able to piece together the ubiquity of the cattle along with the anxieties of separation that surrounded border lives in *chars*. I briefly recount an angry argument with Kamal, Khairun's husband. Kamal, who worked as a supervisor in a garment factory in Dhaka, traveled to Rowmari once every two months to see his wife Khairun and their children. From the time of his arrival with a big sack of biscuits and cakes, he attempted to compensate for his long absences. He often did so by trying to exert his authority and win every argument.

One winter afternoon, Kamal had returned from the Rowmari market where villagers were angry about delays in the cattle supplies from India. Rezaul and I had also returned from the market a little earlier. In tea stalls where village elders and traders convened regularly, the bilateral relationship with India was a common topic of discussion. People regarded cattle flows as a barometer of the neighborly friendship. When cattle supplies were smooth, Bangladeshi villagers interpreted it as a gesture of India's neighborly goodwill. From a bus that regularly plied between Rowmari and villages that connected the *chars* and the foothill villages, travelers often pointed toward the Garo Hills. "See the hills on your right—that is where all the cows come from . . . or else what will we eat? India sends them to us." As the bus traveled from the plains to the foothills, everyone gazed in admiration at the hovering Garo Hills, unaware that Indian traders had to secretly shelter cattle there.

Given that the religious festival of Eid—when huge bulls were in high demand at rich Dhaka houses for sacrificial slaughter—was only a few weeks away, villagers were concerned about delays in cattle supplies. I was aware that preparations for the celebration of India's Republic Day on 26 January had escalated border security in Assam and the Garo Hills, temporarily stalling cattle supplies. In Rowmari, however, villagers linked the delays to preexisting quarrels. Kamal attributed the vagaries of the cattle business to bilateral friendships and rivalries. He was adamant that unless Bangladesh was importing cattle legally, the twenty-six animal corridors could not operate so smoothly. He angrily questioned Rezaul and my intellectual credentials for not being able to distinguish legal from illegal trade. Additionally, he stated that he found my probing of Rowmari's historical connections—like the old Rowmari-Tura road—a complete waste of time. He compared my endeavors to his younger daughter Ameena's aspirations to study history in a college, a subject that he dismissed as useless. His judgments filled in the void of his long absence from the village where he could not secure a regular income. His loud assertions could not compensate for the pain that this distance invoked.

Kamal's beliefs on cattle trade made visible the force of time and cattle's ubiquity in this region. More than a century ago, British veterinary officers eagerly awaited large consignments of cattle with massive humps from northern and western British India to arrive in Rangpur, a district in British Bengal. Cattle were in high demand in Bengal's riverine regions where smaller domestically bred cattle were unsuited for plowing and pulling carts. Traders transported cows, bulls, and buffaloes on railways and roads to arrive in Rowmari's local markets and cattle fairs.[28] The historical sensibilities of Rowmari residents that first pointed me in the direction of the road recalled an important fragment of the cattle-related history of this region, through Ali's ox-cart route.

Cattle trade persisted despite anticolonial agitations and the harnessing of the sacred potential of the cow as a revered mother by Hindu nationalists in the late nineteenth and early twentieth centuries. In mobilizing the differential location of cows as alive and sacred for Hindus and sacrificial and food for Muslims, Hindu nationalists rallied against cow slaughter. The cow came to represent the universal "mother" and united an otherwise dispersed Hindu community, adding momentum to nationalist protests against the British colonial state.[29] They invested cows with divine qualities that signi-fied a "proto-nation," the animals came to embody a Hindu cosmology that also politically represented Hindu identity and nationality.[30] As religious and nationalist struggles intersected in the late nineteenth and early twentieth centuries, violent cow-centered riots broke out.[31]

With the Partition of India in August 1947, new legislation in India re-stricted and banned cow exports, as well as restricted slaughter and trans-port, even within the country. Indian export policies came to be framed to ensure that trade licenses for livestock exports were never issued.[32] The bor-der affirmed the divisive role of religions, leaving the century-old cattle trade route that had relied on railways and roadways in disrepair. Yet, every-day territoriality revolved around making a living out of locally bred cattle for trade, food, and leather, even along a border that divided people by reli-gion. For low-caste Hindu and Muslim border societies who made a living as butchers, tanners, and musicians, cattle and their products (beef and leather) were the only means of sustenance. Official correspondence be-tween India and East Pakistan in the 1950s records transborder cattle rus-tling, like rice wars, as far more than localized struggles to cope with uncertainties that the partition's confusing boundary lines had prompted in the devastated *chars*.[33] Angry exchanges of official letters between bureau-crats in the regions that joined Rowmari, Assam, and the Garo Hills departed from the sacredness that guided national discussions on cattle slaughter and exports in India.

Official records listed Hindu herdsmen, low-caste Hindu communities, and Garos as notorious cattle lifters, and deliberations on cattle raids and thefts remarkably escaped religious overtones. Accusatory letters between India and East Pakistan were not about hostile Hindu and Muslim states fighting with each other or representing the interests of opposing border communities whose pious sentiments were violated. Instead, they were about how states and border societies that were dependent upon cattle could gain control over the border and over what had now become a coveted animal. Cattle ranchers, herdsmen, traders, and tanners struggled to maintain their livelihood from cattle and cattle products, and they had to make sense of how a new border could be of use to them.[34] Transborder cattle raids and thefts made cattle more valuable in borderlands where the sacred had a long history of being mundane.

Cattle transactions received a boost in 1971, after Bangladesh emerged as an independent nation-state following a protracted liberation war. Retired Bangladeshi and Indian cattle traders recounted that cordial diplomatic relations had ensured an open border, where cattle exchange consistently occurred despite legal restrictions. Similarly, senior Indian and Bangladeshi border commanders recalled how cordial bilateral relations led to frequent visits at border villages. However, India did not legalize cattle exports. Transborder trading fluctuated between 1974 and 1979. After 1979, due to political instability in Bangladesh and the emergence of an anti-foreigner agitation in Assam, it became permanently unstable. Increasing political attention to unauthorized migration from Bangladesh to Assam dislocated cattle flows, and Indian border guards arrested and imprisoned the Bangladeshi traders who traveled to cattle markets that interspersed the low-lying border *chars*.

Construction work on India's new border fence with Bangladesh further disrupted prior routes. Yet rivers mediated a flourishing industry of cattle transactions; the Brahmaputra River enabled the passage of cattle across the waters even as India was barricading the land boundary. Rivers have reconfigured geopolitical spaces, productively expanding economic possibilities for villagers, border troops, and state agents. The rise of India's Hindu nationalist party, bans on cow slaughter and beef consumption, and the Hindu vigilante groups lynching those suspected of cow smuggling and trading have made the journeys of small-scale cattle traders and transporters such as Alibaba uncertain and extremely risky. In Rowmari, the majestic arrival of bulls, sometimes swimming across the river tied to a boat with a proxy Indian flag, instills cautious hope among locals that border fencing and bilateral trading will reestablish Rowmari's historic ties with Tura. Here, some villagers can only aspire to trade in cattle—but no one can afford to sacrifice them and consume beef.

Frustrated at our insistence that the cattle trade was all fang-fung, Kamal marched into the house from the courtyard where we were arguing. Taking out his harmonium, he broke into a melodious song. Singing disrespected the presence of his priestly father-in-law, Mahfuz, who regarded it as un-Islamic and who, unlike Kamal, could spend time with Khairun and the children. Kamal's soulful rendering of a river song soothed his anger and vented his desperation for paternal recognition. As riverine music seamlessly joined the world of love and loss, Ameena, upset with Kamal's insults, swept the courtyard.

Meanwhile, for Eid, Khairun had unilaterally decided to slaughter the mother goat. Her decision, as she later conveyed to me, was prompted by a combination of piety and prestige that the slaughter of bigger animals afforded. Naveeda Khan powerfully centers the entangled fates of humans and animals in Bangladesh's nebulous *chars*, where *char* dwellers consider farm animals such as cattle to be goods that can be sold and objects of ritual sacrifice. The poor *char* dwellers could rarely afford to eat or sacrifice these animals. Should they be given as a gift to God in sacrifice, people held that the animal had been saved from hardship.[35] Khairun emphatically stated that the sacrificial slaughter of the biggest animal would establish her actions as pious and result in blessings for her household and for those she distributed the meat to. However her piety was primarily driven by a sudden desire for status, which her husband's long absences had eroded. The lifeworlds of ordinary people inhabiting the borderland *chars* were situated in uneven relationships driven by complex notions of prestige and status relating to cattle traffic and migration.

In the days that followed, Rezaul gently questioned the value of his mother-in-law's decision, respectfully calling her attention to the cries of the baby goats who were still dependent upon their mother for milk. Ameena and I continued to experience their anguish; I woke up every night to their nocturnal cries and the frenzied rattling of their tails.

CHAPTER 4

Kinship, Identities, and "Jungle Passports"

As in Rowmari, in Assam's *chars* too, there was no escaping conversations on Tura. Located on the Garo Hills, in the neighboring state of Meghalaya, Tura was only twenty-six miles from the *char* in Assam where I resided. Although the India-Bangladesh border and internal administrative boundaries divided the *chars* from Tura's hills, the cattle route and the mobility of labor migrants, including undocumented Bangladeshi laborers, made this region continue to be a densely interconnected borderland. I traveled on the Rowmari-Tura road, both to follow these connections and to escape the *chars* during tension-ridden moments of smuggling. In the Tura district court, Garo farmers filed complaints against their neighbors for sheltering Zebu cattle in the hills, soon to be smuggled to Bangladesh. The sheltered animals, confused and hungry because of their long journey, had destroyed the crops. From Tura, I traveled and lived downhill, following the construction of India's new border fence with Bangladesh in the far-flung foothill villages in Meghalaya's border and, later across the border, in villages in the adjoining plains of Mymensingh and Netrokona districts of Bangladesh.

Subimol, a Garo youth who regularly transported me from the *chars* to the foothills in his auto-rickshaw during my initial fieldwork in 2007, often turned his wrist as if to check an imaginary watch. I soon recognized this as a signal that I should conclude my conversations because he was in a hurry. That afternoon, his gesture interrupted my teatime conversations with Shefali and Jonaki, elderly Garo Bangladeshi traders who arrived every morning in Meghalaya to sell "export-reject" clothes. Bangladesh is the world's second-highest exporter of ready-made garments.

The surplus of manufactured garments with minor defects traveled to Meghalaya via Shefali and Jonaki's border crossings from northern Mymensingh and Netrokona districts of Bangladesh.[1] It was the labor of primarily Bengali Muslim women who worked in the these factories that enabled the elderly Garo Christian women to arduously cross the heavily militarized India-Bangladesh border. As I mentioned in the previous chapter, Kamal, Khairun's husband, worked as a supervisor in one such factory near Dhaka. Shefali and Jonaki's journeys made the remote rural borderland a pathway for global circulation; clothes that were a rejected surplus in Bangladesh transformed into cheap essentials for border villagers in India.

Sitting at a tea stall in a *haat*, Shefali asserted that she traveled by a "jungle passport." This expression, commonly used by the Garo border villagers, indicates the use of forest camouflage to cross the border. Both Garo Indians and Bangladeshis used this expression to convey meaning to border crossings without passports and visas. The term circulated in conversations and was openly used and justified as a way to maintain cross-border kinship ties, subsistence trade, daily-wage labor, and even access to health services. "Jungle passport" journeys joined the intimate domain of Garo transborder matrilineal clans (the *Mahari*) and Christian religiosity with that of state rule, smuggling, and a non-indigenous world. Indian and Bangladeshi border forces, primarily Hindu and Muslim, respectively, mediated these spheres.

I ask why, in times of ever-escalating border patrolling and infrastructure building, was it not only possible but also necessary for Garo Christian Bangladeshi women to cross the border? In seeking to answer this question, I suggest that the relationship that Garo kinship and Christian religion has with nation building in Bangladesh has been fundamental to the working of the Garo borderland society and economy. "Jungle passport" journeys brought into sharp relief not only the long-term consequences of state violence and difference but also the importance of transborder affinities in structuring space, kinship, and livelihood. Shefali and Jonaki's moral claims to "jungle passports" as Garos legitimized not only their border crossings, but also their lives. Women traders, as Garos, Christians, and married women and mothers, claim the transborder land for trade and livelihood. They assert their rights to land in Meghalaya as Garo indigenous traders while not claiming land as political territory. Hence, the border forces do not regard them as threats.

Kinship and Conviviality

At borders, notions of community and belonging transcend national citizenship.[2] Here the values of reciprocity—as exchange, trust, dependency, and protection—have both political and spatial implications for mitigating un—equal relations. At the Northeast India–Bangladesh border, kinship, as an all-encompassing moral sphere, stretches and adapts to make life livable and collective beyond the perpetuation of indigenous lineage. Reciprocities that transcend kinship's prior boundaries offer new ways to situate political possibilities at the nation's margins without overdetermining the border's violent ability to impose difference and rule. These possibilities extend reciprocity's analytic potential by relocating questions of interdependence in social theory from the narrow confines of received exchanges among kin to include strangers.

Let me briefly recall a recent debate in anthropology surrounding the publication of Marshall Sahlins's "What Kinship Is." Sahlins posits that lo—cal configurations, whether by birth, social construction, or a combination of both, make people interdependent. He calls this the "mutuality of being," arguing that such connections linked bodies, feelings, and experiences and represented a "manifold of intersubjective participations." This mutuality not only applied to people connected by blood and descent, but, following Eduardo Viveiros de Castro's work in Amazonia, he argues that they also struc—tured people's relationships with strangers and animals. In extending notions of kinship beyond bloodlines and property toward a focus on the "mutality of being," Sahlins includes connections surrounding love, food, land, marriage, and adoption—thereby incorporating multiple ways of participating in collective life into kinship. Even more provocatively, he arrived at the con—clusion that "all means of constituting kinship are in essence the same."[3]

Among the debates inspired by Sahlins's engagement with kinship were criticisms of his failure to account for the pitfalls that undergird mutuality. Janet Carsten counters that although the "mutuality of being" privileges kin—ship's positive values, it eclipses the negative and disruptive qualities as well as the hierarchies and exclusions that informed it. Drawing on her work in Malaysia, Carsten argues that the inclusive qualities of Malay kinship do not override their coercive connotations.[4] Veena Das's work on the partition of the Indian subcontinent in August 1947 lucidly portrays kinship's disempow—ering qualities in the aftermath of a violent bordering process. In *Critical Events*, Das argues that, for women who were abducted during the partition, the values of purity and honor were central to the regulation of women's sexuality and identity within kin networks. For India, these values came to be closely linked to national policies and citizenship: India forcefully "recovered" abducted women who had set up families in Pakistan. Such processes rescaled kinship norms by legally codifying and transplanting them into the domain of the nation-state.[5] In analyzing the ruptures that re-ordered kinship, Das unbounds kinship from being enclosed within intimate spheres of affinity and control to establishing its connections and, by extension, its violence to the scale of the nation-state. She shows how India's nation building aggressively incorporated the gendered values surrounding kinship into the folds of national citizenship.

In relocating the outcomes of the partition as a series of border-making moments, I suggest that the partition's violence not only constrained but also politicized kinship by extending the implications of relationality at the nation's margin. The lives and journeys of Garo Christian Bangladeshi women traders are fundamental to our understanding of South Asia's postcolonial margins, where "partition effects" continue to shape people's identities and predicaments even today.[6] While nations impose borders to exert political efficacy, moral authority, and sovereignty over both territory and people, the lives and journeys across the Garo borderland offer new ways to consider how partitioned borders re-align the political and social prospects of collective life at the nation's edge. Due to the partition the Garo Maharis, or clans—central and extended units that cluster Garo lifeworlds through maternal lineages—came to be divided by the newly imposed border. Yet new transborder relationships and trading enabled the Garos to cope with state violence and land loss who came to first located in East Pakistan and after 1971, Bangladesh.[7]

Between 1940 and the late 1960s East Pakistan targeted Garo Christians in the urgency to establish national citizenship and weed out non-Muslim traitors. Despite this, everyday sociality between villagers who traveled to India to trade and their relationships with Indian border patrols was foundational for coping with the border's abrupt incursion, its ad hoc and confusing nature, and for mitigating the deep mistrust among communities and between villagers and troops. These acts of cooperation and support extended affinity and reciprocity to include the border police, who were initially rural recruits.[8] Indeed, as much as mistrust and hostility, convivial exchanges between villagers and newly appointed border police sustained relationships to shape collective life in the early postcolonial period.

Today, convivial exchanges between Garo Christian Bangladeshi women traders and the mostly Hindu Indian border troops provide new ways to think about the importance of conviviality in structuring belonging amid difference. For more than a decade, scholars have foregrounded conviviality as transience, translation, negotiation, and protection to deepen their engagement with the human condition. In exploring the various ways in which people come together and the changing dynamics that inform diversity and difference, scholars have shown that reciprocal exchanges as well as conflicts inform collective life.[9] Two interrelated lines of enquiry that I find especially valuable emphasize conviviality's enduring and tension-ridden qualities. Paul Gilroy and Ash Amin famously situate conviviality as a "social pattern" and "enduring social form," respectively, that emerges as urban groups, despite racial and cultural differences, live in close proximity. Conviviality is central to the fabric of urban life, as it facilitates access to collective resources amid fields of anonymous difference.[10]

However, the relationships that reciprocity has with freedom and collective life are equally imbricated in power. These make conviviality fraught with frictions; convivial relations also exemplify the precariousness of living together with urban exclusion and inequality.[11] In fact, exchanges in cities prone to violence make people's quest for protection urgent and dependent upon establishing congenial exchanges across differences.[12] Here, not only does the other side of conviviality show its face, but reciprocity also becomes essential for survival and sustenance. The dynamics of conviviality that support Garo Bangladeshi women's transborder trading shift attention away from the strivings of urban cosmopolitanism and tolerance. Instead, "jungle passports" depart from both a narrow reading of how urban conviviality provides a social glue amid diversity and inequality or situate reciprocity to query the limits of kinship and religion. The value of exploring conviviality at the nation's margin lies in the border's capacity to facilitate meaningful exchanges—no matter how uneven—across what are imagined as socially and politically distinct, self-contained spheres. The Northeast India–Bangladesh border is a productive location to investigate how kinship, as an all-encompassing moral sphere (as Sahlins underscores), stretches and adapts to make life livable and collective in remote rural regions.

The flourishing of Christianity among the Garos on both sides of the border, Bangladesh's nation building and emergence as a global exporter of garments, and India's border development policies in Meghalaya, with special focus on developing infrastructure in remote Garo villages, have gendered "jungle passport" journeys. While exacting gendered costs and maternal burdens, these journeys fostered affinities and generated a sense of moral well-being that enabled the borderland Garos to cope with political turmoil and scarcities. Garo Bangladeshi women's transborder ties and the relationships of trust and conviviality that they have established with Indian border troops have facilitated the circulation of garments and household goods that were first received as Christian religious aid and later purchased as export surplus to be sold across the border. Before I elaborate further, let me describe an incident during one of my journeys with Subimol that demonstrates how kinship and border militarization intrinsically gendered transborder livelihoods.

Reciprocities Among the Mahari and Beyond

In August 2007, Subimol and I stopped for tea near a border *haat* in Meghalaya. Shefali and Jonaki, the elderly Bangladeshi traders whom I was meeting for the first time that day, asked me for a ride to the foothill village where I resided in Meghalaya. Exhausted from long hours of walking and carrying two big sacks of garments, they anxiously waited for a bus that had been indefinitely delayed. From the village where I resided, Shefali and Jonaki would still have to walk half a mile to cross the border and another mile to reach their village in Bangladesh.

Seeing them enter his auto-rickshaw with their big sacks, Subimol quickly jumped out of the driver's seat. I too jumped out and followed him. We stood under a tree at a distance as he loudly argued with me, insisting that offering a lift to traders, even if they were Garos and women, would compromise our safety. Subimol was as concerned about my safety, as a woman researcher, as his own. He was an undocumented Garo Bangladeshi migrant in his early twenties who had resettled in Meghalaya. He had only recently procured an Indian voter identity card. His maternal uncle, who had earlier resettled in India provided him with identity documents. Subimol was worried that Shefali and Jonaki, who had traveled from Mymensingh, might identify him as a Bangladeshi Garo. After a heated exchange during which I finally convinced him that they would not compromise our safety, he started his auto-rickshaw.

Much to my surprise, at the conclusion of our journey, Subimol jumped out of the vehicle, folded his hands, and bowed his head in respect. He apologized to Shefali. From our conversations during the journey, he had realized that Shefali belonged to his clan, the Retchil *Mahari*. Filled with remorse for disrespecting an elder from his kin group who lived only a few villages away from where he had lived as a child in Mymensingh, Subimol solemnly requested her forgiveness. Shefali would recall Subimol's respectful gestures toward her on many occasions, even as she reminded me about her exhaustion from the physical demands of transborder trading. Our conversations would invariably begin and end with the *Mahari* as she emphasized her matrilineal clan's importance in her life, whether in helping to build new economic opportunities, in offering credit or a place to rest near the border after a tiring day.

Along the foothill borderland, I rarely had a conversation without Garo families and Garo Christian priests invoking the *Mahari*. The Garo extended kin group—the *Mahari*—also includes all men and women who have married into the clans. Highlighting the importance of the *Mahari* in Garo collective life, a Catholic priest in Bangladesh explained, "No matter what the difficulties are and how tough the border is, the Garos will cross borders to see their families and relatives and for making a living. No fence can stop the Garos from moving." The Garo women who organized the biannual daylong feasts along the foothill borderland affirmed his views. They took their role of bringing together their transborder clan very seriously: they regarded it as laying the moral foundations of their collective life. On these occasions, Garo Bangladeshi women could be seen dragging goats and carrying live poultry and vegetables to contribute to the communal kitchen on the Indian side. During *Mahari* meetings and feasts in border villages, I found Indian and Bangladeshi soldiers sitting and casually watching over the proceedings as large gatherings near the international boundary demanded their supervision. Although the families offered them tea and meals, the troops declined as official rules prohibited them.

In fact, it was the *Mahari* association leaders—who were always women—who enabled transborder trade to flourish by establishing meaningful relationships with the outposts where Indian and Bangladeshi troops resided. They regularly lent furniture, crockery, and cutlery for official meetings at the border outposts, enabling the border forces of India and Bangladesh to function in remote rural locations with limited supplies. Structurally combining dwellings with military preparedness and fortress-like functions, the outposts defined access to the border. They were sites of rest and collective worship, with temples (in India) and mosques (in Bangladesh), and equipped

Figures 16. A border outpost in Meghalaya, Northeast India. The graffiti on the wall says, "Long live Mother India" (translated from Hindi). (Photograph: author)

with kitchens. Villagers were well aware of the hierarchies within the outposts and how senior authorities had to be appeased, and they even helped the troops stationed in their villages make favorable impressions on their seniors. Their relationships with the outposts in turn facilitated their clan members' travel by "jungle passports" for trading, logging, and maintaining kinship and religious ties. These exchanges ensured regular visits of Bangladeshi Garo villagers to collect and trade in wood—an important commodity for fuel and furniture that was abundantly available on the Indian side but rare in Bangladesh.

In explicit recognition of local political authority and respect for Garo indigenous hierarchies, Indian border commanders visited Garo *nokmas* (village headmen) and elders in Meghalaya, while Bangladeshi commanders paid visits to Christian priests in Mymensingh and Netrokona. Indian and Bangladeshi commanders persuaded the Garo *nokmas* and priests to keep a

Figure 17. A border market in Meghalaya, Northeast India. (Photograph: author)

watch over who arrived and left border villages. The commanders routinely asked village elders and priests to see that the villagers followed their instructions, especially on days when their senior officials visited. In this sparsely populated zone, Indian and Bangladeshi troops were dependent on the cooperation of border communities to ensure that things remained calm and peaceful at the international boundary. New battalions were inducted into these old patterns of mobility, facilitating "jungle passport" journeys.

Indian and Bangladeshi commanders readily arranged medical transport for the villagers, offering their patrol jeeps to take critical patients to hospitals. Bangladeshi and Indian troops sat in the outer courtyards of Garo houses while patrolling. Houses with large courtyards even accommodated the tractors that flattened the unruly landscape for India's border fence construction. Garo Catholic priests were in regular contact with the Bangladeshi outposts, ensuring that commanders were tolerant toward religious travel. When Bangladeshi border troops detained and tortured Garo youth for unauthorized travel to Meghalaya to work as coal miners, priests negotiated their release, especially during their return home for Christmas.

While official mandates prevented India and Bangladesh's border forces from establishing personal relationships with civilians and routinely transferred them, the troops who were without their families and had only irregular telephone contact with them eagerly sought out villagers for conversations.[13] Indian troops had even established ties of friendship and romantic love that resulted in marriages with Garo women in Meghalaya's foothills. The young Indian troops who facilitated Bangladeshi women's journeys not only adapted to the requirements of transborder trade and religiosity but also benefited from these exchanges to mitigate their geographic and social isolation. The relationships of trust and dependency between troops and traders, which redeemed the isolation of the border forces, transformed the border into a governable space.[14] The troops regulated Bangladeshi Garo women's border crossings by warning them in advance when higher officials would be visiting—and therefore when border passages would be restricted. Since secrecy defined these transborder arrangements, camp commanders withheld their details from senior visiting officials. After the official visits concluded, border crossings resumed.

The value of the relationships that underpin "jungle passport" journeys extend far beyond trading transactions. Rather than being instrumental, fleeting, or superficially transactional, reciprocity structured dependencies that were essential to social and moral life in a rural borderland. Scholarship on smuggling situates women traders as powerful economic actors who mobilize village and ethnic ties to make a living from volatile borders. Women traders skillfully adapt to new regulations and trade routes as they adeptly negotiate passage with border troops.[15] Local communities and states actively create and maintain borders, in ways that facilitate women's transborder mobility for smuggling and trade without disrupting preexisting cultural norms.[16] The associations that Garo clan leaders and Christian priests have with border commanders in outposts scaffolded the broader set of exchanges that make reciprocity intrinsically political and the border fluid. Despite national mandates that demand a clear division between military and civilian spaces and restrict contact, dependencies straddled demarcated sites. Such convivial exchanges that ensure Garo women's trading did not involve bribery, despite the lack of official documents. Reciprocity was integral to both security and affinity. Indian border troops sporadically check their bags and baskets, but they do not prevent Garo women from crossing the border for trade—even as both states continue to escalate national security at the border. Indian border troops who facilitate "jungle passport" journeys are thus an integral part of the borderland society.

Developing the Border

On *haat* days, Meghalaya's far flung border villages magically transformed into bustling hubs. Indian border troops walked in and out of the *haats* with their wireless radios. Indian camp commanders negotiated with grocery stores for supplies. Border markets had temporary stalls and newly constructed permanent shops. The makeshift stalls, constructed from plastic sheets and bamboo poles, indicate the persistence of informal trade along the Garo borderland. Inside the *haats*, Indian and Bangladeshi subsistence traders squatted in designated places, spreading out their merchandise. T-shirts with American flags, colorful leggings, striped brassieres, woven stoles, ornate melamine crockery, vegetables, and soaps manufactured in Bangladesh lay next to piles of ginger, tubers, and oranges grown in Meghalaya. As foreigners, Bangladeshi traders were not allowed to rent market stalls. They either supplied items manufactured in Bangladesh to Indian retailers or squatted in designated areas. The traders rotated between various border markets located within a few miles of each other and scattered on both sides of the international boundary. Markets took place twice a week on specific days and resulted in transborder trading and associated activities for a whole week.[17] Since Indian Garo traders owned and rented out shops at border markets in Meghalaya, they seldom traveled to Bangladesh to procure goods. However, similar to Bangladeshi Garos, Indian Garos frequently traveled to Bangladesh for shopping and to maintain kinship ties.

The permanent shops in Meghalaya's border markets are an outcome of the Indian government's schemes for border development; these investments are intended to improve infrastructural connectivity and generate employment in regions close to the border.[18] Sanjib Baruah and Bengt Karlsson have incisively shown how India's development funding functions as a device of control and governance in Northeast India. Baruah avers that as extensions of India's military apparatus, these initiatives seek to contain insurgency and bring dissident regions and people within the fold of the Indian nation. India's development programs "nationalize space" in frontier locations in ways that impose a sense of ornamental federalism rather than generate an even distribution of power and resources.[19] Karlsson underscores that despite development funding, people continue to experience a lack of development and express feelings of resentment as the intended schemes benefit only a small section of society in Meghalaya.[20] Widespread corruption and mismanagement of infrastructural projects in the Garo Hills continue to ensure that even newly constructed roads were in varying degrees of disrepair while the contractors built concrete extensions to their houses.

Meghalaya's border markets were far more than just the product of India's center-state federal relations that sought to impose specific forms of governance and border rule. India's developmental logic and its disciplining of frontier populations, as well as Bangladesh's selective control over the mobilities of the Garos, gendered border crossings in unanticipated ways. Jonaki and Shefali's "jungle passport" journeys productively contributed to creating new markets for goods in Meghalaya; the clothes that they sold were half the price and of greater variety than the ones that arrived from the district headquarters in Tura. Garo Bangladeshi traders asserted that when Garo Indian traders labeled them as unauthorized Bangladeshi border crossers in order to drive down the prices of garments, Shefali and others defended their presence in Meghalaya on the basis of their Garo identity. They justified their border crossings by reiterating their *Mahari*'s presence in Meghalaya, as well as by emphatically stating that the Indian border forces facilitated their journeys.

In Meghalaya, as in the rest of India, the stereotype of the Bangladeshi "infiltrator and terrorist" is primarily Muslim and male. In that sense, Garo women are seen as less suspicious. Like the neighboring state of Assam, Meghalaya's concerns about Bangladeshi "infiltration" have led to the setting up of forty-seven "infiltration checkpoints" manned by the police.[21] At the same time, the resettlement of non-indigenous societies in Meghalaya has also generated violent interethnic conflicts.[22] Since 2009, the Garo National Liberation Army's demands for the creation of sovereign Garoland has led to greater surveillance of *haats*. Still, in recognition of the remoteness of foothill villages from the administrative centers, Meghalaya has consistently demanded that traders from Bangladesh be allowed to travel to border markets without passports. India and Bangladesh therefore sanctioned four bilaterally funded border markets along the Meghalaya-Bangladesh border in 2011 and 2019, where traders can officially travel without passports and trade less than U.S.$50 per day duty free.[23] However, as Shefali and Sorola's journeys show, transborder trading is widespread.

"Life is tough," Sorola mused, as cross-border trading entails walking long distances. A Bangladeshi Garo trader in her thirties, she occasionally wiped her child's sweaty forehead as the afternoon sun peeped in through the roofs of the grocery shops. However, the need for income was always there, with some days being better than others. Normally, Sorola and other traders earn U.S.$1 to $3 per day, and earnings increase during the festival seasons. Because subsistence traders are neither discouraged nor prohibited to travel, when questioned about their passage from Bangladesh to India women look surprised—believing that travel would *always* be allowed—as they were not smugglers. By reiterating that they were not smugglers, small-scale traders situated themselves within the moral compass of subsistence travel by "jungle passports."

Bangladeshi Garo women traders asserted, "We are *Banglar manush*" to morally justify their presence in Meghalaya. While the Bengali expression *Banglar manush* generally implies people who belong to Bangladesh, along the foothill borderlands, the invocation of this expression is specific to a sense of shared Garo ethnicity and claims to transborder geographies and resources. Rather than establish a difference between Bangladeshi and Indian Garos, women traders mobilized their identity as *Banglar manush* and their *Mahari* connections as moral sanctions to cross the border. It is this sense of malleability that Janet Sturgeon elucidates in her writings about the lifeworlds of Akha farmers who live along the Thailand-China border. The Akha farmers negotiate a complex landscape and environment to secure their livelihood, responding to emergencies and state extractions to produce and profit from markets. She designates the Akha's ability to adjust and readjust to state plans and local needs, as well as to respond to the possibilities that the border affords, as "landscape plasticity." Combined spatial and temporal knowledge, "landscape plasticity" gives the Akha resilience both in negotiations with states and in the extension of land use patterns across the border.[24] Sara Shneiderman has shown how the members of Central Himalayan societies who lead transnational lives as traders between Nepal and India simultaneously locate their political claim making in multiple nation-states while remaining culturally committed to the "ungoverned" aspects of their identities. She argues that performing identities are fundamental for securing ethnic recognition and the conditions needed for cultural practices to flourish.[25] For Garo Bangladeshi women traders, the border that fragments their clans and families simultaneously makes their claims to shared geographies and livelihoods legitimate on the basis of their Garo *adibashi* identity. Their "jungle passport" journeys revolve around making a living from the borderland; Garo women traders reiterate a sense of sameness rather than difference from

Meghalaya's Garos. Their assertions are historically grounded in the ad hoc ways the border has separated shared lands and lineages.

The expression *"Banglar manush"* held vastly different connotations for Bangladeshi Garo men and youth. In Bangladesh, "going to India" is perceived as a "crime," especially for Garo youth, whom both India and Bangladesh arrest and torture for crossing the border without authorization. Bangladeshi and Indian troops perceive their presence as threatening to national security because of the goods they are suspected of trading in, alcohol and arms. To save money for higher education and move to urban centers in Bangladesh, poor Garo youth are compelled to engage in dangerous border crossings and take up low-skilled labor in Meghalaya.[26] When intercepted by border troops, Bangladeshi Garo coal miners working in India face harassment and torture. The troops often confiscate their earnings. The border outposts impose conditions on Garo Bangladeshi men's regular border crossings for daily wage work: Bangladeshi laborers are required to purchase their "jungle passport" journeys by working one day a week without wages in Indian border outposts in physically demanding tasks, such as clearing thickets, loading and unloading heavy goods, and cleaning the outpost compounds. On the way back to Bangladesh, they collect fuel wood from the forests to give to the Bangladeshi outposts as tribute. The Indian troops reward them with a week's passage.[27]

For Subimol, *Banglar manush* held a different meaning. Every time we stood near a police infiltration checkpoint in front of a relatively large border market in the foothills, I sensed his anxiety. While Shefali and Jonaki would stand right next to the checkpoint without any fear or inhibition about being identified, Subimol would hide in the shadows. One afternoon we all watched a policeman standing outside an infiltration checkpoint that had a mandate to identify unauthorized Bangladeshis. The policeman in charge had chained a captured monkey and was making it dance to the tunes playing on his radio. His actions entertained the small crowd that had gathered near the *haat*. Although Subimol had the support and backing of his maternal uncle, this did not diminish his concerns that the police would either falsely classify him as a Garo dissident or deport him as an unauthorized Bangladeshi. Unlike Subimol, Shefali, Jonaki, and other women traders did not leave their homesteads to relocate to Meghalaya. As Garo women, their presence seemed far less suspicious both to the policemen at the checkpoint and to Indian troops, who did not suspect that elderly married women would resettle in India. Still, Garo women's invocation that they were *"Banglar manush"* had a deep sense of irony because their transborder journeys attested to their marginal position in Bangladesh in ways that I explain subsequently.

Traversing Nations

Bangladeshi Garo traders conveyed a sense of timelessness, claiming that border trade was "eternal"a turn of phrase that reflects the connections between the Garo Hills, the foothills, and the adjoining plains. "Jungle passport" journeys derived legitimacy from this sense of shared history and Christian religiosity where, despite the construction of new barriers, moving from one part of the borderland to another is not seen as transgressive by either nation-states or the Christian communities. The Garo borderland's historical and productive capacity shows the fluidity of ethnicity beyond the marking of two distinct ethnic categories among the Garos in Mymensingh and Meghalaya. In fact, as anthropologists have shown, in Northeast India fluid and multiple identities are widely prevalent. Here people draw a sense of identity from their village, lineage, clan, religion, and religious denomination, as well as broader ethnic classifications.[28] Rather than being fixed and static, people's attachments and self-identifications as well as their wider social affirmations across scales enable them to shift from one identity to another.[29] Even people's demands from nation-states in South Asia, as David Gellner, avers is diverse. For some border societies, these rest on an acknowledgment of the nation-state along with demands for special recognition and protection from it, while others resist the pressures of modern governmentality.[30]

In the early postcolonial period, India and East Pakistan's contrasting policies on indigeneity rearranged kinship in distinct ways on either side of the Garo foothill border. India followed a complex interventionist policy in Northeast India. After 1947, autonomous district councils were entrusted with matters relating to land in the Garo Hills with the intention of protecting customary practices such as safeguarding clan landholdings by placing land in the custody of the *nokma*.[31] Affirmative action and supporting customary practices reinforced the primitiveness of the Garos as a scheduled tribe, but the implications of maintaining collective and customary life were far more political and spatial along the Garo foothills and plains. East Pakistan, on the other hand, removed protectionist policies in northern Mymensingh and other regions and labeled the Garos as traitors. In Mymensingh, the

Garos lived in proximity to other groups whom the East Pakistan government regarded as communist revolutionaries. As I have shown in Chapter 2, when the Garos crossed the border into India to meet their families
and trade in markets, East Pakistani authorities suspected them to be communist spies with pro-India loyalties.

The serpentine border, which cut across this sparsely populated landscape,
however, ensured that villagers and troops were enjoined in relationships of
dependency. Through the 1950s, the border police, who were rural recruits
themselves, and villagers formed complex alliances to gain control over land,
as well as to survive an isolated region. Despite their suspicion of border societies, outposts were rarely cut off from villages. Agrarian territorialities
shaded into nation building. The police relied on Garo villagers; they set about
collectively producing the border with them. Despite official claims to the
contrary, the border police used transborder kinship ties for state espionage.
India and East Pakistan encouraged villagers to act in the interests of the
state, either through formal employment or by assisting the police, with
whom they shared ethnic and religious affinities. These further complicated
territorial struggles. State dependencies on villagers, especially the Garos,
whom India and East Pakistan classified as "scheduled tribes" and "aboriginals," made the border central in regulating collective life. East Pakistan vac-
illated between regarding the Garos as villagers who could be entrusted
with guarding the border while persecuting them as Christian infidels. While
dependency and suspicions politicized kinship, its expanded affective horizons came to include troops and transborder spaces.

A series of events in 1964 disrupted the balance of authority between East
Pakistani state agents and Mymensingh's Garo villagers. That year, in response to riots in India over the disappearance of a holy relic from a mosque
in Kashmir and new legislation that deported Muslims from India as foreigners, East Pakistan unleashed a reign of terror, dispossessing the Garo Christians. When East Pakistan's persecution of the Garos resulted in dispossession
of their lands and threats of forced conversion to Islam—events that I have
elaborated on in Chapter 2—Garo women's border crossings came under
scrutiny. Garo elders and village headmen protested against women's cross-
border travel to markets, fearing that Muslim East Pakistani border troops
would assault and abduct them at the border. Village elders held that, in
response to the land lost from displacement due to the resettlement of Bengali Muslim refugees in their lands, land and property inherited through
women and the norms of matrilineal kinship had to be carefully protected.

Intermarriage between Garo Christian women and Bengali Muslim men who had resettled in the area further escalated the anxieties surrounding land loss and kinship boundaries. Youth groups monitored the movement of Garo women near the border. As a senior Garo Catholic priest who had lived through those turbulent times, explained, these trade routes were rumored to be used for contraband and arms. Villagers feared that the allure of money and interactions with non-Garos would morally corrupt Garo women. As a consequence, women's border crossings for trade were temporarily stalled. While some families left for India in fear and relocated there as refugees, encouraged by the special status that the Garos had as "scheduled tribes," village elders closely guarded the moral boundaries of kinship for those who remained behind. It did so in ways that circumscribed it within the boundaries of the very nation that was perpetrating violence against them.

In 1971, Bangladesh emerged as an independent nation-state after its Liberation War with Pakistan. There was remarkable reversal in border dynamics. Border troops continued to guard the international boundary, but cordial diplomatic relations between Bangladesh and India made the border a fluid, convivial space. Border villages were more open to transborder visits without passports, while traders and families could easily cross from one state to the other.

Meanwhile, in a significant development, the conclusion of the 1971 war also prompted the arrival of goods via Christian missionary aid, mainly in the form of household subsistence items. The Christian missions in greater Mymensingh provided relief goods to enable their laity to cope with the war's devastating aftereffects. The lives and journeys of the women traders closely followed the growth of Christianity among the Garos of Bangladesh. During the time that I resided with Shefali in Mymensingh, she recounted how Christian missions had wide-ranging influence in mitigating state violence directed at the Garos. The Christian aid and charity that facilitated transborder trading provided Garo women with the means of coping with state repression and scarcity. As Christian Garo households in Bangladesh received more relief items such as clothes, sheets, and warm blankets than they required—and, in some instances, even when they had just what they needed—Garo women decided to sell them to members of their *Maharis* situated just across the border in India. By now, they were officially Bangladeshi citizens, and their religious identity as deserving Christians in postwar Bangladesh and their transborder location as Garos with families and kin in India ensured the circulation of goods. The war, ironically through land loss, and religious aid reversed the status of immobility that had prevented Garo women from crossing the border in the 1960s.

Shefali recollected the caution with which they had proceeded to trade in charity items, almost whispering the details to me. Initially, they took a few blankets and warm clothes to their clan members' houses across the border to see if they would be interested in purchasing them. They sold them very cheap, keeping profit margins very low. Since these goods were part of a charitable surplus that Garo Christian households had received, the women were morally inclined to keep profits at a minimum. While their Christian identity meant they received the goods in the first place, their identities as Garos enabled them to carefully transform charitable items into tradable goods. The inherent domesticity of the goods encouraged the women to mobilize transborder women kin to supply them to local markets. Women's actions—connected through lineages across the border—gradually transformed Christian aid from a charitable subsistence to coveted household products that circulated beyond Christian families. The ambiguity of being a Garo and having members of their kin already present in the Garo Hills facilitated assimilation as well as employment in the new state of Meghalaya, which was carved out of the state of Assam in 1972. If Garo women's location as peripheral border subjects implied that sustenance and livelihood in the villages would increasingly rely on their "jungle passports" journeys, it also ensured that the border and the indigenous zone that lay beyond in India, rather than the nation itself, was necessary for surviving both state repression and neglect.

The role of Garo women as economic actors amid state repression and nation building has not figured in the rich feminist historiography that has shown the gendering of nationalism in Bangladesh.[32] Their location as ethnic minorities in Bangladesh, as well as their contribution as mobile traders, fell outside the nationalist notions of both honor and shame that Bangladesh had ascribed to Bengali women. Their kinship structures and distinctiveness that made them ethnic minorities in Bangladesh and "tribes" in India established them as worthy subjects of anthropology but not historiography that takes gender as its point of departure. Bangladeshi border forces still put more effort into preventing Muslim Bengali women from crossing over to India. For instance, when women, especially young Muslim women, engaged in conversations with members of the Indian Border Security Forces (BSF), they were reprimanded by the Border Guard Bangladesh (BGB). Even seemingly casual conversations with Indian border forces were seen as violating national and religious norms and local norms of honor, resulting in warnings laced with tones of reprimand and protection. Shefali, on the other hand, stated that the BGB easily relinquished their responsibility toward the Garo Christian women traders, making it clear that the responsibility for their travel rested with them. They emphasized that Bangladesh would "do nothing" for them should they be caught or ill-treated by the Indian border officers. Bangladeshi border troops pointed in the direction of India's new border fence to indicate that travel to another country without a passport and trade permit was not legal.

Since Bangladesh continued to settle landless Bengali Muslims on Garo lands in the 1970s, some foothill Garo families relocated to India while others continued to rely on the border for sustenance. In the mid-1970s, the Garo foothill border zone emerged as a site of armed rebellion following the assassination of Bangladesh's prime minister, Mujibur Rahman, and the military coup in Bangladesh. The Kader Bahini, named after their founder, Kader Siddiqi (a freedom fighter in the 1971 Bangladesh war of independence), resisted the imposition of military rule in Bangladesh. They waged a prolonged armed struggle against the Bangladeshi border troops (Bangladesh Rifles). The Indian Border Security Forces (BSF) aided the Kader Bahini's forays from the southern and western Garo Hills by providing arms and sheltering the rebels in the Garo Hills. Garo border villagers recounted how gunfire, hunger, and terror dominated their lives; the Bahini conscripted Garo youth. Rivers and streams that had functioned as fluid zones of connection between India and Bangladesh transformed into burial grounds. In the exchange of gunfire between troops and rebels, the slain bodies of Garo youth were dumped in the river. They recalled how both the Kader Bahini's young fighters and the Bangladeshi border forces looted them to survive and dominate a remote region. The protracted nature of the conflict and India's role in aiding the Bangladeshi rebels further militarized this zone.

Violently displaced and fearing for their lives, Mymensingh's Garo youth whose families were made destitute by the rebellion arrived as exiles in India. Although issues of land alienation and unauthorized Bangladeshi migration to states in Northeast India strained diplomatic ties between India and Bangladesh, the Meghalaya-Mymensingh borderland remained a negotiated space. Christian village headmen in Meghalaya enabled Garo Bangladeshis to acquire homestead land and Indian citizenship. Under India's affirmative action policies, Garo youth acquired jobs as schoolteachers, police, and forests guards. Garo women who had lost land in Mymensingh played a central role in regaining homestead land for their family, even purchasing agricultural land in Meghalaya. Although larger political transformations had shattered their lives, they soon acquired legitimacy as Garo Christians and Indian citizens in Meghalaya while maintaining transborder relationships. When the Kader Bahini rebellion ended in 1977, young Garo men were absorbed into the Bangladesh Rifles, adding to the material prosperity of the border belt. As Ellen Bal recalls, this was Garo men's first opportunity to formally participate in nation building as Bangladeshi citizens.[33] Even historically, border militarization and the border's porosity had gendered repercussions, in this instance offering recognition to Garo men.

Exchanging Surplus

In the 1980s, the economic reforms funded by the World Bank and the International Monetary Fund inter alia, led to Bangladesh's emergence as a global exporter of manufactured garments and created new items for transborder trade. The garment factories established in Dhaka, as well as the export-processing zones outside Dhaka and in Chittagong, expanded the ready-made garment manufacturing sector eleven fold from early 1983–1984 to 2016–2017, employing four million people and comprising 81.4 percent of Bangladesh's total export earnings in 2018.[34] The majority of the production is geared toward low-cost casual wear products, and 80 percent of the factory workers are women.[35] Industrial production relies on the intensive and repetitive labor of female workers who are supervised by men such as Kamal.[36] The laborious work of young Muslim women from rural areas in Dhaka's factories has enabled Bangladesh to attain global recognition as a leading garments exporter. This has also led to the simultaneous redistribution of export surpluses within and beyond Bangladesh's land borders.

The wide-ranging availability of export-rejected garments ensured that the Garo Bangladeshi women who regularly crossed the border would start trading in garments. In Mymensingh, Bangladesh, I accompanied Shefali on her procurement trips to a wholesale market. She scrutinized each garment carefully, opening and turning them inside out. Over the next hour, she minutely checked for visible defects in the T-shirts and trousers. As export surplus products, the garments were unbranded and only labeled with blue and red flags. At home, Shefali rearranged the big consignment of T-shirts by neatly compressing them into huge plastic bags. In between, she attended to her small vegetable garden. Her daughter Lily and grandson resided with her. Lily, who had earlier worked as a housekeeper in an elite expatriate household in Dhaka, where Christian Garos are preferred, had returned to the village as soon as her husband was employed in a "good job" by a foreign embassy. A Christian mission had provided Lily's husband with schooling, including teaching him the English language. These factors had enabled him to gain employment in Dhaka. Her husband was a security officer, who manned the gates. Lily's presence and her subsequent motherhood, which prevented her from working in Dhaka, finally relieved Shefali of the domestic chores that she had performed for many years alongside transborder trading. Lily insisted that Shefali did not need to trade anymore, but Shefali was determined to continue. Lily's discouragement was partly because Shefali was aging and partly because her husband disapproved.

At a Christian nongovernmental organization (NGO) where Shefali and I ate lunch one afternoon, a dining hall staff echoed Lily's concerns. As he served us lunch, he insisted that despite all of the hardships, their family had achieved "status" in the village since her son-in-law obtained stable employment. He conveyed to Shefali that her transborder trading had compromised her son-in-law's social position in the village. Although he resided in the village for only short periods of time, Shefali's long standing profession, which had lasted thirty-five years, was compromising his newly gained status. Shefali's family and other villagers not surprisingly discounted her labor and entrepreneurship, while living off her income.

Dina Siddiqui's powerful analysis of Dhaka's export-oriented garment factories, in which a large labor force of mostly rural women stitched garments, reveals the complex contours of domesticity and factory work. In her reading of the relationship that the women have to the machines and to the conditions of laboring under male supervisors, Siddiqui argues that despite mechanization, the garment factories exude an atmosphere of a "highly policed, mechanised domesticity." She shows how both the nature of the products—that is, fabrics that surround women, who then transform them into garments—and the gendered aura of the sewing machines that are foundational to the production process make women's relationships to the machines ambivalent.[37] The gendered and distributive power of garments transcends the confines of the factory floors. The substance of the commodity—surplus garments—and their everyday use as clothes contributed to their moral value, making travel by "jungle passports" legitimate. As rejected and surplus garments became rural transborder essentials, the border

crossings they demanded seeped into familial relationships. Trading reinforced Garo women's maternal and kinship authority over transborder
geographies while simultaneously escalating their domestic burdens. Jonaki
lived through protracted uncertainties while coping with widowhood, while
Shefali dealt with intermittent periods of being a single parent until her husband finally left her. Both women singlehandedly raised their children while
making a living from transborder trade.

Banter at Borders

By reiterating that they were not smugglers, small-scale women traders situated themselves within the moral ambit afforded by their ethnicity to travel
by "jungle passports." Even as Garo Christian villagers guarded the commercial boundaries of "jungle passport" travel by imposing obligations on traders to keep quantities at subsistence levels, market forces overrode these
compulsions. Traders reiterated that poverty was the defining moral condition justifying their journeys, even as I traveled with them to wholesale markets in Bangladesh where they purchased bulk goods that required more
than modest investments. Many traders could hardly be called poor, but the
language of poverty still justified their exploitation of market forces to re-
channel rejected garments into desired commodities.

The ethics of poverty reiterated by traders did not prevent them from
being lured by the desire to sell bulk items to make high profits. Jonaki
and Shefali both vociferously claimed that they "do not fear," as they are
"not smugglers." Their assertions were as much about reassuring themselves
as about the difficulties and unease of crossing borders with large volumes
of goods—and, when they could afford it, hiring laborers to carry the
heavy consignments to the border. If silence and hurrying defined the disposition of small-scale traders such as Minoti, then laughter, smiles, and
anxieties defined bulk traders. For the latter, travel by "jungle passports"
involved coordination and "stocktaking"—a term used by traders to refer
to congregating at a selected spot at the border and distributing goods
among themselves. As women exchanged goods, each trader was left with
a collection of items. "Stocktaking" at the border ensured that Indian
troops would not perceive any trader to be a specialist in one commodity.
"Stocktaking" also involved rest and leisure, sometimes after walking
many miles.

As skilled entrepreneurs, women traders stretched the moral contours of subsistence trade. Sometimes Indian troops initiated conversations with women traders, especially those who traded in bulk commodities, to unsettle their confidence as border crossers. Such conversations happened with the knowledge that the women often engaged in much more than subsistence trading. Shefali narrated one exchange with an Indian border patrol who told her, "So, grandmother, see the fence it is coming up nice and strong—look at it . . . how will you travel to India? Very soon you cannot travel anymore, and then what will you do?" Indian border troops cackled as they made these remarks and teased the elderly Bangladeshi traders. In response, Shefali and others challenged them by flaunting their extensive knowledge of the terrain. They retorted with mocking smiles, "You do not know what we know . . . we know hidden forests, paths, rivers and streams, we know and see what you cannot see . . . we will come anyway, go construct your fence." These conversations between male Indian border troops and Bangladeshi women traders deflected the anxieties that surrounded bulk trading. In such instances, travel by "jungle passports" acquired impish implications that exceeded moral thresholds. The laughter of bulk traders, their sheepish smiles, and their banter with border guards reinforced the importance of the convivial relationships of trust and legitimacy that afforded access to transborder spaces. Humor deflected and greased friction: it was essential for surviving and making a living from the dangerous border.

Like my tea drinking at Indian and Bangladeshi outposts, these playful exchanges made a heavily militarized borderland convivial without displacing the border's menacing edge. My border interrogations were harsh, but camp commanders and intelligence agents ensured that, as their "guest," I seldom left the outposts without drinking tea—no matter how angry or upset I was with their interrogation. One attempt to seek permission from a Bangladeshi outpost to travel to a village where I could meet Bangladeshi families led to a longer interrogation than usual. When I handed over an official letter from my university to the camp commander at the gate of the outpost, he called upon his colleagues. Although we shared a common language and ethnicity as Bengalis, my Indian nationality and presence near the border made my intentions suspect. Five soldiers casually surrounded me while I responded to the camp commander's questions. At one point, the camp commander insisted that my university letter was fake. "Where is the signature on the seal? This signature is not genuine!" he thundered. Exhausted from walking two miles on an empty stomach from the village where I was living to the outpost, I snatched my letter from his hands and attempted to leave. In a loud voice, the camp commander ordered me to sit down, emphasizing that while I had approached the outpost on my own, he was the one who would decide if and when I could leave. I grabbed the handles of the red plastic chair in a serious effort to conceal my trembling hands. In no time, steaming cups of tea arrived with snacks and biscuits; the intelligence officer who had earlier questioned me ferociously whispered an apology. The camp commander smiled and insisted that I could not leave the camp without tea and snacks. One of the border commanders strolled away toward a senior officer who stood with a small mirror, dyeing his beard. Soon, three young men from India arrived to pray at the small mosque located within the outpost's compound—the only one in the foothill zone, where churches were more prominent. The tea, snacks, and congenial conversations failed to sugarcoat the camp commander's harsh interrogation of me as an Indian national. It ensured that I could not leave the outpost, unilaterally reaffirming the commander's authority over the border under his jurisdiction, similar to what I had experienced at the Indian outposts. Subsequently, his men accompanied me to the border villages to ensure my safety as a female Bengali researcher under their jurisdiction.

For Bangladeshi Garo women, laughter and exchanges with Indian border troops had deeper implications that exemplified the precariousness of living together with exclusion. For instance, the laughter that women traders engaged in with the BSF did not prevent the troops from seizing their goods. When traders conspicuously carried big consignments, the Indian border troops confiscated the bulk goods to protect their own reputation. In 2005 and 2007, Shefali and Jonaki incurred heavy monetary losses of 10,000 and 7,000 taka (U.S.$100 and U.S.$70), respectively. The Indian troops conveyed that since the quantity of goods exceeded the agreed-upon thresholds, not confiscating the garments would cast aspersions on their ability to manage the border. Although Shefali and Jonaki incurred financial losses, the troops did not harm them or prevent them from again traveling to Meghalaya.

The Margins of Passports

Along the foothills and plains of Mymensingh, the impact of Christianity and education led to state repression as well as offered a sense of sanctuary to the

Garos to cope with violence and poverty in East Pakistan and later Bangladesh. These political transformations provided the context for Garo women to transform objects of Christian religious aid into commodities. Today, Bangladesh's policing of Garo youth as traffickers of illicit alcohol and India's containment of Garo male dissidents who seek a separate Garo homeland converge at the border to feminize border crossings. While the border itself splits and engenders their identities in noticeable ways, women's "jungle passport" journeys attest to the importance of reciprocity and kinship in making the border a negotiated space. Contrasting notions of indigeneity as they coalesce around the border make Bangladeshi Garo women mobile but also easily dispensable citizens.

On both sides of the border, Garo women's "jungle passport" journeys were informed by the perception and concomitant profiling of a political category of national inconsequence. The ambiguous location of Bangladeshi Garo Christian women and their presence near India's new border fence did not challenge national security in India, because the Indian BSF perceived them as harmless women rather than as Bangladeshis who threatened India's territorial integrity. Instead, their mobility derived meaning from their cultural and religious distance from Hindu and Muslim women, as well as from the predominantly Hindu and Muslim border troops. Unlike the Bangladeshi troops, who neither controlled nor relinquished control over "jungle passports" and oscillated between knowing and not knowing and seeing and not seeing, the Indian troops actively facilitated and gained emotional benefits from Garo women's journeys.

One night just before she went to sleep, Shefali suddenly announced to Lily and me that she would quit trading. Shefali loudly asserted that she would stop "all this walking and dragging clothes to India." Lily was relieved that her mother would finally retire. The next morning, however, Shefali woke up at dawn and set about packing garments in a gunnysack. "Where are you going?" I asked her. "Where else?" she responded. The fog had enveloped the border and it was bitterly cold, but the weather did not deter her. Inside her room, the gunnysacks occupied most of the space. In fact, her presence in the house seemed fleeting: it related to looking after and sorting textiles, taking quick baths and meals, and playing with her grandson. Totally absorbed in arranging her consignments, she chose to ignore the promise she had made the night before. Despite her aching bones, her body gained a purposeful momentum.

Herein lingered the lasting imprint of political and social circumstances that had come to shape Shefali's life and her mobility. The relationships of trust that facilitated travel by "jungle passports" limited the border's violent ability. However, despite seeming to claim the borderland through the world of kinship and trade, Shefali's relationships to the two nations she traversed and whose fortunes and misfortunes made her cross the border, also reinforced her sense of displacement.

CHAPTER 5

Fear, Reverence, and the Fence

Wiping his mouth after a funeral feast in a village in Bangladesh's foothills, the retired Garo Bangladeshi border commander Achin stated, "India is building a wall, like the Great Wall of China. We hear that it will be charged with electricity. Although I have guarded this border for many years and feared our Bangladeshi villagers as much as the Indians—you know some are dangerous, they have arms and others smuggle—the news that electricity will pass through the wall scares me." Achin was worried that his daughter Valentina, who had relocated to Tura after marriage, following the dictates of Christianity instead of the Garo tradition of matrilocal residence, would no longer be able to travel on a "jungle passport" to see him in Bangladesh.

Just that winter morning in 2008, Ali had warned me that I was traveling too close to India's "new wall." Ali, a Bangladeshi youth, was transporting me on his cycle rickshaw to the border village where I was invited to attend the funeral feast. As we neared the village, he pointed at the direction of India's new fence, which was still under construction. He cautioned, "Be careful, the wall should not be scaled—there are guards who shoot and kill. Anyone who comes into contact with the wall will die." As a Bangladeshi Muslim, he especially feared the Indian border troops. We looked from Bangladesh's foothills toward the emerging infrastructure of barbed wire and iron pillars. Seeing us approach the border from a hillock in Meghalaya, Indian troops grabbed their binoculars.

By this time, loud construction noises had disrupted the elephant corridors in the Garo Hill borderland. Distressed tuskers descended from the degraded forests in the hills and trampled rice fields and the pillars of the new border fence. Crossing over to Bangladesh, they destroyed houses and

Figure 18. The Indian Border Security Forces guarding the border in Assam, Northeast India. (Photograph: Shib Shankar Chatterjee)

injured villagers. In the *chars*, the installation of floodlights instilled fear in undocumented border crossers, especially Muslim men, that their border-dependent livelihoods might cease. The gradual appearance of an intimidating enclosure that India periodically announced would be electrified made Indian and Bangladeshi *char* dwellers assert, "One never knows this border." Along the Garo foothills and the riverine border, travelers frequently told me, "We fear the border troops and their guns." The border's new configurations escalated the anticipation of torture. Death haunted even the most skilled border crossers, who reminded me that I might not see them again.

Infrastructures of Fear

Globally, the unequal relationships between nations, as well as between nations and impoverished border crossers, translate into detentions, deportations, torture, and death. Limiting human mobility in the name of national security, illegality, and sovereignty harden territorial boundaries and normalize border enforcement. Writing about the U.S.-Mexico border, Joseph Nevins states that the nationalization of territory and society establishes a "global apartheid."[1] In another rendition of the nation-state's power to demarcate territories, Eyal Weizman has underscored Israel's brutal architectures of occupation in Palestine. Such infrastructures both occupy surfaces under the ground and control the airspace, and result in a "creeping apartheid."[2] I am interested in the porosity of an incomplete border that is cloaked in fears of torture and death at the hands of border troops. At the Northeast India–Bangladesh border, barbed wires, metal pillars, and concrete outposts are perennial objects in the making and fear-distributing objects. Their shifting arrangements delimit violent events to a singular political form and temporal frame.

The visibility of excessive force at borders illustrates Giorgio Agamben's emphasis on the state of exception. For Agamben, the tensions produced by the alternating suspension and imposition of laws create zones of legal void in which bodies are often reduced to "bare life," stripped of human qualities and political forms. In conditions of such extreme social and political dispossession, killing is not regarded a crime.[3]

But violence is much more than the "physicality" of force, assault, and infliction of pain.[4] Sovereigns rule not only by imprisoning and killing but also by their *sheer presence* and *capacity* to torture and kill. It is the anticipation of violence and its slipperiness, as Pradeep Jeganathan states, its visibility in the "cusp of things"—its fleeting qualities embedded in fields of recollection and anticipation—that make violence a force to reckon with.[5] Yet as I show in the following pages, even as nations alter landscapes and discipline bodies, fears harness senses, bodily vigilance, and social agility. Mistrust, animosity, and dependency forge vigilant minds and bodies. At the Northeast India-Bangladesh border undocumented travelers frequently glance over their shoulder, clutch rosaries and charms, and anticipate the footsteps of troops. Indian and Bangladeshi border troops reproduce fear when they vacillate between benign control and military ruthlessness, as well as when they struggle with their own unsettling isolation and stress.

People's responses to navigating lethal borders, such as the absolute terror in which border crossers run across the Northeast India–Bangladesh border, realign territorial and bodily boundaries and the boundaries between humans and animals. The fear of torture and death rapidly alters prior relationships of trust, deference, and civility between border villagers, troops, and animals—ushering in spatial and temporal disorientation. Along the Garo borderland, India's new border infrastructure disunited people and elephants in distress. This rupture gradually transformed the all-knowing and all-powerful elephant from a revered cohabiter of a shared landscape into a metaphor for a fearful nation. The complications of human-animal relationships are far more than just imputing either animal passivity or animal cunning onto migrants and brokers. Dense relationships of fear and trust are shared by humans and animals in this landscape.[6]

Like villagers' altered relationships with elephants, the encounters between villagers and troops degenerate from relationships of rural and transborder civility into ones of terror.

Let me recount a series of fearful journeys with Chandra along the Garo foothill borderland in 2007 and conclude in 2015, by which time India's new barriers had segregated the borderland and lives outside the established trading networks of "jungle passport." I will begin this chapter in the Garo borderland and return to the borderland *chars*.

Disorientation

Starting in autumn 2007, Chandra and I bicycled through the forests that interspersed the Garo borderland. I lived in Chandra's village, located along Meghalaya's border with Mymensingh, Bangladesh. Unable to make sense of the routes on maps, I sought Chandra's help during the school vacation to access remote border villages. These I subsequently chose for fieldwork. The assertive Chandra made a living from selling snacks outside a high school. She had an equally busy domestic schedule: she fostered her deceased sister's children and cared for her elder sister, who suffered from depression.

Garo Christian and Bengali Muslim villagers, border patrol agents, intelligence officers, and wild elephants cohabited the 300-yard demarcation zone between Bangladesh and Northeast India. The terrain crept with the hovering presence of people, animals, trees, and the metallic pillars planted for fence construction. As we cycled through this zone Chandra and I moved between Indian and Bangladesh territory. From boundary pillars 2275 to 2290, we passed by the Ronkha and Chring Rivers, rice paddy fields, forests, and border outposts. Pillar 2275 was a concrete triangle with "India" inscribed on one

Figure 19. Indian Garo women laborers mining sand for India's border fence construction, Meghalaya, Northeast India. (Photograph: author)

side and "Bangladesh" on the other. On our west was India's partly constructed new fence.

As we started our journey in the morning, Garo sand miners—women and children—walked across the river to fill their baskets and sacks with sand. The engineer had recruited them to mine wet sand from the river to make the concrete foundations of the fence. By autumn 2007, the contracted laborers who worked on building the new fence had already dug trenches, and they had measured the metal pillars and weighed the barbed wire that would encircle it. The Garo Indian women resented the presence of the non-Garo migrant laborers the firms were mandated to hire, who earned far more than they did. They desired to make a living by building the fence, aware that it might displace their homestead land and enclose their village separating them from their kin who lived in Bangladesh.

Rusted wires—remnants of the old fence—were barely visible, peeking out from the foliage that sometimes fell on our right and sometimes on our left. As we cycled past a bamboo grove, a barely discernable rectangular boundary pillar emerged. Smaller pillars jutted out between paddy fields and houses, some chimney-like and square, others T-shaped, with one side facing India, the other Bangladesh.

From pillar 2280, we cycled downhill across a narrow stream and passed by forests with huge trees that shaded the border road. Chandra, cycling in front of me, suddenly announced, "This is Bangladesh." "Where?" I asked. "On your left," she screamed, cycling ahead. A few minutes later, Chandra remarked, "We are back in India." As we cycled through Aina village, old border fences covered by foliage emerged on my left. Minutes later, Chandra, still ahead of me, shouted again—"Bangladesh." Across the fields, we occasionally saw men waving away the birds that nibbled on the rice paddy. As the mud road meandered, we continued to cycle along fields and through forests. I looked for the old border fence but failed to locate it. I was unable to distinguish between Indian and Bangladeshi territory. I struggled to keep up with Chandra. My spatial disorientation contrasted with her knowledge of the forested landscape. Not only did she know the precise location of every boundary pillar as well as a border guard, but she also crossed over to Bangladesh with ease.

A few minutes later, the old border fence emerged once again on our right in the form of barbed wire covered in foliage, disorienting me even further. In the stretches that were forested, it was dark even during the day. The shadowy presence of Indian border troops and intelligence agents dominated this landscape. Border patrolling jeeps that sped by forced us to cycle downhill next to the paddy fields that bordered the broken road. As Chandra and I cycled along the international boundary, she extended an arm and a leg over the boundary so that her outstretched limbs were in Bangladesh and her body in India.

Although I regularly cycled with Chandra along the Ronkha River, I frequently glanced over my shoulder, having a sense of being trailed. By autumn 2007, I had lived with armed scrutiny for six months. Alibaba, Chandra, and other villagers had trained me to sense the border, to test its temperature. On many occasions during my early fieldwork, they had prevented me from accessing the border when they sensed danger. Despite Chandra's presence, I constantly looked forward and backward as we bicycled. I thought about the intelligence officers in striped pink shirts, white T-shirts, and patchy green uniforms who suddenly appeared and disappeared.

Let me briefly recount an incident from early in my fieldwork that will better situate my anxiety. On a hot May afternoon in 2007, I was looking at India's newly constructed fence and at large consignments of fruit juice imports arriving from Bangladesh. I had arrived at the outpost with the intention of seeking permission to see India's new border with Bangladesh. This outpost was exceptionally large, as it was an official immigration and export corridor. The Indian troops stationed here were distant and formal, unlike the smaller outposts where Indian commanders casually boasted over tea that every undocumented Bangladeshi was shot at sight.

That afternoon, the local head of the civilian administration had just left the outpost after proudly showing a new colleague the stretches of the border that India had already fenced off. As they drove off in their jeep with flashing lights and the sounds from their siren became faint, one of the three patrolling officers who stood next to me suddenly became suspicious. Aggressively snatching my bag, he uncovered my camera and a banking machine that provided me online access to my bank account. He pressed a button on the bank pass and, mistaking it for the remote control of a bomb, yelled in panic, "Where is the bomb?" He quickly spoke on the wireless radio, and within minutes, a senior commander arrived. In the long interrogation that followed, I produced the university letter that I had shown at the gate to request permission for entry to the outpost. I took out my bank card, inserted it in the machine, and explained how Internet banking worked. After what seemed like several hours, the commander finally agreed to let me go, but not before he had asked me a series of questions in sequence and in reverse sequence.

This incident set a precedent for the rest of my fieldwork. My presence amplified the border troops' fears of indigenous dissidents and journalists who could report their deficits. Some suspected my intentions. I started fearing the troops. As I cycled with Chandra through the buffer zone, the wavering meaning of protection corresponded with the shifting landscape, which alternated between light and darkness even during the day. The border had also restructured my sense of time. The long exhausting hours that entailed negotiating distinct times for different kinds of trans border trading blurred the boundaries between days and nights. Even within the confines of the village homes where I resided, late at night, the noise of animals and the loud purring of transporting trucks filtered into my consciousness. As I cycled with Chandra, I checked whether my pocketknife was still in my cloth bag. I could never discern whether the presence that watched over us was a pair of human eyes, an animal, or a patch of trees in the forest.

"Ambi Acchu" and "Mama"

Like me, Chandra also frequently glanced over her shoulder. She hurried me on, insisting that we needed to reach home before the *ambi acchu* ("grandparents" in Garo language) crossed our paths. During our first conversation, I asked, "Elephants, you mean?" She barked back, "Don't take names—then you disrespect them. In our tradition, you do not anger them. You respect them. You do not call them by names, ever! They are everywhere. They can hear us; they can see us. They know everything. They sense if we disrespect them, even if you are far away. Be careful. If they cross our path, remember to fold your hands and bow down. Say *ambi acchu*, please let us pass."

As we cycled fast, passing through several border outposts and observation towers, we saw elephant footprints along the sandy road. Chandra nervously asked every border guard on duty, "Have you seen the *ambi acchus* come?" Sensing our anxiety, a border guard joked, "Not yet, but maybe it is time now."

Reverence coupled with fear and avoidance defined the relationship that Garo border villagers had with elephants. Due to the elephants' massive size, the abundant resources that they needed to survive, and their capacity for destruction, the Garos placated and respected them.[7] The borderland Garos do not refer to large animals by their names but by the features and characteristics that define them. For instance, elephants are known as *Dalgipa* ("the big one"), and tigers are *Miksugijapa* ("the one who does not wash his face"). Such forms of deferential nomenclature, even in the animal's absence, invoked its powerful presence in their lives and established the trust and deference that was required to share a habitat with them. The relationship that people have with animals shapes their dreams. The soul's psychic potential provides humans with the power to embed themselves into animals. Shapeshifting is nocturnal; it is the human self that activates the animal form in sleep. Garo shapeshifters are attributed with special powers of premonition.[8]

Chandra and other foothill villagers held that if one spoke against and insulted an elephant, it would comprehend the insult. Villagers spoke with immense reverence about elephants since they believed that the intelligent animals were skilled at understanding human language. While younger Garo borderlanders referred to elephants as grandparents, Garo Bangladeshis also called them "big uncles" or *mama*. The term *mama* means "maternal uncle" in Bengali (the term *chra* is used by Garos) and combines both affection and authority.[9] These words of affectionate respect were also attributed to elephants' gentle disposition toward humans, despite their strength and power.

In Tuli, a village that the Ronkha River bisected, splitting it between India and Bangladesh, the human-elephant boundary was as real and as blurred as the national boundaries. Occasionally, my journeys with Chandra ended at Tuli, where I spent time following the timber loggers. The international boundary ended clumsily either in a courtyard in Tuli or in the Ronkha River. Villagers had placed bamboo benches in their courtyards for the border troops to sit on during their patrols. Here, troops and travelers were tangled in coded courtesies—Indian border troops often mistook Garo Bangladeshis as docile Garo Indians. Convivial conversations sustained border crossings.

One morning at a house on the Indian side of Tuli, James, a Garo Bangladeshi laborer in his mid-forties, engaged an Indian border troop in conversation by addressing him as *mama* (maternal uncle). The international boundary ran through the courtyard of this house; James, a regular border crosser who felled logs, often rested at this house in which his *Mahari* members resided. An Indian border-patrolling officer arrived, swinging his gun as we shared betel nuts and lime. He took a seat on a bamboo bench. Placing the gun next to him, the guard carefully glanced at everyone. James picked up his betel leaf, folded his hands, and bowed in salutation. He gently addressed the guard in Hindi (the guard's mother tongue), "*Mama*, how are you?" The guard responded pleasantly to this obvious display of respect: "*Mama*, I am well." He lined his betel leaf with lime, placed it in his mouth, sat for a while chewing it, and then retreated to the forest on the edge of the foothills. A few hours later, James emerged from the forest with wooden logs and successfully crossed the dried Ronkha River back to Bangladesh.

Through this exchange, James acknowledged both the authority of the Indian border troops over the landscape and the forest resources upon which he depended for a livelihood. Like other Garo Bangladeshi villagers, he had established meaningful associations with the Indian troops in order to mitigate danger. Respect established the border's central role of sustaining everyday life amid the otherwise prevalent atmosphere of fear. Instead of being instrumental or superficially transactional, the deference that villagers demonstrated toward the troops, which found expression in coded vocabularies of coexistence, arose from a sense of respect out of fear and shared dependence on forest resources.

Across the border, along Bangladesh's foothills, apprehension and reverence multiplied through the rituals associated with such coded existence. Here, Garo villagers silenced me every time I referred to Indian border forces by their official name, the BSF. They asked that I be courteous, just like with elephants. In sequence, they insisted that I should bow down, fold my hands, and greet the *mamas*. Like the powerful elephants, the guards would be pleased and let me pass. I often lost track of conversations and wondered who, exactly, was being feared, as *mama* was used so frequently. Garo coal miners clarified for my benefit—*pahari mama*, or the "uncle from the hills," meant elephants, while *mama* alone referred to the Indian troops. The semantic overlap between elephants and the Indian border forces articulated not only the established hierarchies but also the increasing fears and uncertainties that emerged from the rapidly changing terrain and new forms of border enforcement. As villagers repeatedly stated, "You see the gathering, it has increased over the years"—using the word "gathering" to refer to the heavily armed border battalions. Chandra's resounding words about wild elephants, "They can see us; they can hear us," also reverberated across Bangladesh's foothills. Elephants were like proto-nations in this borderland.

The Elephant Nation

By 2015, India's new fence had encircled forests and grazing grounds in the Garo borderland. From a diversely barricaded landscape comprising old fences, plastic flags that indicated the international boundary, mud paths between rice fields, or tarmac roads separating agricultural land, this zone had transformed into one that Indian and Bangladeshi federal border forces and specialized-weapons teams forcefully patrolled. Although the civil engineers and construction workers who were building India's new fence had departed, the terrain still resembled a large construction site. Trucks arrived and dumped sand and gravel for renovating old border outposts. India had also sanctioned plans for constructing new outposts to accommodate increasing troop deployment. In response, Bangladesh too built new outposts.

Indian and Bangladeshi outposts had morphed from small observation posts with the occasional large barrack into sprawling complexes over the past decade. Inside the residential barracks were furnished television rooms, badminton courts, handball courts, and regular supplies of water, electricity, and rations that the surrounding villages lacked. New constructions and the increasing deployment of troops gradually undid the relationships that had been fundamental to life and livelihood in this zone.

Despite the flurry of construction activities that came with the promise of electrification of India's new fence, villages plunged into darkness at dusk. The only visible lights were from the bulbs of the Indian outposts that flickered due to low-voltage electricity. At dusk, the sounds of bellowing elephants interrupted church bells, the loud devotional songs in praise of Hindu deities emanated from Indian outposts, and prayer calls emerged from a few mosques located in Bangladesh's foothills. From autumn to the early onset of winter, these pious callings failed to comfort the rice-farming villagers. Elephants had destroyed their harvests. The distraught animals trampled India's new fence. Crossing over to Bangladesh, they injured householders. The disruption of a shared habitat and the relationships of fear and respect that cemented it caused elephants to suddenly appear, just like the Indian troops.[10]

India's new fence intervened between the boundary pillars 2275 and 2290 in January 2015. India stepped up the patrols of its international boundaries with Bangladesh and Pakistan in preparation for U.S. president Barack Obama's visit. In the days leading up to 26 January 2015, when India celebrated Republic Day, internal and external security threats converged. By then, Indian troops had concluded a series of armed operations that resulted in the killing of Garo dissidents and the capture of kidnappers who had, among others, abducted a local school teacher and an Indian engineer in charge of floodlighting India's border fence. These events had led India to deploy additional commandos and specialized weapons teams in the Garo foothills.

In March 2015, India's National Security Guard commandos stood stationed a few yards away from each other in groups of six along the Garo foothills of Meghalaya. Their black clothes, headbands, face masks, and helmets enhanced their anonymity. By then, patrolling jeeps had reduced unmetaled village roads to dirt tracks that spiraled dust and flattened elephant dung. The chaotic reordering of this zone made my journeys from one border village to another even longer. Since we could no longer cycle, Chandra and I had no option but to walk from boundary pillars 2275 to 2290 to reach Tuli.

Soldiers strictly patrolled the black iron gates that led from India to Bangladesh. They noted our names and informed the next gate that we would be arriving. We walked through the two gates, passing by rice fields located in

Bangladesh. Soon after the second gate, I could no longer see the new fence. By now, the security teams and troops who dominated the landscape were also monitoring villagers from makeshift bamboo towers in the treetops. The new arrangements had ensured that agriculturalists were denied access to the border. Although the fenced land was legally open for cultivation, Indian troops either prevented Garo Indian farmers from cultivating the land or intentionally opened the gate only at midday, when the hot afternoon sun prevented them from farming. This compelled Garo cultivators to keep their lands fallow. At the same time, Indian commanders pointed in the direction of Bangladesh, comparing the enterprising Bangladeshi farmers who cultivated the land until the edge of their national territory to the "lazy" Indian villagers.

Garo villagers who were displaced by India's new border fence were paid very little financial compensation. The monetary compensation was measured in terms of the exact amount of land that the new barrier appropriated and did not include the land that was made inaccessible outside the barrier. Villagers complained that they had not even received partial compensation to rebuild the homes that they had been forced to demolish.

Completely confused by the changing terrain and the large presence of troops, I asked Chandra where we were. She asserted, "Still on zero point," implying the buffer zone between India and Bangladesh. "But where is the new fence? Which side? Why can't I see it?" I asked. "Look carefully," she said, "the fence is hidden in the forest on your right; see there," Chandra said. I strained my eyes and looked carefully through the trees before I could see the new multilayered barrier.

Chandra and I walked through the forest for two miles, passing a forest camp and two newly constructed border outposts. As in previous years, in 2015, Chandra constantly looked behind her as we walked from one village to another along the border. She feared the Indian troops more than the elephants. She said, "They are everywhere now. They sit silently on the trees, inside the jungle, and by the roadside. The newly posted ones especially sit in locations from where you cannot see them, but they can see you."

Like her, I barely made eye contact with the black-attired commandoes. Instead, I looked closely at the fence as we walked past it. I noticed the sharp edges and numbers on the metal pillars of the structure and how two rounds of coiled barbed wire overlapped the spaces in between. From a distance, the thickness of the fence's angular metal frames stood out, rendering the thinner barbed wire invisible. As we walked closer to the fence, however, the razor-sharp, stretched edges seemed more brutal. Even without touching it,

I felt its spikes. I looked away, scared that staring at the fence might make the commandoes suspicious.

A few minutes later, I again lost sight of the fence as we passed by the lush paddy fields. After walking a few meters, I momentarily forgot where we were and took out my camera. Chandra screamed in fear, "Are you mad? Does this paddy field matter? Did I not tell you we are walking on zero point—zero— this means the *jawans* [soldiers] can come and do anything to us, you hear me? You cannot see them, I told you, but before you know, they jump on you with their guns—can't you see they don't trust us anymore! There is so much of struggle now—just to walk through the three-mile stretch of the forest— even for children to pluck gooseberries in this stretch is a struggle."

As we walked, Chandra continued, "The soldiers hide behind gooseberry bushes and trees, jump at people, they startle us—like the elephants that always arrive unannounced and are just as greedy these days." Since trees were being cut for fence construction and people had to make a living through logging, the elephants now appeared to be greedy rather than deserving of the rice paddy. Garo villagers fearfully compared the new soldiers who patrolled their lives and the Garo dissident groups who demanded ransom from them to the raiding elephants. Their capacity to destroy livelihoods had made elephants a proto-nation in the past in the form of border troops who could be respected and placated. The new "elephant nation" however, had made its presence felt through India's escalated patrolling and the increasing deployment of specialized weapons teams.

Foucault's invocation of the panopticon to emphasize the perennial visibility of people and their control by the state, even in the physical absence of state agents, provides a glimpse of the inner workings of state power.[11] The panopticon at the Northeast India–Bangladesh border takes distinctive forms. Indian state power is perpetuated through unstable and erratic governance, and constrained state capacity, which often fed into deliberately perpetuated rumors of electrification of the fence. Media releases of new digital surveillance such as night cameras and drones reinforced rumors. Aided by their wireless radios, troops frequently monitored the movement of villagers in ways that provided as well as impeded access to the border. This intended unevenness in a resource-scarce border had reduced people's ability to "sense" the border. The increasing national scrutiny and rumors—especially in the states of Meghalaya and Assam—exhausted villagers.

People's relationships with one another along and across the border and their anger at elephants and border troops heightened their struggles. From familiar forces of destruction, Indian border troops and elephants had morphed into unstable forces who damaged landscapes and destroyed livelihoods. The troops who tortured border crossers and the greedy elephants that arrived unannounced and trampled the fence, rice fields, and houses—as well as the anger that accompanied these newfound fears—exacerbated the instability that dominated border lives. Chandra's domestic burdens had increased. It was rumored that, completely unable to lay her eyes on a lover in Bangladesh who had jilted her, Chandra's elder sister had sunk into grave depression. As her sister lay emotionally incapacitated, Chandra did all the household work in addition to caring for her nieces and nephews.

When I reached Tuli in Meghalaya, I realized that the fence had placed a prominent burial ground outside the Indian territory. In 2015, Indian soldiers watched over the Christian mud graves, only reluctantly allowing villagers to pray beside them. The outposts no longer relied on villages for rations and furniture. Inside the residential barracks were furnished with television rooms, badminton courts, handball courts, and regular supplies of water. The larger outposts had diesel generators for electricity that the surrounding villages lacked. Border troops, now watched over by special commandoes, were disinclined to visit headmen, and villagers hesitated to converse with troops. If the danger emanating from guns, uniforms, and fences further heightened my own consciousness of the border apparatus, for the Garo Christians, new forms of forbidding state power had gradually fragmented the relationships that people had built through trust and exchange with the outposts.

The mistrust was evident just a few days after I returned from Tuli to attend the Catholic Church's annual *sabha* (congregation) in a border village in Meghalaya. This event enabled villagers who could not travel for baptism and confessions the opportunity to partake in mass devotion. As the largest annual meet of its kind, priests, choirs, and the laity were all present in a newly harvested field. The field adjoined India's newly fenced border. Unlike other years, Indian troops forbade Christian Garos from Bangladesh to cross the border for this holy event. Catholic priests called Indian outposts but failed to negotiate passage. Given the recent rise in transborder abductions, Indian troops did not want to take the additional responsibility for Bangladeshi Christians. The outposts' powers to demarcate and control border crossings, which were earlier confined to prevent Bangladeshi Muslim pilgrims from traveling without passports to visit Sufi shrines in Meghalaya's foothills and Assam, now extended to include Christians. Garo women and children stood in large numbers across India's new border fence, watching their kin members and extended families on the other side for hours. They were not willing to give up hope that the troops might relent later in the day. The stationed troops, however, ensured that Garo Bangladeshi Catholics could not cross the border.[12]

Twisted Wires, Twisted Bodies

Navigating India's new border fence and troops entailed an increased risk to life for both Garo Christians in the foothills and plains and Muslim workers in the *chars*. Before crossing the border, transporters honed their senses to understand darkness and light, silence and noise. They listened for the slightest footfall of border troops before taking the final plunge across the border. Border crossers waited in silence, not too close to each other, but also not too far away. They emphatically stated that at the actual moment of crossing, there was no stepping back. The anticipation of death and apprehension that their livelihoods, which relied on the border, might cease, pushed bodies into motion. The new fears of strong pillars, electrified fences, and armed guards created emotional and spatial disorientation. But they also reinforced anxious mobility.

As a recognizable landscape transformed into an unpredictable place and dangers escalated, religious charms and heavenly protection were increasingly incorporated into the newer and more dangerous modes of border crossing. For Sumoti, the chairperson of a Garo kinship association, crossing the border was now a fearful experience. The anticipation that armed troops would brutally stop her, at best, or beat and kill her, at worst, made Sumoti's body shiver. Shaking her body vigorously in exaggeration, she recounted the following sequence of events to me in her house:

> We recite a prayer before we leave the house and clutch our rosaries. At the border, I look right, left, and then right again and then break into a fast run. I run for my life, the rosary damp in my hand. I run as fast as I can to the nearest house across the border. Sometimes, if my uncle, who lives on the other side, is standing close by, I even run past him. Only when I reach a house do I look back to see if the others have made it. As soon I make it, I kiss my rosary and kiss the ground. I thank Jesus (she bows down and touches her lips to the ground); when I cross back, I do the same.

Before Chand, a small-scale cattle trader, and Lal Mia, a fisherman—both Bangladeshi and Muslim—left for India, their families recited prayers for their safe journeys. Their hands and nails were freshly painted with bright orange henna (a plant dye) to make their journeys auspicious; amulets with plant roots from spiritual healers were tied to their arms. Lal Mia, who had seasonally traveled to Assam as a fisherman for the past thirty years, no longer traveled by boat in a large group. Cross-border firing, especially by Indian border forces, ensured that the journeys that border crossers had earlier regarded as travel between neighboring provinces became radically altered.

Alibaba, the cattle transporter, invariably displayed signs of nervousness before and after border crossings, often breaking into a depressive monologue. He and his transporter friends constantly spoke about death: "I don't know if I want to continue with border business . . . I fear death these days." Even the most daring, youthful, and jovial border crossers reminded me every time I met them that I might not see them again: "Who knows this border? Let us see if we ever meet again." Despite using the metaphysical powers of objects to grant safe passage across the lethal border, the transporters also pointed out that the best possible preparations might not be enough to help them cross safely. Mondol, one of Alibaba's transporter friends, announced one afternoon in a loud voice that the green uniforms of Indian troops, now seen in larger numbers than before, constantly startled him. As we chatted that afternoon in Alibaba's house a few yards from the border, his son Badshah shouted, "Big guns! Big guns!" While the Indian border forces intensely combed the village for smuggled cattle, Alibaba's wife Nasneen held the excited Badshah. We sat silently until they left.

Reece Jones has shown how India, in its fight against terrorism, amplifies differences between Hindus and Muslims. Among their outcomes at the India-Bangladesh border is India's classifying of Bangladeshis as "pre-modern" Muslim enemies.[13] Chand, Alibaba, and other Muslim border crossers especially feared torture and violent deaths at the hand of the predominantly Hindu Indian border troops. When Indian troops indefinitely closed border gates, the border's violence and its reverberating effects lingered in the form of prolonged unemployment and hunger. With the border gates closed for three months, Chand lost money and his youthful cheer. As we sat in his courtyard in a remote *char* in Kurigram, Bangladesh, he depressingly stated, "The border is a strange place these days; everything has shut down for Bangladeshis, we don't know who to trust anymore." From a very known place that Chand had crossed regularly, where he had arranged chairs for Bangladeshi and Indian troops during official meetings, the shutting of border gates made the boundaries of religions significant. Chand's failed deals and monetary losses in India meant that he could no longer purchase wooden shutters for the windows of his new house. Instead, tin sheets covered the gaps. Since he was unable to travel to Assam, Chand's Indian collaborators claimed the advance that he had provided them without honoring his cattle consignment. As his wife Dilshad lamented while lighting a clay oven and placing a pot of rice to boil, "They [his counterparts in India] now turn their face away when he arrives; security is also high these days . . . they no longer host him." From their courtyard, we could see India's emerging border fence with its newly planted metal rods.

Torture, detention, and incarceration of Muslim cattle workers at the hands of Indian Hindu troops released time's coercive forces. These unsettled the transborder relationships that had earlier realigned notions of national territory and national times. The consequences of violent times were evident in bodily bruises and scars, partly constructed houses, and empty kitchens and stomachs. In Assam, Alibaba went to the market every morning to see if he could earn a few cents from loading and unloading goods, failing which, he sat at the roadside looking vacantly at the sky. He waited for more trucks to arrive with goods in the afternoon.

Chand and Alibaba anxiously waited for the border gates to reopen. Time stretched indefinitely. As a political predicament, waiting had rendered them unproductive.[14] Political and legal regulations unevenly distribute insecurity, danger, and hope in ways that force people to wait indefinitely for employment and sustenance; time expansions push people into forms of "nonbecoming."[15] Waiting imposes a sense of boredom that is related to chronic poverty and cruelty.[16] Enduring unemployment prolongs time, placing people outside the horizons of modernity and preventing them from achieving even the socially desired status of adulthood.[17]

Alibaba and Nasneen's son Badshah frequently stopped playing to run inside the house and demand food when I arrived from another village to visit. I had temporarily left Alibaba's *char* and was residing in a Garo village since disruptions in cattle flows made my otherwise well-established domesticity with traders and their families edgy. Nasneen's voice cracked as she spoke to me, covering her bruised jaw with her palm. Embarrassed about the visibility of her bruise and the lack of tea, she asked if I wanted to pay a visit to her sister-in-law Nakhoda, whose eldest son also traded in cattle. Alibaba walked in the opposite direction to sit in the local market; he was neither concerned nor apologetic about the violence that he had perpetrated on Nasneen.

After purchasing a packet of tea leaves, sugar, and biscuits from a local shop, Badshah, Nasneen, and I walked to Nakhoda's house, the last one along the border, which functioned as a transit point for traders, brokers, and even legal travelers who paid for meals and rest. Seeing Nakhoda's adolescent son lick the last morsels of rice and lentils from his fingers, Badshah immediately demanded a plate of rice. Nakhoda admonished me for bringing the tea leaves while brewing tea for us with the same leaves. For the next hour, Badshah regularly interrupted our conversation, asking his aunt for rice. Nakhoda smiled lovingly at her nephew but did nothing.[18]

We chatted a while, waiting for Nakhoda to attend to Badshah—leading me to realize that, knowing that her sister-in-law had greater resources, Nasneen had intended to get Badshah a meal. Nakhoda continued to verbally engage him with affection while being totally unmoved by his hungry cries. As we walked back, Nasneen softly cursed her sister-in-law while Badshah momentarily forgot his hunger and broke into a run. We returned home that afternoon with rice, eggs, and oil. Nasneen and I hurriedly cooked. Badshah ran into the kitchen demanding an entire egg for himself—it otherwise would be divided between him and his two elder siblings.

Alibaba's dispiritedness caused by prolonged unemployment and hunger compelled him to cross the border despite the increasing threats to life. Alibaba and Mondol conveyed that body suppleness was central to crossing the border. Unlike the old border fences that could be more easily dodged or cut through at the damaged parts, the material toughness of India's new border fence ensured its fearfulness as an infrastructure. Alibaba and Mondol's emaciated bodies met the demand for skilled physical navigation by walking, running, and crawling longer distances as escalated patrolling ensured that the routes constantly changed.

Transporters jokingly warned each other, "You are getting fat; you will soon be thrown out of business." Alibaba spoke about angels who guided travelers, speaking in clear voices from the trees under which they rested and consoling transporters at the dead of night. He referred to these voices and hazy bodies that magically spoke and guided border crossers as *farishtey* or "angels." The angels who protected mobility, appearing as old men dressed in white, emerged from the mist, showing the way to travelers who had lost their way. To the border crossers, they were as real as the border forces.

Along the boundary pillar 2275, this time with the word "Bangladesh" facing me, I witnessed the Bangladeshi troops guarding the border. I had accompanied the BGB at the start of their evening patrol shift. I had requested that they direct me to the old boundary pillars. The mud path on which we walked was the international boundary. Beyond us was the Ronkha River. Next to pillar 2275 on our right were small patches of grazing land and on the left the forests through which Chandra and I had bicycled and walked through. At a distance, hazy human and animal figures were visible through the winter mist. Borderlanders went about grazing cattle and crossing the border with bags full of vegetables and chickens. As the troops shouted in mock aggression and waved their guns, everyone broke into a fearful run. The men grazing cattle immediately goaded their sticks sharply onto the backs of the animals. The guards did not change their pace or their posture. Watching the men run, they indicated to me how much their military uniform, which blended into the landscape, was feared.

Veteran fence cutters such as Moi Ali, who I first met in Aladdin's house, proudly narrated how easily he had cut through India's old border fence with Bangladesh. The single-layered old fence was lying in varying states of disrepair with rusted pillars and brittle barbed wire. Despite his macho boastfulness and warnings that "everyone fears us. After all, we are *tar kata manush*" (men who make a living by cutting border fences), Moi broke into nervous laughter at the mention of India's newly built barrier. Nervousness soon replaced his theatrical laughter. He anxiously stated, "We hold pliers with shaky hands . . . we are scared to go near it." By not mentioning the "new fence," Moi reinforced its ominous presence in his life. Like the elephants and border troops, it could not be referred to.

I had seen migrant workers from Assam's *chars* carefully constructing the new barrier in the Garo foothills of Meghalaya. They carefully insulated each metal pillar with copper plating and then welded it at an angle to secure the coiled barbed wire. The engineers supervised the slant—where the welding did not meet the requirements of the angle, they discarded the pillar. The slant was important for securing the barbed wire. The engineer in charge in one zone demonstrated to me how he carefully weighed the wire and tested its sharpness. Under his instructions, I touched the coils and tried to gauge which would work and which would be discarded. Workers twisted the ones that did and rearranged these to create a lethal buffer. Finally, they double coated the iron barbed wire with anticorrosive paint, making it gleam and easier to coil around the pillars. From the outer margins of the fence to its inner confines, neatly configured barbed wire circles filled the matrix.

As Reviel Netz states, barbed wire operates at "the level of flesh," slicing across spatial and biological boundaries. The global proliferation of barbed wire relied on its forceful capacities to perpetrate pain; the relationship between iron and flesh that the razor-sharp wires fostered intimately connected the predicaments of humans and animals.[19] The twisted form and corrosive textures of barbed wire *make* the nation's margin a lethal location; the land's changing contours chronicle the nation's irredeemable presence in the lives of its suspects and citizens. The layout, measurement, and weight of India's new fence generate a sense of extreme power asymmetry; its material textures reinforce terror and hunger. The nation surfaces in the form of twisted wires and emaciated rural bodies; adults and children alike. With every rotating jeep tire, gust of wind, and soldier's footstep, the villagers encounter the nation's disruptive presence in their lives.

Even after I had left the border it continued to reshape my mind and body. The border had numbed my skin of its sensory capacities. Franck Billé argues that the correspondence between skin and national borders is both somatic and a political phenomenon that can productively enrich border ethnographies. Inspired by Serres, he suggests that scholarly engagements with topology benefit from a close reading of the elasticity and textures of the skin in ways that clearly establish the palimpsests of sovereignty.[20] I jumped out of my skin at the sight of patchy-uniformed men—even when they were not border troops and soldiers. In my trauma dreams, the nights were as bright as the days. Sometimes an imaginary light from the high-intensity floodlights replaced a bright shining moon. I had seen a few floodlight posts being constructed on the Indian side of the border. These were situated in Garo villages that constantly plunged into darkness because of erratic electricity. In the foothills, nurses and health workers struggled to keep medicines and vaccines refrigerated. In a clinic run by a Catholic church in Meghalaya where I volunteered, newly posted young Indian soldiers—primarily rural recruits from other states of India—regularly stopped in to request medicines for unexplained body pains and headaches. Needing to ameliorate the pain of their isolation in a remote region, they chatted with the Catholic nuns and engaged other patients in conversations. The free paracetamol offered them a magic cure for a few days. Then, they would appear again.[21]

State surveillance made me doubt relationships of trust. This was evident in a heated exchange that I had with Manik, who, along with his wife Polly, had befriended me since 2007. Manik was an undocumented Garo Bangladeshi who had relocated to India two years earlier to join his Indian wife,

Figure 20. An Indian soldier stands at the international boundary that cuts across Meghalaya and Mymensingh. Behind him is a pillar on which is written "josh," meaning patriotic fervor. In the distance is a cone-shaped boundary pillar indicating India, beyond which is Bangladesh. (Photograph: author)

following the dictates of Garo matrimonial residence. Since it was unsafe for him to resettle in Polly's village, he had temporarily resided for a year in another village, during which time a contractor recruited him to work as a laborer on India's fencing project. Manik had helped build India's new border infrastructures and, after a few police interrogations, came to resettle in his wife's village. It was the last house on Indian territory.

One afternoon, Manik and I walked through a forest to reach the house of a retired teacher and communist revolutionary who had lived in India as a political exile since the early 1950s and whom I wanted to interview. Manik, who was walking slightly ahead of me, turned to glance at me. Smiling, he lit a cigarette as he often did. This act of lighting a cigarette in the forested border coincided with strange and unfamiliar sounds. I suddenly suspected that Manik intended to assault me. Frightened of his presence and of the sounds I could hear, I screamed in panic, accusing him of getting me lost inside the forest. To make matters worse, instead of being angry, Manik laughed at me. I tried to retrace my steps and broke into a run. Completely unsettled by the faint sunlight that filtered in from the trees, I was unable to find my way out. Manik caught up with me and said, "Let's walk together." I walked next to him fearfully until we reached the village, where I completed my interview.

Later that evening, I tried to compensate for my angry outburst by eating rice and gravy at their house. On our way back, Manik had chased a wild rabbit, and the day ended with the killing of the rabbit in a corner of the courtyard away from my view. Exhausted from the day's events, I could neither speak nor eat. We sat in their courtyard watching Indian troops return from their evening patrol shift. Other troops strolled about, resting in white vests and khaki shorts. I sat in silence as Polly's mother, who was still upset with me for not having converted to Christianity, started abusing the Hindu goddess Kali, who she blamed for all of her miscarriages. Manik was preoccupied with his own worries. He remarked on the troop escalation in India, which had made his journeys to see his aging father in Bangladesh very difficult. I tried to cope with my fear; he spoke about his fears and sadness.

Barbed wire not only disrupted the relationships of civility between troops and villagers that had earlier been fundamental to the production of an unknown border but also entrenched remoteness as a violent precondition, making even hardened soldiers depressed. This was evident in the Brahmaputra's *chars*. As I sat sipping tea one monsoon afternoon at an Indian border outpost in Assam the commander pointed to the rising waters of the Brahmaputra. He was worried about the river engulfing the outpost. In the long depressing conversation that followed over tea and biscuits, he mentioned neither unauthorized Bangladeshis nor Muslim Indian villagers. His depressed tone as he stated, "Once the river floods, everything will end" reinforced his sense of isolation and dystopia.

I had heard resonance of the same depressed tone in the words of the border constable who had feared my banking machine at another Indian border outpost and who subsequently telephoned me regularly in the months that followed my initial fieldwork in Assam. The outpost's presence in my life continued in the form of his despondent voice. Initially, the conversations were about the constable routinely checking on my whereabouts. Within a month, the tone changed, and the telephone calls became sad monologues. His queries now related to enquiring after me and my family's well-being. In fact, he would hardly wait for my response before launching into his sense of

loss because he was apart from his family. As surveillance shifted
cus on national security to isolation, it instilled anonymity and dep.

Mutilated Bodies

Sitting within the confines of Khairun's home in Rowmari, Bangladesh, I had a very different sense of Indian border troops. In Khairun's household, the Rowmari-Tura road and the "war of Boroibari" filtered into everyday conversations. Boroibari is a disputed territory near Rowmari town, one of the many border locations where territorial issues between India and Bangladesh were unresolved. While India maintains that there is a lack of authentic information about the areas under dispute and advocates for surveys, Bangladesh demands that the areas be immediately handed over to the respective states.[22] In their perception, this territorial conflict was a war, and not just a random confrontation. The Indian border troops were the clear villains.

On 17 April 2001, the Indian and Bangladeshi border forces clashed over this uncertain territory. Unknown to those in Rowmari, the Indian forces were retaliating for another territorial dispute in which Bangladeshi border forces had surrounded an Indian outpost in Pydwah, Meghalaya. Confused, Indian soldiers asked a boy for directions to the nearest Bangladeshi border outpost. He intentionally misled them—an act for which Bangladesh generously gifted his family a water pump after the war ended.

For Rowmari's residents, "the war" seemed to continue for months. They faced incessant shelling from India. Families huddled together in their mud-walled and tin-roofed houses in fear, deafened by the sound of gunfire that effortlessly filtered through cracks in the walls, windows, and door screens. When they mustered the courage to come into their courtyards, the intensity of the high-voltage floodlights from India unsettled their sense of time. "It was very bright . . . it seemed to be day even at night. We were all confused, the roads were bad and the additional troops took a while to reach Rowmari!" Mahfuz, Khairun's elderly father, exclaimed. Young men on both sides of the border forgot their transnational connections, becoming eager and ready to take up arms and aid the border forces in the fight.

One evening, Mahfuz and his grandnephew Khokon, who had come to visit him, emphatically stated that not all Indian soldiers had been able to reach the Boroibari outpost to attack it. When Bangladesh's border forces found an Indian soldier who had lost his way in the rice fields, Rowmari's youth were ordered to decide his fate. Sitting at a distance from the triangular boundary pillar in Rowmari, the same pillar on which he had once sat with his adolescent friends to tease Indian border guards, the university-going Khokon recounted the graphic mutilation of the Indian soldier's body. "You should have seen his size, the Indian soldier was massive with a turban and a huge beard—his body was over seven feet tall—our troops half killed him and then they handed him over to us, the youth. He had no way to escape. Then we started . . . you can imagine what we did to him . . . before his slow end."

Khokon left the graphic brutality of what followed to my imagination. His exaggeration of the size of the Indian soldier's body was similar to his description of Mir Jumla's body. A governor of Bengal under the Mughals, Mir Jumla's legendary exploits are immortalized on his tomb. His tomb was rumored to be specially constructed to accommodate his huge body. These rumors were accompanied by narrations of regret and resentment. Indian troops prevented villagers from Bangladesh from visiting Mir Jumla's tomb, which is located just across the border in India. In recounting the war, Khokon forgot his teasing of Indian border commanders and his gifts of perfume and cigarettes. He also forgot my Indian nationality and his Indian friends just across the border, his "*dostos*," as he affectionately referred to them on other occasions.

The same Indian friends, mostly Hindu tanners, butchers, and daily wage workers, had earlier conveyed to me their interpretations of the Boroibari war in Assam's *chars*. They had volunteered their services to Indian troops to take up guns and shoot the Bangladeshis. Indian youth recollected loitering in the evacuated villages, insisting that they would help Indian troops in their fight against Bangladesh. As Robi and Sujal, who worked as plumbers, stated: after all, "we eat India's rations (subsidized food)." Disappointingly, however, the Indian border forces only ordered them to climb coconut trees and supply the combatants with safe water. "The soldiers ate nothing, but only drank coconut water," Robi continued. "They consoled us. They said that unlike troops who died in combat, our death would not elicit state compensation in India."

In the same *char* in Assam, the aged and frail Bilkis Begum who regularly traveled to Rowmari to see her eldest son, a politician, was relieved when the war ended. She received news that her son was safe, and as soon as the Indian soldiers left, she again occupied her room. "You should have seen the ample rations that they left me—rice, lentils, and oil—I did not have to ask my youngest son for food for the next few months."

Soon after the conflict ended, Bangladesh returned seventeen mutilated bodies of Indian soldiers, including the body of the reportedly "lost" Indian soldier. Instead of handing over these bodies to their families, India hurriedly concluded their cremation in Tura, where the Rowmari-Tura road had once started. Since the war in 2001, a heavily barricaded border outpost in Bangladesh was constructed in the perennial anticipation of an attack from India.

In January 2011, just a few miles away from Rowmari at the site of this disputed land, an Indian border constable shot the fifteen-year-old Felani Khatun dead as she attempted to cross India's new fence with her father while being aided by brokers. Felani's father, Nurul Islam, had resided in Assam for several years and was crossing the border for her marriage in Bangladesh. When her dress was caught in the barbed wire of India's new fence, Khatun screamed in fear. In response, Ghosh shot her—her dead, bleeding body was left hanging upside down from the barbed wire of India's new wall for several hours. Once the winter fog cleared, Khatun was visible to border residents, curious onlookers, and journalists—and, soon, to the wider world. Her body came to exemplify Bangladesh's geobody and its unequal relationship with India. Ghosh was acquitted for this crime two years later. State violence ensures that fear circulates, accentuating what Michael Taussig—seeking inspiration from Walter Benjamin's rendering of the state of exception—articulates as "illusions of order congealed by fear." In Khatun's case, both the exception and the rule that her killing exemplified created an "ordered disorder."[23]

Atlases of Fear

As Mahfuz and I walked past the Bangladeshi border outpost in the direction of Tura, armed sentries with machine guns and bullets strapped to their chest interrogated us. A mile away from the Rowmari-Tura road, my halting pen sketched it on a huge brown sheet of paper. Mahfuz, his grandson-in-law Rezaul and his lecturer friends, and the Amin sat with me in a political party's office in Rowmari long after the party workers had left. Since the Amin had failed to procure a map with the road everyone insisted that I should draw one instead. I struggled to map the road. My young, assertive friends imposed distances and measurements that challenged the Amin's measurements. They argued endlessly with each other about the location of the boundary pillars. Ignoring them, the Amin silently calculated with his fingers on the sheet of paper. I continued drawing according to his imagined scale. A mile and half in the direction of Tura, he asked me to stop and draw a circle to indicate a Bangladeshi border outpost. Then he asked me to sketch a line with a series of little crosses indicating India's border fence. Mahfuz and I had stopped precisely in this location while walking on the Rowmari-Tura road. Here, two border outposts faced each other across the new barrier.

From Bangladesh, India's new barrier surfaced as a fence rumored to be charged with electricity. Just across the border from Rowmari, Indian villagers who came to shop in a market near the border excitedly asked me, "Have you seen the new fence? You can see Bangladesh through it, on the other side." Fears of electrification generated an architectural marvel. India's fence construction ensured that the word "Bangladesh" was taboo, especially in the Muslim-populated *chars*. Here, border villagers shied away not only from any connections with Bangladesh but at the mere mention of its name, anxiously recovered land documents from old tin trunks.

Fear protects people from the ultimate risk—the risk of death. At the Northeast India–Bangladesh border, fear and reverence along with the troops as an integral part of border societies had historically ensured that the risk of death was allayed. As terror diffused throughout the landscape, it made grazing grounds, rice fields, and forests into zones of disorientation without displacing the motif of mobility that made borders productive and unstable locations. At dawn and dusk, India's fence with Bangladesh provided a lethal backdrop for a mass of frenzied humans and animals. Fear blurred the bodies—sarong clad and thin—of citizens and foreigners. It rendered indistinguishable the bodies of women who ran across the border from men—all running at the sight of border troops. Fear divided those who dared to cross the border from those who were rendered immobile in anticipation of an electrified fence. It joined the predicaments of those who swore to never make a living out of the border with the ones who swore never to leave it.

Fear ensured that the teasing taunts that the troops hurled at Chandra and me, their half-dressed attire of white vests and khaki shorts as they relaxed outside Manik's house, the wet uniforms and Bangladeshi T-shirts that Indian soldiers dried on the barbed wire of the fence felt ominous. Fear failed to normalize this landscape of lush green rice fields and forests.

CHAPTER 6

Bangladeshi "Suspects" and Indian "Citizens" in Assam

As soon as the bus from Dispur, Assam's capital city, entered Melkiganj, a loosely suspended sign welcomed visitors. The frequent stopping of the overcrowded buses by India's security forces ensured that the usual ten-hour journey to this far-flung border town took another four hours. The troops frisked selected passengers, asked them to produce identity cards, suspecting them to be either unauthorized Bangladeshi migrants or political dissidents in Assam. The border signpost expressed gratitude to travelers for visiting India, announcing the end of Indian territory even before visitors could enter the town's bureaucratic enclave. The enclave was a short distance from the bus depot.

Inside the enclave were Foreigners Tribunals X1 and X2, two of the hundred tribunals adjudicating the borders of India citizenship and the illegality of Bangladeshi migrants in Assam.[1] From the narrow corridor of Tribunal X1, situated on the ground floor, family members who accompanied the petitioners could peep inside the trial chamber. They could also see police escorting handcuffed men into the narrow alley behind the tribunals that led to the district prison. Although mundane bureaucratic allotments had ensured the tribunals' proximity to the prison, this sight of handcuffed prisoners made those who had been summoned to the tribunal even more nervous. One of them was the frail, approximately sixty-five-year-old Nehar Bibi, who resided in a village that bordered Bangladesh in Assam. She was not aware that the border police had identified her as a Bangladeshi "illegal" migrant, and the court summons had never reached her. It was a year later that Nehar finally arrived at the doorstep of Tribunal X1 with her lawyer, clumsily clutching a deportation notice to her chest. Exhausted from the long journey from her village and from fasting during the holy month of Ramadan, Nehar almost fainted in the courtroom.

Judicial trials aim to deport Bangladeshi immigrants who have arrived and resettled in Assam without authorization after the legal cutoff date of 25 March 1971. The surveys conducted by Assam's specially constituted Border Police and, since 2015, the updating of the National Register of Citizens have set this process into motion. The police scrutinize new names on electoral registers and new arrivals, especially in districts of Assam that border Bangladesh. Once the constables submit reports to the tribunals, the tribunals summon the accused, who appear with documents to prove their Indian citizenship. The accused arrive with their lawyers and submit petitions. They perform Indian citizenship through paperwork—parentage, education, residence, and property documents—while state prosecutors sift through the original documents, scrutinize them, and interrogate the suspects. When the identity papers finally reach the judge, he publicly scrutinizes them. Once the trial concludes, the judge sits alone in his chamber reviewing the paperwork and testimonies before finally adjudicating the terms upon which Indian citizenship would be ascertained.

While some nervously entered the premises of the tribunals, others loudly and indignantly insisted that they were Indian citizens. As I started observing and noting the judicial proceedings in the nondescript two-storied house that accommodated Tribunals X1 and X2, the borders between Indian citizens and unauthorized Bangladeshis constantly blurred. Sometimes, silence descended as the summoned suspects mysteriously did not turn up. Neither police interrogation nor a legal summons from the tribunals could impel people to attend the tribunals. Before I elaborate on how both the commotions and silences generate doubts about people's relationships to places and paper identities in Assam, let me briefly foreground the specific histories and politics that guide these trials and make the contours of Indian citizenship even more shadowy in the state of Assam.

Citizens and Suspects

Indian sources estimate that of the twenty million Bangladeshis suspected to have resettled in India without official authorization, six million reside in

Assam.[2] Although both India and Bangladesh consider migration after 25 March 1971 without official authorization to be illegal, neither diplomacy nor the implementation of a legal cutoff date has resolved issues of divided households and transborder labor migration.

Legally, Indian citizenship is defined by exclusions. As Anupama Roy states, the legal locus of the "migrant outsider" has been indispensable to the crafting of the Indian citizen. The different configurations of migrants as refugees from Pakistan and later Bangladesh have informed the ideological premises and the institutional manifestations of Indian citizenship. In India, Muslims are suspected perennially of being immigrants, noncitizens, and outsiders.[3] Neerja Gopal Jayal has shown how, over the years, Indian citizenship came to be ascribed with qualifications that entailed constitutional classifications as well as exceptions. These exceptions, she argues, operate in the sphere of the "political state" and closely follow the religious difference between the Hindus and the Muslims in India.[4] In December 2019, the long history of religious fault lines of Indian citizenship was further reinforced through the Citizenship Amendment Act (CAA). This offered Indian citizenship to Hindus, Sikhs, Buddhists, Jains, Parsis, and Christians—who had "illegally" migrated to India from Afghanistan, Bangladesh, or Pakistan on or before 31 December 2014. This legislation has led to widespread fear that with one broad stroke, the governmental machinery could strip many Muslims of their existing Indian citizenship.[5]

Madeleine Reeves argues that migrant (il)legality operates in "a space of relations" rather than being a precise distinction between legal and illegal migration. She shows how ambiguities define the lifeworlds of migrant laborers in Moscow, where it is equally difficult for migrants, employers, and law enforcers to implement the classificatory logic of the state.[6] In many nation-states, especially corrupt ones, political membership and citizenship remain fuzzy as unauthorized migrants easily procure citizenship documents.[7] In India, the procurement of identity documents mediates this in-between space. Those who occupy zones of licitness are, however, embedded in a constant struggle for legitimacy and claims to political membership.[8] In the absence of official policies to regulate labor migration between India and Bangladesh, India's security-centric discourse and electoral politics have linked undocumented Bangladeshi migration with threats of "infiltration" and Islamic "terrorism." Such claims are fraught with uncertainties. Indian political parties continue to vacillate between enabling Bangladeshi immigrants to fraudulently acquire identity documents to vote in Indian elections and demanding the speedy deportation of these "Muslim illegal immigrants."[9]

In India, national citizenship can materialize in and through acts of corruption.[10] Corruption of identity documents and papers facilitates ordinary people's entitlements to basic necessities and a sense of community. In fact, the production and verification of identity documents enable claim making for both poor Indian citizens and undocumented Bangladeshis.[11] State complicity in corrupt practices and facilitation of fake identity paper render the boundaries of citizenship and migrant illegality even fuzzier.[12] Veena Das and Deborah Poole have shown that the state at its margins is "experienced and undone through the illegibility of its own practices, documents and words."[13] The fabrication of identity papers is fundamental to both the production and manufacturing of Indian citizenship and the incorporation of the Bangladeshi migrant. Yet, the overall assumption in India is that as noncitizens, undocumented Bangladeshi migrants exceed the morally accepted thresholds of documentary corruption that Indian citizens normally engage in.

In Assam, the main concerns surrounding unauthorized Bangladeshi migration relate to land loss and conflicts over ethnolinguistic identities. For these reasons, the boundaries of Indian citizenship have been monitored in unique ways. In Chapter 2, I have elaborated on the contentious nature of the crafting of colonial boundaries between the British provinces of Assam and Bengal, the immigration of Bengali peasants to Assam for land settlement, and the resettlement of Bengali Hindu refugees following the partition. Starting in the 1960s, a political discourse focused on "infiltration" from Bangladesh led Assam to demand the construction of a border fence.[14] The reader may recall that in 1964, "mobile" courts were set up next to police stations, and those detected as "Pakistani foreigners" were hastily deported. Anxieties surrounding the political patronage of illegal voters and the potential loss of land to unauthorized Bangladeshis led to a widespread anti-foreigner agitation between 1979 and 1985, known as the Assam Movement. The movement demanded the speedy identification of unauthorized Bangladeshis in the state of Assam, their disenfranchisement as voters, and their deportation. In response, the central government in New Delhi passed the Illegal Migration (Determination by Tribunals) Act (IMDT) in 1983. IMDT tribunals were set up to try suspected "illegal" foreigners through the due process of law. The provisions of the Act ensured that Indian Muslim minorities were not to be harassed in the name of detecting Bangladeshi foreigners. However, there were few deportations under the IMDT Act.[15]

Figure 21. A widely circulated poster in border districts of Assam warning citizens against new arrivals from Bangladesh. In bold writing, the poster requests residents to report the presence of any suspected and unknown people in the area to the police. (Photograph: Shib Shankar Chatterjee)

The All Assam Students Union (AASU), whose members led the Assam Movement, has demanded that the names of all "illegal" Bangladeshi foreigners be deleted from the electoral rolls. The AASU regards Bangladeshis as immigrants who have a nefarious design to increase their numbers, eventually to take over political power in Assam and destroy India's territorial integrity. From the early 1990s, the AASU started demanding the annulment of the IMDT Act (1983) because of its ineffectiveness in deporting illegal Bangladeshis.[16] In comparison, the Foreigners Act of India (1946) that was enacted in British India was perceived to be more "deportation friendly."[17] The Foreigners Tribunal Order (1964) allowed for the creation of tribunals such as X1 and X2 under the Foreigners Act. Coming into operation in 1946, this act called for "complete control" over the movement of foreigners. After independence, the Indian state retained this stringent Act, which can exclude people through provisions intended for war situations.[18] In response to Sarbananda Sonowal, who was a former president of the AASU and had filed a public interest litigation, the Indian Supreme Court cautioned that large-scale Bangladeshi immigration threatened both the state of Assam and the rest of India—expanding the meaning of "external aggression" to include economic aggression.[19]

The AASU regularly conducts large-scale protests and strikes against what they perceive as India's handing over Assam's lands to Bangladesh.[20] In a voice that reverberated down the neat corridors of AASU's headquarters in Guwahati, AASU's advisor Samujjal Bhattacharya stated to me, thumping his fist on the wooden table, "Bangladeshi illegal immigrants want to earn their living in Assam, and they get political patronage, as politicians here need Bangladeshi vote banks. Earlier these illegal immigrants only wanted to vote but now Bangladeshis even plan to send their representatives to contest elections in Assam. Considering the large numbers of migrants who are flowing in through a porous border, a Bangladeshi will soon be the Chief Minister [the political leader of a state] of Assam."[21]

However, in 2016, it was Sarbananda Sonowal who led the Bharatiya Janata Party (BJP) to form the state government in Assam. Three decades after the Assam Movement, the rise of Hindu nationalist politics under the BJP has fractured the political field in Assam by further sharpening ethnic, linguistic, religious differences, and hatred toward the "illegal" Bangladeshis. Prior to the 2016 elections, the Assam Border Police had identified 150,000 voters as doubtful citizens and prevented them from casting ballots.[22] In 2015, under the BJP-led government in New Delhi, Assam started updating the

National Register of Citizens, which aimed to detect unauthorized Bangladeshis and has excluded 1.9 million people from the citizenship list. In the process, it has rendered them stateless often on dubious grounds.[23] Sanjay Barbora underscores that initially, in 2015, the National Register of Citizens was perceived to offer legal and political avenues to resolve the contentious issues of autonomy and social justice that have shaped political mobilization in Assam since the mid-twentieth century. In contrast, he suggests that India's Citizenship Amendment Act of 2019 reaffirmed India's colonial relationship with Assam and the rest of India, demonstrating a disregard for the political assertions of Assamese and indigenous people.[24] Assam's opposition to India's Citizenship Amendment Act emphasizes how the inclusion of Hindu Bengali refugees from Bangladesh—some of whom were excluded from the National Register of Citizens—destabilizes Assam's demographics, language, and culture.

Today, under Assam's BJP-led government, both religion and ethnicity frame public debates on Indian citizenship in Assam. Religion, which was on the backburner in Assam, has been brought to the forefront. Political parties, civil society groups, and the public at large all mobilize these categories to craft demands for inclusion and exclusion of certain groups of people. Assam's fluid boundaries with Bangladesh, as well as its complex boundaries with India and contemporary electoral politics under the BJP, generate bureaucratic practices that specifically drive people into foreigners tribunals.[25] The police surveys, verifiable forms, judicial deliberations, and finality of court orders that seek to identify "illegal" Bangladeshis and deport them manufacture suspicion to unsettle familiar and familial bonds in Assam. As the borders of legality and illegality are transplanted into the judicial domain in Assam, police surveys and judicial trials generate and perpetrate doubt. By leaving unclarified the contentious issues of land loss and identities in Assam, judicial processes make suspicion, rather than legal and procedural certainty, fundamental to the manufacturing of Indian citizenship in Assam.

Registers and Files

Assam's Border Police walked in and out of the offices of Tribunals X1 and X2, heaping interrogation reports on the desks of the clerks Sujala Das and Samar Bhoumik. They were the custodians of the most important document at the tribunal—the register of records that contained the dates of court hearings. Their notings in this register would set into motion the judicial proceedings that would decide the citizenship claims of identified suspects. Unlike Bhoumik, whose location on the first floor and handling of a small number of cases ensured that few people surrounded him, Das's massive blue register was always open for her to list police reports. She was constantly interrupted by people who gathered around her table for hearing dates.

Das drew neat lines with a plastic ruler, measuring each column before filling in the details. In the blue register, she noted, from left to right, serial numbers, dates, names, addresses, gender, and the status of the cases. From this register, Das calculated case statistics for the Assam Border Police and identified the court summons and the dates for trials and judgments. The judge's signature and seal endorsed each entry. As Das attended to the case files, she intentionally ignored the people who gathered at her table. She also maintained a cautious distance from her colleagues, keeping her widowhood and the location of her residence in Melkiganj secret, lest they engaged in gossip.

Case files comprised police interrogation reports, case diaries, court summons, and petitions submitted by those the Assam police had accused of being illegally resident foreigners. The order sheet that covered each case file chronicled the summons, hearings, and adjournments. The petitions drafted by lawyers and copies of identity documents that were subsequently added made the files bulky. The petitions were standardized, mostly typed in English. Without exception, the petitioners submitted that they could neither read nor write, had not received notices from the police, and requested more time for the procurement of documents. Proof of Indian citizenship rested on being able to produce a range of mandatory identity papers: electoral lists, land registration records, citizens' registration papers, and birth, marriage, and school-leaving certificates. Das folded each of the papers and placed them date-wise in light pink paper files, tying them all together with a thread.

Writing, filling forms, and creating case files were central to adjudicating the border of Indian citizenship in X1 and X2. These were far more than the repetitive and routine bureaucratic acts and processes that make societies legible.[26] The bureaucratic actions and paper documents that state agents and people provide, acquire, submit, classify, manage, and retrieve all recall the centrality of state machineries and their influence on democratic functioning and practices. In generating complex paper economies, these not only support state actions but are themselves constitutive of the state.[27] As

Figure 22. Indian border residents show their voter identity cards to the Indian Border Security Forces for checks before parliamentary elections at the India-Bangladesh border. (Photograph: Shib Shankar Chatterjee)

Nayanika Mathur emphasizes, official papers are entities that come into being through bureaucratic practices. These, she argues, are both uncertain and violent, and yet have life-giving properties.[28] A sense of dual indeterminacy shapes identity documents; anomalous laws and conflicting forces that produce the legality of identity documents and the fact that all documents have be linked to people mediate political subjectivities.[29] Official documents and files that move between local governments and populations shape the force of politics as well as developmental projects.[30] What remains critical to these "paper truths," to invoke Emma Tarlo's phrase, is not so much what they convey about rules and procedures but what they reveal about the relationship of people to rules.[31]

Petitioners and lawyers constantly interrupted Das's work. Some pleaded for more time to procure identity documents. Others mistook her desk for Bhowmik's, upon which she brusquely directed them to the first floor. When lawyers urged her to provide a hearing date, Das put on an air of importance. She took longer to draw the columns and rows. Stretching out her hand to retrieve her small green diary, she opened it and shook her head slowly.

A sharp bell from the trial chamber regularly interrupted her tasks and performances in the tribunal's office. The bell was a signal for divisional assistants such as her to enter the chamber. Das often tripped on the upturned old carpet at the entrance, just like the others who were entering the trial chamber for the first time.

Begum Versus Bibi

Upon her entry, Das presented a case file to the judge. One day, the file pertained to Sultana Begum. Tribunal X1 had summoned Begum to the court on the suspicion that she was a dubious Bangladeshi voter who was illegally residing in Assam. Das handed Begum's heavy case file to the judge. Begum's petition was detailed, stating that she has been married for ten years to Khaliduddin, who was a politician. The petition stated that she had relocated from her village to her husband's village, which bordered Bangladesh. I spoke with Begum as she waited for the judge to summon her to the courtroom. She emphasized that police harassment and delays had unsettled her life for several years. During this period, she had traveled several times to her father's village to retrieve her school certificates from her brother's house. She also conveyed that the label "Bangladeshi" had brought her family into disrepute and had impaired her position as a local politician's wife. As soon as the police arrived and later when the court summons reached her, rumors spread that her husband, a well-known politician, had taken a Bangladeshi as his second wife. Her husband's political opponents took every opportunity to malign their reputation, and the protracted legal process ensured that her neighbors and other villagers also continued to doubt her Indian credentials. The postponement of her court hearing for five years—because the previous tribunal had been understaffed and later dissolved in 2005—led people familiar with her to suspect her identity even more.

Rumors about Begum being an illegal Bangladeshi had reached the village school in which her two sons studied. While her elder son, who attended secondary school, endured his friends' taunts that his mother was a foreigner, the younger son was curious. He asked her, "Why are you being called a Bangladeshi? Are you really from Bangladesh? What does that country look like? Will we be sent to Bangladesh? Please, will you take me there?" Like the insults that her elder son faced, her younger son's persistent village gossip–influenced curiosity anguished Begum. Begum conveyed that she had confined herself to caring for the children and their education, keeping away from her husband's political activities. She served guests who came to her house but always kept clear of village gossip. Her attempts, like Das's, did not prevent their neighbors and colleagues from gossiping; rumors about the former's identity and the latter's manner of dressing in bright colors that her male colleagues regarded as inappropriate for her age persisted.

Begum's trial animated Das's case files. Writing about land documentation in Islamabad, Matthew Hull makes a compelling case for reading the file as a "complex graphic genre." As artifacts whose histories are repeatedly inscribed on them, files are conferred with "event-like" qualities.[32] For Hull, not only does this attribution define the role that files play as unique graphic artifacts, but it also demonstrates their relationships to people, space, and time.[33] Illuminating the file's powerful material properties in the Indian context, Akhil Gupta draws a similar analogy, foregrounding files as objects that attain "a life of its own"—larger than the people who act on it.[34] As soon Begum made an appearance, the papers came alive through the performance of Indian citizenship, transcending their prior confinement as texts in files. In the trial chamber, Begum faced the judge and the state prosecutor. Both her high school education and her identity as the wife of a local politician had given her confidence. She clearly answered the questions that the state prosecutor asked her. Her lawyer presented a series of identity documents that established her claim to Indian citizenship. As state prosecutors pulled police survey and interrogation reports, official documents that the tribunals had sent out, and the original identity papers that the defense counsel had presented, the connections between the papers and her identity as an Indian citizen were established.

In Begum's case, the state prosecutor carefully matched her identity documents with those of her husband and father. While verifying these papers, the state prosecutor theatrically bit his tongue in embarrassment. The silence in which Begum's identity documents were retrieved from neat plastic folders, verified, and shared reflected the consensus that her case was one of police misidentification. Beyond an occasional biting of the tongue or a shake of the head, police surveys and interrogation errors seldom surfaced as an issue during the formal proceedings of the court.

Begum broke the silence that had descended in the courtroom. She raised her voice to the judge: "Sir, the notice is wrong. These are all fabrications. I am a citizen of India. I do not have any relatives in Bangladesh, not even ancestors; I have been harassed for so many years." Smilingly, the judge responded, "So you do not want to go back to Bangladesh?" Everyone in the courtroom broke into smiles. Begum confidently held her pen and signed documents that established her as an Indian citizen. Outside the courtroom, during the recess, she whispered to me that she would press charges against the police for maligning her reputation.

Unlike Begum, women of modest means with few or no identity papers and thin case files faced aggressive cross-examinations. The frail Nehar Bibi was completely oblivious that the police had identified her as a Bangladeshi and had summoned her to Tribunal X1. The village teacher had approached her after seeing a notice in English pasted on the walls of the village primary school. Behind her was her lawyer, who had earlier appealed to the tribunal to make a special consideration and re-open her case. Her submission to the court held that she was aged and uneducated and that she had not received the notice personally.

When her name was announced, Bibi entered the courtroom wiping her face with a green handkerchief. Exhausted from fasting for the holy month of Ramadan, she slowly grabbed the arm of a plastic chair by the door with her bony hands. She made an attempt to sit. At once, her lawyer stopped her; the court typist glared at her from under his glasses. In the absence of the state prosecutor, who was late, the judge asked Bibi to present her case. She mumbled. The judge tried to facilitate the process and asked her a few questions. She failed to answer. Straining her ears to listen, she fiddled with her umbrella as she spoke to the judge. Confused, she made eye contact with her witness, a neighbor named Bari, who presented himself before the court.

It was only during Bari's testimony to the court that the state prosecutor barged into the trial room, profusely apologizing to the judge for his delay. Folding his hands at Bibi theatrically, he bowed in an obvious display of respect. He requested as that as an elder, she forgive him for the questions that he was obliged to ask. With this apology, he hurled a torrent of questions at Bari, Bibi's witness—to compensate for his late arrival. Giving Bari only a few seconds to think, the prosecutor constantly confused Bari and demanded that he present his birth and marriage certificates before the court. Dumbfounded, Bari looked helplessly at the lawyer and claimed that he was not asked to procure his own documents before coming to the court. Seizing upon the moment of confusion, the state prosecutor announced to the court that Bibi and Bari had worked on a series of carefully crafted lies to acquire

Indian citizenship. Looking at the judge, he declared in a booming voice: "Bari is a Bangladeshi national and is falsely supporting the claims of another Bangladeshi national, Nehar Bibi."

Subsequently, the state prosecutor cross-examined Bibi, during which he took advantage of her feeble hearing skills to switch the names of villages and years to further confuse her. He also asked her to recall names of prominent politicians in her village, giving her almost no time to comprehend his questions. Bibi lacked identity documents except for a voter identity card. It was inadmissible as evidence of citizenship as these were often falsely procured. Furthermore, she did not have a registered marriage certificate. The legal question was whether Nehar Bibi had enough evidence to prove that she was her father's daughter. Although her father's name, Asub Ali, appeared in the 1965 electoral rolls, there were no documents to prove that Bibi was his daughter. The prosecutor interpreted her uncertain and jumbled responses, and the lack of documentary evidence, as sufficient reason to believe that she was an illegal Bangladeshi. Gloating at having proved a "suspect" to be an "illegal Bangladeshi" the prosecutor pointed at her to loudly announce, "You, Nehar Bibi have come to India after March 25, 1971, you have entered here illegally and you are a Bangladeshi." Since she could not sign, the typist quickly asked Bibi to put her thumb impression on a court document that stated her case has been examined. With a smug smile, the state prosecutor patted the visibly flustered defense counsel on his back.

It is not surprising that Sultana Begum and Nehar Bibi's court trials followed completely opposite trajectories. Their socio-economic distinctions and differing political affiliations provided them with unequal access to identity papers. Begum, an articulate high school–educated woman, had gathered identity documents from her family and school. Her impeccable case file, a bulky one with order sheets noted in several appearances and petitions supplemented by sheets of photocopied identity documents, decisively situated her as an Indian citizen. Her appearance in court as an educated woman whose husband owned land and was a politician, as well as her claims of police harassment, made her the perfect indignant citizen whom the Assam Border police had erroneously identified. Bibi, on the other hand, was the perfect suspect. Her police report emphatically classified her as a Bangladeshi who had migrated from a neighboring village in Bangladesh. She was flustered and failed to answer the state prosecutor's barrage of questions. Furthermore, she had very few papers to prove her claims and had failed to appear earlier despite multiple court summons. Their contrasting circumstances show how national interest and regional identities converge on the scrutiny of the foreigners, who are repeatedly required to assert their own legitimacy in a process that is both unpredictable and dramatic, one that relies on the duplicity and courtroom performance of lawyers more than the determination of settlement histories and issues such as marriage migrations.

Although Begum and Bibi's appearances before the court and the theatrics that accompanied their trials illuminate how papers and performances reinforced one another, the final official paper—the judgment—did legitimize Bibi's presence. The judge took note of Bibi's statements about her father's compulsions to constantly migrate as a landless laborer to seek work and her relocation to her husband's house upon an early marriage. He emphasized that Bibi disagreed with the state prosecutor's claims and stated that the police had not conducted adequate enquires. He recorded that she submitted her father and husband's electoral documents in original and certified copies from village authorities. The judgment stated that although the state prosecutor doubted whether Bibi was the daughter of Asub Ali and the wife of Sohan Ali, he was unable to provide any evidence to the contrary. Furthermore, Bibi had provided evidence of her name in an older electoral register, along with that of her husband's, endorsed by village authorities. The judge therefore delivered the verdict that Nehar Bibi was not a foreigner; she was an Indian citizen.

Both judgments were exactly two and a half pages long, but textually, they stood apart in form and content. In Begum's neatly typed judgment, which had only one minor handwritten correction, the tribunal established her as an Indian citizen and then concluded by emphasizing that she was not a foreigner. By contrast, the typewritten judgment for Bibi's case only asserted that she was not a foreigner; in the final version, handwritten corrections stated that Bibi was an Indian citizen under India's Citizenship Act of 1983. The judgments' contrasting forms, which reinstated Bibi as an Indian citizen, highlight the imprecision of Indian citizenship in Assam. Although both judgments reinstated Bibi and Begum's Indian citizenship, suspicions surrounding their identities will continue to haunt them.

In between hearing cases, the judge called my attention to the regular flow of labor migrants from Bangladesh to Melkiganj. Rumors abounded that Bangladeshis laborers surreptitiously swam across the river that functions as a boundary between India and Bangladesh. With every high tide, when the river waters toppled floating border pillars that demarcated the two states, anxieties about illegal migration heightened. Senior border police officers conveyed that constables escorted those deemed as unauthorized Bangladeshi settlers to "pushback points" at designated locations, the nearest located about 5 miles away. From there, the police would physically push illegal foreigners over the border into Bangladeshi territory—an extralegal measure that is a widely accepted practice in India. Bangladesh has consistently prevented "foreigner intrusion" from India and refused to accept ousted and stranded people as Bangladeshi citizens. As a response to India's "pushback" strategy, Border Guard Bangladesh (BGB) developed "counter-pushback" functions. Although crude physical actions of territoriality happen, police officers in India would casually mention that those pushed into Bangladesh would reside there for a week or two before walking back and returning to India. Since 2015, the National Register of Citizens has, with its policy of detentions inside district prisons and special centers that were especially set up to isolate those deemed as "illegal Bangladeshis," disrupted this extra-legal process of pushbacks.[35]

Begum and Bibi's struggles of legitimacy further testify to the gendered gradations of Indian citizenship in Assam. The border police routinely accused Muslim women of being Bangladeshi migrants who married Indian men to fraudulently acquire Indian citizenship. The hunt for "illegal Bangladeshi" Muslim women exposes the contradictory use of official documents such as electoral list. The judiciary regards electoral lists as unreliable document because Bangladeshi migrants can easily insert their names into these registers. On the other hand, the judicial process demands the electoral histories of families through records in electoral rolls as evidence of citizenship. In their survey reports for the tribunals, Assam's border police listed Muslim names such as Mumtaz Begum, Sona Bibi, and Asma Bibi, identifying them as Bangladeshis who had come to reside in Assam without official authorization. The reports were ambiguous in stating whether Indian men had traveled to Bangladesh for marriage or the accused Bangladeshi women had traveled to India. In Mumtaz Begum's case, a border police inspector had questioned the election commission officer's former endorsement of her as an Indian citizen. The inspector's letter stated that during a house enumeration survey, the police had identified her as a resident of the village. While the election commission officer did not doubt her authenticity as an Indian citizen based on her father's electoral records, the Assam Border Police suspected her credentials. In the police report, the inspector noted that although there was evidence that her father had voted in past elections, the tribunal needed to verify that Mumtaz Begum was his daughter.

Begum and Bibi's judgments established the legality of their residence in Assam, their marriages, and their Indian citizenship on the basis of paternity. By preventing Muslim women from voting in elections for extended periods, police actions such as these ensured that their names were struck off from electoral lists. State actions ensured that adult women became infantile political subjects, and their marital relationships and mobility also came to be delegitimized for extended periods as they waited for the tribunals to reinstate them as legal subjects.

Sonarband Colony

Among the petitioners who gathered around Sujala Das's table were the residents of the Sonarband refugee colony. Displaced by the partition of the Indian subcontinent in 1947, Assam was compelled to resettle Hindu Bengalis who arrived from East Pakistan as refugees. In the newly independent India, Bengali Hindu refugee arrivals from East Pakistan added to Assam's burdens. In 1948, Assam classified Bengali Hindu refugees as "non-Assamese" and "non-indigenous." The state government ensured that, in addition to the refugees, other nonnatives of Assam would also be disenfranchised and barred from voting, even though they had resided in Assam and owned land and homes.[36] Although many Indian states opposed Bengali Hindu refugee settlements, in Assam, this was aggravated by linguistic issues around Assamese and Bengali, leading to large-scale riots in 1960 and 1961. Time has not resolved this controversial issue. Bengali Hindu refugees' claims to Assam's land as Indian citizens are as controversial today as they were in British India and early postcolonial Assam.

Eighty-year-old Renu Dey and her two sons, Subir and Soubhik, faced the state prosecutor in the courtroom. Their lawyer presented their petitions, which stated that Renu and her husband, Prafulla, had migrated to Assam as refugees in 1950 from East Pakistan (Bangladesh since 1971). They registered as Indian citizens under the 1956 Citizenship Act of India. As a Bengali Hindu refugee in Assam, Renu had carefully stored her citizenship papers. Slightly frayed at the edges, these papers had been encased in a thick and dusty plastic envelope. Subir furnished his parents' citizenship registration form. The citizenship certificate mentioned Sonarband colony as their address.

After scrutinizing the document, the judge remarked that the ink and the signature looked too fresh for an old document. The bright blue ink stood out in the faded certificate. The defense counsel promptly responded that inks used fifty years earlier were of superior quality compared to the inks that were manufactured now. Unconvinced, the government prosecutor held the documents against the light to verify the official seal. The state prosecutor handed the citizenship certificate and housing loan papers to the stenographer, who in turn passed them to the judge. Turning to Renu's sons, the state prosecutor constantly interrupted them as they tried to answer his questions. He insisted to the court that Renu and her sons had entered the state of Assam recently and illegally. In a final move to assert his claims that the Dey family members were "illegal Bangladeshis," the state prosecutor presented a handwritten document—a confession—with Soubhik's signature. In this, Soubhik had apparently stated, "I have given my name and address. My age is around forty years. I am giving the statement that I have come to reside in this place for the last few years and that I do not know the year in which I was born. I also do not know where I was born. I have nothing much else to state."

Soubhik was dumbfounded. In the following months, several such confession statements surfaced from case files during cross-examinations. While a few statements were obscure and vague, others were impressively detailed, outlining the names of villages and towns in Bangladesh from where migrants had traveled. Occasionally, confession statements written in English affirmed the information that police had provided in their interrogation reports. While some were missing signatures, others were handwritten. In many cases, witness statements supplemented such confessions. Often, these witness statements indicated that those accused of being illegal Bangladeshis had arrived in Assam and grabbed land.

In Melkiganj's tribunals, the accused were often stupefied when state prosecutors presented confession statements. Despite discrepancies and the obvious attempts of the border police to falsely impose a sense of order and meet their Bangladeshi identification targets, the state prosecutor turned the act of reading out the confessions into a flamboyant performance. Holding a sheet of white paper in his hand, he read the statements aloud for everyone to hear, not only those present in the trial chamber but also the audience of family members who stood outside, peeping into the chamber through the open window. Unlike acts of bureaucratic legibility, where police interrogation reports and confession statements textually synchronized, the prosecutor's exaggerated enactments of both obscure and detailed confession statements sensationalized the otherwise mundane judicial trials. Breaking the monotony of legal dreariness, his dramatization of written confessions made petitioners jittery and confused—acts that provided him scope to make even more vocal claims about them being illegal Bangladeshis. Although everyone in the judicial chamber was aware that police confessions were not legally admissible as evidence, by persistently staging these written texts, the state prosecutor also mocked the efforts of the Assam Border Police to fabricate confessions. Finally, his loud cross-examinations served to establish his indispensability as the protector of Indian citizenship in Assam.

Setting aside the confessional dramas and despite the freshness of the ink, the judge accepted the Dey family's identity and land papers as genuine. He delivered the verdict that the Dey family members were Indian citizens. In the weeks that followed, several other residents of the Sonarband refugee colony were legalized as Indian citizens. Among the exceptions was Manik Roy, the son of a resident of the Sonarband colony. Roy was born in the Sonarband colony. Like Renu Dey, Roy's father migrated to Assam after the partition. He had settled in the Sonarband colony and procured a housing loan. A man in his late forties and a shopkeeper by profession, Roy presented several documents before the tribunal. These included his father's refugee card, citizenship certificate, housing loan cards, and land documents. He also provided his school-leaving certificates. The state prosecutor examined Roy and his witness, a neighbor who knew his father. The state prosecutor argued that there were discrepancies in the information provided by Roy and his witness about the year in which his father migrated, where his father resided, and the year that his father had died. Based on the cross-examination, the Tribunal held that the paper evidence that Roy provided was tampered and "created."[37]

In his verdict, the judge affirmed that Roy's signatures on the copies of his father's refugee card, citizenship certificate, and the receipt of loan tax were not identical. The only document that could prove Roy's Indian citizenship was his school-leaving certificate; however, the judge doubted the signature of the headmaster. Furthermore, the land documents that Roy provided were certified copies and not original documents. Based on the inconsistent information and weak paper evidence, the tribunal declared Roy to be a Bangladeshi foreigner. Unhappy with the verdict, Roy approached the High Court in Assam. The High Court held that the tribunal had based its opinion on the similarity of his signatures on the basis of comparison and observation. Thus, the tribunal relied on its own opinion to establish the authenticity of the evidence, instead of calling an expert for verification. The High Court set aside the order of the tribunal and referred Roy's case for a retrial. However, the High Court did not indicate whether the documents that Roy had furnished were authentic. Such decisions on the legitimacy of the papers further prolonged the trials of many others.

The systems of disclosure upon which the police surveillance relied had the effect of turning families against each other. Among those who sat pensively in the back office was Monmohan Das. He claimed that in his village, the police had encouraged people to come forward and disclose the names of "illegal" Bangladeshis. Monmohan, who was in his mid-seventies, sat exhausted near Sujala Das's table, fanning himself with a court order. He insisted that his brothers were taking advantage of the new laws to dispossess him of his share of his father's property. He emphasized that his younger brother had notified the police that he was a Bangladeshi to ensure that he was so embroiled in the tribunal's proceedings that he would not have the time to fight another court case to make a claim on his father's land. Since doubts surrounded the identities of people such as Monmohon Das, who were accused of assimilating into refugee colonies as new migrants from Bangladesh, no one at Melkiganj's tribunals paid any heed to his claims about family conflicts.

Historical animosities over border territories and refugee populations cast a looming shadow not only over court trials but also outside the tribunals' premises. Just outside the gates of the tribunals, Hindu Bengali politicians gathered to address journalists from local newspapers, claiming that the Assam Border Police targeted Bengali Indian citizens in this border district in the name of detecting "illegal" Bangladeshis. Among the politicians was Shyamoli Sarkar. Trained as a lawyer, she asserted that police detection drives and judicial trials targeted low-caste Hindus such as her who were formerly refugees but—since the early 1950s—were legal Indian citizens. Sarkar represented the interests of her constituency to the press, noting their grievances.[38] Thus, despite the Melkiganj tribunals' assertion that Sonarband colony's residents were Indians, as Bengalis, their presence continues to be controversial.

The next day, local newspapers carried stories about Indian citizens in Assam being maligned as suspected Bangladeshis. The judge calmly glanced at the news reports and put them aside. The staff went about their routine duties, disregarding the new commotion from the press conferences that started in the afternoon. Das mechanically checked the new interrogation reports that the border police heaped on her table and noted them in her blue register.

"UT": The Untraceable

Intermittently, the din died down. When the identified suspects who the tribunals had summoned failed to appear, silence replaced the frenzied rustling of petitions and files, as well as the clamor of voices. The empty offices and trial chambers—which enabled the divisional assistants and peons to take long afternoon naps—called attention to the hunt for elusive Bangladeshi foreigners in Assam and the desperation to locate the state's invisible populations. Despite police surveys and court summonses, Assam's missing populations were neither legally nor physically identifiable. As subjects who eluded police mapping and legal verification, their absence added to the ever-evolving dynamics of suspicion along borders.

Sujala Das filed cases of missing people under the label "UT," the acronym for "untraceable." Between 1988 and the end of 2007, the number of cases tried at the tribunals equaled the number of "UT" cases. Among those who failed to arrive were Mumtaz Begum and Asma Bibi. Suspected to be Bangladeshi women whom the police had accused of illegal residence in Assam, Mumtaz and Asma mysteriously disappeared. The border police, who had initially identified and interrogated them as suspects, could not trace their whereabouts, so they could deliver the court summonses. In Asma Bibi's case, the police located a young man with her husband's name, but his identity did not match the documentary details that the police interrogation report had provided. When villagers insisted that the only Khalid who had ever lived in the village was this young man, another mismatch between police surveys and suspected Bangladeshis surfaced. The missing suspects evidenced how the police were confused about Assam's border geographies. Yet, their reports meticulously documented Bangladesh's border geography, even noting the names of villages and towns in Bangladesh. These also detailed routes through which Bangladeshis had secretly arrived in Assam.

Other "UT" cases included the Ghosh family, who had come to resettle in a village near Melkiganj. The police identified the family as Bangladeshi Hindu migrants who had arrived in Assam in 1992. The investigation report stated that they had fled Bangladesh on account of religious persecution against Hindu minorities during retaliation for widespread communal violence against Muslims in India, which was prompted by the demolition of the Babri mosque. The family made an appearance before the court in 1995. Only one member of the Ghosh family was able to furnish a written statement to the court, in which she requested more time to procure identity documents. In 1996, the entire family went missing. The Assam Border Police could not trace the family and were unable to ascertain whether they had migrated back to Bangladesh, elsewhere in Assam, or other Indian states.

The judge used the free time that missing suspects created in the courtroom to review more "UT" case files stored at the tribunal's office. On one such silent afternoon, he read aloud the case of X2 case 191 to me to explain the dilemmas of identifying suspects in order to deliver summons to them. He complained that when a sub-inspector had arrived at Mashila Police Station to deliver a court summons, the massive village divided into ten subzones had thoroughly confused him. He was not able to cover the entire village in a day. In another case, the police could not locate Kamila Bibi in Nayapaltan village, which was divided into three large subdivisions. In these instances, like several others, sub-inspectors returned without delivering the court summons to suspects that their colleagues had previously identified.

One among the Assam's border police constables was "investigator 012"— whom I have named after the esoteric manner in which he classified his reports. His case diaries illustrate the varied ways in which detection serves to entrench suspicions along borders. Like other state agents, investigator 012 had the daunting task of identifying suspects in a large jurisdiction of Melkiganj. His handwritten reports, like those of his colleagues, were extremely legible. He penned equidistantly positioned words in straight lines. His interrogation notes disregarded the column headings of the case diary that was recycled from cases under India's Criminal Procedure Code. On the first quarter of the page, these included subtitles—"arrested and sent up," "arrested and released on bail," and "at large." His writing cut across this matrix. In the remaining two-thirds of the page, 012 followed the three stated column headings—number and hour of entry, place of entry, and synopsis of entry.

Investigator 012's field trips were extremely thorough. Over six months, 012 reported arriving in the village of Cachari at precisely 9:15 every morning. At 10:00, he left for his preselected destination—the house of the "suspect"—arriving at exactly 1:00 in the afternoon. For an hour, he employed various interrogation techniques and gathered intelligence about the suspects from their neighbors. By 3:00 in the afternoon, the expedition was complete;

he folded his survey sheets and left for the local police station. At 6:00 in the evening, 012 ended his day. For the six months that he investigated suspected foreigners in the village of Cachari, 012 reported traveling three times to the same house and baiting several suspects belonging to the same family.

Although carefully penned surveys kickstarted the papers into motion, in several instances, they failed to push people into the Foreigners Tribunals. Instead of firmly locating people in specific places, 012's meticulously handwritten notes reinforced registers of imprecision. Writing about the replicability of forms, Akhil Gupta conveys how the ability to standardize information and generate statistics are ways of situating the world.[39] However, in this instance, "routinized performances" establish far more than the bureaucratic capacity to replicate.[40] The question of replicability that the police report forms displayed affirmed the intertwining of electoral politics and bureaucratic action. Investigator 012's actions and his suspiciously precise identical notings derived momentum from the electoral politics that supported populist notions of undocumented Bangladeshis taking over Assamese territory.

The police constable's inability to deliver summons to previously mapped suspects led senior delegations of the Assam Border Police to arrive in Tribunals X1 and X2. Their seniority demanded that they traveled by jeeps with flashing red lights and sirens, although the offices of the Assam Border Police were round the corner. During such meetings, two armed police constables stood at the entrance of the trial chamber. The border police set the agenda. Everyone sat upright, shook their heads, and nodded vigorously at the issues that the police commissioner listed. In every meeting, Namita, a peon, quickly took out delicate porcelain teacups from a locked cupboard, efficiently brewed tea, and handed a cup to everyone, including the stenographer, who was busy typing the proceedings. During these occasions, the stenographer quickly gulped the tea, forgetting his high-caste identity, which prevented him from accepting tea from Namita otherwise. If Shyamoli Sarkar's public insistence that the Assam Border Police were persecuting low-caste Bengali Hindus in Assam reinstated her importance as a lower-caste Hindu politician in her constituency, the presence of high-ranking police officials made Namita's low caste momentarily irrelevant.

These meetings were mostly about difficulties in tracing suspects. During one border meeting, the senior delegation emphatically asked the judge where the police should paste court summons on public premises to ensure visibility. What was the most efficient and legally permissible way of summoning suspects? In these meetings, faulty surveys and misidentifications remained undiscussed, as did lazy naming and gender confusion when migrants initially identified as young men turned out to be aged women. Among the outcomes of one meeting was the agreement that court summons and deportation notices could be pasted in community spaces such as schools and post offices to ensure visibility. When the police started pasting such court summons on local school walls, it led Nehar Bibi, among others, to arrive at the tribunal.

In other instances, court summons did not yield the desired outcomes. Each time Das and Bhoumik labeled a "UT" case as "Filed" or "Dead," they tied them together in one compressed bundle with metal clips and threads. Given the large number of cases she handled, Das compressed files in increasing numbers. The act of file compression created a temporary legal archive that could be reopened if the police provided the tribunal with new information. However, such information was rare.

Faced with a large number of "UT" cases in one week in autumn of 2007, the Tribunals resolved sixty "UT" cases by declaring that the untraceable people were "illegal Bangladeshis." All judgments were in absentia. The people affected included Dhiren Das's family. In their absence, the judge decided that the law had waited long enough for the family to prove their credentials. A verdict was delivered, stating that all members of the Das family were "illegal Bangladeshis" who had arrived in India after 25 March 1971. Although the Tribunal ordered their deportation, the police could not serve the deportation notices, as those now labeled as foreigners could not be located. Das once again bundled several files—her routine actions cementing the ambivalence of Assam's invisible foreigner population while leaving the state's Bangladeshi dilemma unresolved. "Secret sources" continued to leap out from the pages of police interrogation reports, their anonymity making them as powerful as the uniformed police constables they supported. State deportation statistics show that until 2015, only 2,448 deportations were carried out among the 38,186 people who had been classified as Bangladeshi foreigners.[41] From 2016 to 2017, a total of 359 Bangladeshi nationals were deported.[42]

Despite their inability to deport those deemed to be illegal Bangladeshis, the reports that police constables continually heaped on Sujala Das's table testified to how electoral politics in Assam was driven by "illegal Bangladeshis" and spread the state's tentacles in everyday life. The cases of missing suspects—as a mass of floating unidentified and undeportable populations—

added to the dominant political imagination that "illegal" Bangladeshis in Assam were elusive criminal subjects. Sometimes, suspects who lacked identity papers, such as Bibi, transformed into Indian citizens; at other times, even when petitioners produced identity papers and certifications to prove their citizenship claims, they were kept in limbo.

Citizenship and Illegality

What are the rights of citizens and suspects who have been made stateless in Assam? How do marital and property rights, including the value addition of labor, fit into citizenship rights? In Assam, people with documentary evidence of Indian citizenship have been rendered stateless on the grounds that their paper identities are fraudulent, sometimes just on the basis that it is easy to procure documents. Others, who assert they are Indian citizens, do not have the necessary papers to prove their claims to land as property, their marital relationships, and, by extension, their claims to the membership of the nation itself. Instead of resolving issues on unauthorized migration and land loss, the ethereal presence of Bangladeshi suspects in law and life accentuates Assam's dual predicament as a perennially repositioned internal and external frontier of Indian democracy. Even judgments at the tribunal do not necessarily obliterate confusion and social suspicion.

For the Muslim peasants of Bengali origin, the partition, India's aggressive evictions and deportations, and the Assam Movement pushed many into East Pakistan and Bangladesh. Yet, these did not generate the intended outcome of slotting land and lives; identities and notions of loss across the riverine islands that have witnessed a long history of rice raids continue to unfold through the surveillance of unauthorized Bangladeshis in Assam. The imposition of judicial borders through police surveys, court trials and detentions, and now digital surveillance of night cameras and drones generates a panoptic of fear. The Indian state today has a plethora of identity cards, property papers, and more recently biometrics to prove citizenship, but rather than resolving questions of land loss and identity, end up further confusing issues. Suspicions shape the politics of belonging and fail to determine the legal thresholds of either Indian citizenship or Bangladeshi migrant "illegality." Laws encourage vigilance; suspicion weaves in and out of intimate spaces and turns family, friends, and neighbors against each other. The policing and judicial systems of modern states presuppose suspicion in ways that foreground uncertainties and ambiguities.[43] Suspicion becomes a device to decipher the boundaries of citizenship by harassing people, extorting money, manipulating papers, and settling scores. In Assam, the label "Bangladeshi" maligns, ridicules, and dispossesses people in the name of Indian citizenship. It polarizes society by stoking fears of being swamped by undocumented Bangladeshis.

Afterword

This book originated in my fieldwork at the Northeast India–Bangladesh border in 2007. I intended to follow the journeys and lives of undocumented Bangladeshi migrants. My fieldwork, however, took a life of its own when India started constructing a new fence along its borders with Bangladesh around the same time. As I continued to explore the its shifting forms, I realized that border fences and walls symbolize neither national sovereignty nor the failures of nation building.

My book sought to show the manner in which India's border fence acquires a metaphorical charge and transforms into a potent political register, even as it struggles to impose neat territorial divisions. In this region, even roads and rice have been segregating devices. Now more than ever before, cows are markers of borders and boundaries. Hence the temptation to physically mark the segregation of societies, to build fortifications and make infrastructures of surveillance bigger and better, will continue in the years to come. These efforts will make walls and fences projects in perpetuity.

Yet, India's barbed wire matrix is not just another obvious manifestation of a barrier, although its structure and design are a sign of the times. "Jungle passports" has shown how people make borders and relate to them in unanticipated ways, especially in regions where ethnicity, religion, language, families, and trading ties spill over the confines of national territories. Here, mobility is a fundamental attribute of life as people's claim on land historically precedes present day national boundaries. Mobility expresses itself in the nervous masculinity and the *fang fung* of cow traders, gendered banter, kinships and the steely determination of Garo women, loggers, people spreading their fares in the *haats*, *Mahari* lunches, and funeral feasts. Mobility also continues to be a compulsion in the time of climate change, a mode surviving in the shifting and eroding *chars*, denuded and encroached elephant habitats, and increasing variability in food and rice production.

Figure 23. A river boundary between Northeast India and Bangladesh.
(Photograph: author)

The border functions as a life force in ways that reorder notions of sovereignty, territoriality, legality, and identity. Despite the violent incursions of
national security and the intention to segregate societies and economies at
the Northeast India–Bangladesh border, ecologies, infrastructures, mobilities, and exchanges gather unevenly. Although border crossings pose risks
to life and economic ruin, the asymmetry of dangers, reverence, and relationships continues to make the border porous. Infact, border infrastructures
and troops are integral to social life, kinship, and smuggling.

India's contemporary populist politics has imposed judicial borders in
everyday life in Assam and along Assam's borders with Bangladesh. Police
surveys, court trials, detentions of unauthorized Bangladeshis, and now digital surveillance of night cameras and drones generate a panoptic of fear.
India's Citizenship Amendment Act of 2019, which seeks to give preference
to non-Muslim immigrants from among India's neighboring countries, also
fans the narrative of the "illegal" Bangladeshi Muslim migrant taking over

land and jobs. It makes religion central to the resolution of citizenship, even in Assam. Women who are landless and without property suddenly find themselves bereft of political identity in Assam. Those who submit themselves to the demands of Indian citizenship in Assam, as well as those who refuse, ensure that the borders between citizens and outsiders will continue to shift.

In this book, I have shown how, through conflicts and scarcity, life is made possible at borders outside the neat logic of nation building and the finality of fences and walls. The fear of ruin and death is heightened manifold, and the new fence, in all likelihood, will take a long time to become regularized. But despite the ramping up of uncertainties and fears and notwithstanding the incursions of violent nationalism from federal to regional politics into people's lives, rural societies will claim and refashion the border. This is because the Northeast India–Bangladesh border divides and sustains far more than just two nations, religions, tribes, ethnicities, citizens, and troops. It is here that people's notions of belonging and their relationships with animals, the *fang fung* economies, and the potency of commodities to forge as well as fracture relationships acquire features that are uniquely *borderi*.

As I pen these lines in October 2020, the COVID-19 pandemic has once again exacerbated the twenty-first-century narratives of "insiders" and "outsiders" and antiglobalization rhetoric. At present, the tide of ultranationalism, populism, and demonization of the "illegal migrant" has found a new ally in a virus. Global border walls and fences have started hardening even more, and we are caught in a border siege and ruled by measures of distance and paranoia. Migrants and refugees are the obvious victims. But so are neighboring provinces, nation-states, and communities.

Today, the containment of mobility and distancing are central to the preservation of life. Yet like never before, this containment and isolation—of which the Northeast India–Bangladesh border is a significant exemplifier—also remind us why mobility is generative of life itself.

NOTES

Introduction

1. All names in this book are pseudonyms. I have also been intentionally vague about the names and locations of border villages.

2. In Bengali, the word goru refers to cows, bulls, and oxen.

3. In the border zones where I conducted fieldwork, *chars*, or river islands that are composed of sand and silt, are formed as well as destroyed by the changing course of rivers such as the Brahmaputra River and its numerous tributaries in Assam and the Jingiram River in Kurigram district of Bangladesh. These *char* lands are then reclaimed for cultivation and settlement. On the hybridity of *chars* as borders between land and water, as well as the precarious lives of the *char* dwellers, see Lahiri-Dutt and Samanta, *Dancing with the River*. On land ownership, cropping patterns, and poverty in Assam's *chars*, see Chakraborty, *Assam's Hinterland*. On life and religiosity in the *chars* in Bangladesh, see Khan, "Dogs and Humans," 245–264.

4. The U.S. land and water boundary with Mexico is 1,933 miles long, extending from the southern tip of Texas to California; Beaver, "CRS Report for Congress." The length of the Israel-Palestine border is 449 miles; B'Tselem, "Statistics."

5. In 2010, Human Rights Watch documented a pattern of grave abuses against both Bangladeshi and Indian nationals by India's Border Security Forces (BSF). It estimated that every third or fourth day over the past decade, at least one unauthorized border crosser had been shot to death by Indian border forces. Ain O Salish Kendra, a human rights organization in Bangladesh, estimates that between 2009 and 2019, Indian border troops killed 455, injured 657, and abducted 518 Bangladeshi citizens. See Human Rights Watch, *"Trigger Happy."* See also Ain O Salish Kendra, "Reports on Border Violence."

6. *Indian Express*, "Two Crore." India's projections of unauthorized Bangladeshis lack empirical basis.

7. Northeast India comprises of the states of Arunachal Pradesh, Assam, Manipur, Meghalaya, Mizoram, Nagaland, Sikkim, and Tripura. Assam, Meghalaya, Mizoram, and Tripura share borders with Bangladesh. I have used the term "Northeast India" to situate the political location of the states of Assam and Meghalaya with special reference to their complicated internal borders with India as well as their distinct relationships with Bangladesh. When I use the term Northeast India, I use it to specifically refer to the borderland zone that I investigated in Assam and Meghalaya. On the militarization of Northeast India and sub-nationalism,

I have relied on Sanjib Baruah's seminal books, *India Against Itself* and *Durable Disorder*. On the Armed Forces Special Powers Act (1958), which is in operation in some states of Northeast India and Kashmir and sanctions armed impunity and suspends democratic functioning, see McDuie-Ra, "Fifty-Year Disturbance," 255–270; Baruah, "AFSPA."

8. Baruah, *India Against Itself*.

9. McDuie-Ra, "Fifty-Year Disturbance," 255.

10. McDuie-Ra, "Violence Against Women in the Militarized Indian Frontier," 330–333.

11. International Organization for Migration, *United Nations World Migration Report 2020*.

12. Portes, Guarnizo, and Landolt, "Study of Transnationalism," 217; Schiller, Basch, and Blanc, "From Immigrant to Transmigrant," 48–63; Appadurai, *Modernity at Large*.

13. Massey, "Power-Geometry," 59–69.

14. India has introduced a Comprehensive Integrated Border Management System (CIBMS), in the Brahmaputra River's *chars* in Assam, with a data network, fiber-optic cables, surveillance cameras, and intrusion detection system. *Economic Times*, "Electronic Surveillance."

15. Beverley, "Frontier as Resource," 242–243.

16. See Jones, "Spaces of Refusal," 685–699.

17. Borders have inspired seminal scholarship on nation and state making, race, labor, gender, and belonging. See, among others, Anzaldúa, *Borderlands*; Donnan and Wilson, *Borders*; Heyman, *Life and Labor*; Vila, *Ethnography at the Border*; Kelly, *Law, Violence and Sovereignty*; Navaro-Yashin, *Make-Believe Space*; Mezzadra and Neilson, *Border as Method*; Jusionyte, *Savage Frontier*; Ibrahim, *Settlers, Saints and Sovereigns*; Peter Sahlins, *Boundaries*; Giersch, *Asian Borderlands*.

18. Deleuze, *Nietzsche and Philosophy*, Nietzsche, *The Will to Power*.

19. Biehl, *Vita*, 394–395.

20. Biehl and Locke, *Unfinished*, 5–7.

21. Singh, "Anthropological Investigations of Vitality," 550–563.

22. Partha Chatterjee, *Nation and Its Fragments*.

23. Bigo, "Mobius Ribbon," 92.

24. Donnan and Wilson, *Borders*, 10.

25. I received valuable suggestions on borders as a life force at a conference that I co-organized with Brenda Yeoh and Sidharthan Maunaguru at the Asia Research Institute, National University of Singapore. I am grateful to all the participants, especially to Sidharthan. I also thank Eli Elinoff, George Jose, and Bodhi Kar for their valuable suggestions.

26. Van Schendel, *Bengal Borderland*, 212.

27. Ministry of Home Affairs, *Annual Report 2005–2006, Annual Report 2006–2007*.

28. Reece Jones has shown how, despite the distinct ecologies of the India-Pakistan border, which mostly runs through deserts and glaciers, and the India-Bangladesh border, which comprises agricultural lands, India's border policies are very similar in both regions. Jones, "Agents of Exception," 888.

29. Larkin, "Politics and Poetics," 327–343.

30. Appel, Anand, and Gupta, *Promise of Infrastructure*, 20.

31. Anand, *Hydraulic City*, 6, 12.

32. Brown, *Walled States*, 24–34.

33. Krishna, "Cartographic Anxiety," 508, 517.

34. Andreas, *Border Games*, 8–18.

35. De León, *Land of Open Graves*, 43.

36. Das and Poole, *Anthropology at the Margins*, 13; Hansen and Stepputat, *Sovereign Bodies*, 27–29.

37. Smart and Heyman, *States and Illegal Practices*, 1, 10–11; Chalfin, "Border Zone Trade," 202.

38. Roitman, "Productivity in the Margins," 222.

39. Cons, *Sensitive Space*, 20–22.

40. Van Schendel, *Bengal Borderland*. See also van Schendel, "Working Through Partition," 393–421; van Schendel and Rahman, "'I Am Not a Refugee,'" 551–584.

41. See Samaddar, *Marginal Nation*; van Schendel, *Bengal Borderland*; Hussain, *Boundaries Undermined*; Jones, *Border Walls*; Cons, *Sensitive Space*, 20–22.

42. On the India-Bangladesh border enclaves, see van Schendel, "Stateless in South Asia," 115–147; Jones, "Sovereignty and Statelessness," 373–381; Cons, "Narrating Boundaries," 37–46; Shewly, "Abandoned Spaces," 23–31.

43. Jalais, *Forest of Tigers*; Alexander, Chatterji, and Jalais, *Bengal Diaspora*.

44. See, van Schendel, *Bengal Borderland* and Hussain, *Boundaries Undermined*.

45. Terms such as "tribes," "aboriginals," and "ethnic minorities" are contested as well as mobilized by those who are placed in these categories in India and Bangladesh. In this book, I have used these terms to reflect state classifications at the appropriate historical periods. On tribes and indigenous people of India, see Beteille, "Concept of Tribe," 297–318 and Xaxa, "Tribes as Indigenous People of India," 3589–3595. For an engagement with the politics of wildness and the emergence of *adivasi* identity in India, see Skaria, *Hybrid Histories*. For two distinct discussions on the analytic potential and mobilization of the term "indigenous," see Karlsson, "Anthropology and the 'Indigenous Slot,'" 403–423 and Kaushik Ghosh, "Between Global Flows and Local Dams," 501–534. See further McDuie-Ra, "Embracing or Challenging the Tribe," 66–86 and Chandra, "Going Primitive."

46. Bal, *They Ask If We Eat Frogs*, 6.

47. Bal and Claquin, "Borders That Divide," 101.

48. I have represented fieldwork locations in the map, excluding the locations of the two foreigners tribunals.

49. Rashid who resided in Guwahati accompanied me in my initial fieldwork in Assam and Meghalaya in 2007. In Meghalaya's foothills, Chandra accompanied me in one specific zone. In Bangladesh, the householders with whom I resided occasionally insisted that their young nephews and nieces accompany me during my fieldwork. I have used pseudonyms to protect their identities.

50. During the time of my fieldwork in 2007 and 2008, Border Guard Bangladesh (BGB) was known as the Bangladesh Rifles (BDR). In January 2010, Bangladesh Rifles was changed to Border Guard Bangladesh. Both the Indian Border Security Forces (BSF) and the BGB federally funded "paramilitary forces." Guards and commanders of these paramilitary organizations are entrusted with border patrolling, preventing smuggling, and controlling terrorism. They are trained in war functions and operate as the first line of defense during wars and border conflicts. The BSF, which protects the international boundary, is conferred with enormous powers to deal with internal dissidence and has been provided with impunity against prosecution for human rights violations. The BGB has similar functions, but unlike the Indian troops, it is headed by a national army commander. See website of Border Security Forces at http://bsf.nic.in/ and Border Guard Bangladesh at http://www.bgb.gov.bd.

51. For a recent case of pushback of fifty-nine suspected Bangladeshi nationals, see Bagchi, "The Curious Case."

52. Ludden, "Presidential Address," 1062.

53. I have written about this in greater detail in Sur, "Dreaming Borders."

54. Anzaldúa, *Borderlands*, 39.

55. Anzaldúa, *Borderlands*, 27–30.

Chapter 1

1. *Financial Express*, "Dutch Bangladesh Bank."

2. Ispahani, *Roads and Rivals*, 2–7.

3. Haines, "Colonial Routes," 537–539.

4. In this instance, the British officers recognized Khasi territorial independence and placed their territory beyond the borders of British India until the last decade of the nineteenth century. Hunter, *Imperial Gazetteer of India*, vol. 5, p. 256; Mackenzie, *The Northeast Frontier of India*, 222–223.

5. Dzuvichu, "Roads and the Raj," 477, 491.

6. Masquelier, "Road Mythographies," 829–831.

7. Dalakoglou, "The Road," 133.

8. Harvey and Knox, "The Enchantments of Infrastructure," 1–16.

9. On how the classification of Scheduled Tribes does not reflect the diversity and struggles of tribal communities in India, see Sundar and Madan, *The Scheduled Tribes and Their India*.

10. Misra, "The Sovereignty of Political Economy," 383, 348. Indrani Chatterji notes that Mughal commanders used the term "Garo" to refer to Tibetan-speaking cotton cultivators and soldiers of Himalayan monastic lineage in the seventeenth and eighteenth centuries; see Chatterji, *Forgotten Friends*, 19, 50.

11. Eliot, "Observations on the Inhabitants of the Garrow Hills," 21–45.

12. Regulation X, "Administration of Criminal Justice in the Garrow Hills," 1822, British India.

13. Watson, *Memoir of the Late David Scott*, 30–31.

14. Barooah, *David Scott in North-East India*, 181.

15. M'Cosh, *Topography of Assam*, 165.

16. M'Cosh, *Topography of Assam*, 165.

17. Sivaramakrishnan, "British Imperium and Forested Zones of Anomaly in Bengal," 245–246.

18. Hunter, *A Statistical Account of Assam*, 136.

19. Act XXII of 1869, in Mackenzie, *The Northeast Frontier of India*, 551–552.

20. Parimal Chandra Kar, *British Annexation of the Garo*, 39–41.

21. Prakash, *Another Reason*, 25.

22. Parimal Chandra Kar, *British Annexation of the Garo Hills*, 44–47.

23. Austen, "On the Garo Hills," 36–40.

24. Hunter, *Imperial Gazetteer*, vol. 5, 27; Hunter, *Statistical Account of Assam*, vol. 2, 157.

25. Parimal Chandra Kar, *British Annexation of the Garo Hills*, 58.

26. Hunter, *Statistical Account of Assam*, 158.

27. Hunter, *Statistical Account of Assam*, 160.

28. Winichakul, *Siam Mapped*, 158.

29. Bodhisattva Kar, "When Was the Postcolonial," 25–49.

30. Jayeeta Sharma, *Empire's Garden*, 61.

31. Hunter, *Imperial Gazette of India*, vol. 5, 26.

32. Kaushik Ghosh, "A Market for Aboriginality," 8–48.

33. General Administration Report of the Garo Hills for the Year 1875–1876, Assam State Archives, Dispur; Hunter, *Statistical Account of Assam*, 165, 168.

34. Kerr, *Engines of Change*, 5.

35. General Administration Report of the Garo Hills for the Year 1875–1876, Assam State Archives, Dispur; Hunter, *Statistical Account of Assam*, 165, 168.

36. Dalton, *Descriptive Ethnology of Bengal*, 248–249.

37. Parimal Chandra Kar, *British Annexation of the Garo Hills*, 60–61.

38. Oldham, *Memoirs of the Geological Survey of India*, 8–13.

39. Oldham, *Memoirs of the Geological Survey of India*, 8, 20–22.

40. Oldham, *Memoirs of the Geological Survey of India*, 258–259.

41. Oldham, *Memoirs of the Geological Survey of India*, 261.

42. Anderson, "The Effects of the Earthquake in 1897," 258–261.

43. Report by Captain A. A. Howell, ISC, Officiating Deputy Commissioner of the Garo Hills, on the effects of the earthquake in his district, No.100 G, dated 24 July 1897, in the *Report of the Earthquake on 12 June 1897, No. 540 9G*, 14.

44. Oldham, *Memoirs of the Geological Survey of India*, 2–3.

45. Howell, *Report of the Earthquake*, 50.

46. Playfair, *The Garos*, 88.

47. Oldham, *Memoirs of the Geological Survey of India*, 14.

48. See further Baruah, "Reading Fürer-Haimendorf in Northeast India," 17–30; Dirks, "The Policing of Tradition," 182–212.

49. Mihir N. Sangma, *Unpublished Reports on Garo Affairs*, 128–136.

50. Parimal Chandra Kar, *Garos in Transition*, 79.

51. Karlsson, *Unruly Hills*, 135. On the protests led by Sonaram, see Kumar, "State 'Simplification,'" 2941–2947.

52. Report of the Arbuthnot Commission in Mihir N. Sangma, *Unpublished Documents on Garo Affairs*, 29, 35.

53. Parimal Chandra Kar, *British Annexation of the Garo Hills*, xiii–xvi.

54. Martinez, *The Border People*, 5, 10.

Chapter 2

1. On the controversies surrounding shifting cultivation in the Garo Hills, which is beyond the scope of this chapter, see Malik, The 'Problem' of Shifting Cultivation," 287–315.

2. On frontier identities in Goalpara along Assam and Bengal's margins and changing British policies on land use, migration, and political control in this region until the 1930s, see Misra, *Becoming a Borderland*.

3. Hartley, *Final Report*, 83–84.

4. Hartley, *Final Report*, 11–12.

5. Interview, Mymensingh District, Bangladesh, 21 December 2007.

6. Dev and Lahiri, *Assam Muslims*, 67–73.

7. Chakrabarty, *The Partition of Bengal and Assam, 1932–1947*, 184–185.

8. Jayeeta Sharma, *Empire's Garden*, 100–102. See also Guha, *Planter Raj to Swaraj*, 166–167.

9. Saikia, *Forests and Ecological History of Assam 1826–2000*, 326–331 and *A Century of Protests*, 87–96.

10. Jayeeta Sharma, *Empire's Garden*, 102–103.

11. Jayeeta Sharma, *Empire's Garden*, 103; Chandan Sharma, "The Immigration Issue in Assam," 291.

12. *Assam Police Weekly Intelligence Reports (APWIR)*, week ending 12 March 1947.

13. *APWIR*, weeks ending 19 March 1947 and 26 March 1947.

14. *APWIR*, week ending 16 April 1947.

15. Syiemleih, *On the Edge of Empire*.

16. van Schendel, "Madmen of Mymensingh," 151–152.

17. Bal, *They Ask If We Eat Frogs*, 169.

18. *APWIR*, week ending 24 May 1947.

19. *APWIR*, week ending 23 July 1947.

20. *APWIR*, weeks ending 15 January 1947, 29 January 1947, 5 February 1947, and 26 February 1947.

21. On the response to the Sylhet referendum in Assam, see Chaudhuri, "God Sent Opportunity?"

22. Baruah, *India Against Itself*, 106–110.

23. Joya Chatterji, "The Fashioning of a Frontier," 185–242.

24. Joya Chatterji, "The Fashioning of a Frontier," 221–224; van Schendel, *The Bengal Borderland*, 46–49.

25. CR [Confidential Report] 1B4–5/52; van Schendel, *The Bengal Borderland*, 123–130.

26. Reid, "Recent Developments in Assam," 57–68.

27. *APWIR*, week ending 17 December 1947.

28. *APWIR*, week ending 24 December 1947.

29. *APWIR*, week ending 31 December 1947.

30. The Immigrants (Expulsion from Assam) Act (1 March 1950), accessed 15 July 2011, www.helplinelaw.com.

31. Reid, "Recent Developments in Assam," 64.

32. *Sangbad*, 10 September 1951; *Azan*, 29 September 1951; and CR 2 A1–1/51 (March 1954), 279–301.

33. Van Schendel, *Bengal Borderland*, 193–194.

34. CR 2A1–1/51 (March 1954), 279–301.

35. Extract from the fortnightly confidential report of the Dacca Division for the first half of June 1951, A. B. Khan, "Delhi Pact: Secret," 18 June 1951.

36. CR 2A 1–1/51 (March 1954), 270–301.

37. Letter no. 65/RC, 30 January 1951, from Ahsan-uddin, Relief Commissioner and Secretary to the Government of East Bengal, Dacca, to A. D. Pandit, Chief Secretary, Government of Assam, Shillong, India.

38. On peasant protests in northern Mymensingh rebellions, see Bhadra, *Iman O Nishan*; van Schendel, "Madmen of Mymensingh," 151–152, 170.

39. Memo no. 1268/Con. Home (Police) P 5R–61/49.

40. Memo no. 1268/Con. Home (Police) P 5R–61/49.

41. From Ali Asghar, Esq., I.C.S., District Magistrate, Mymensingh, to Assistant Secretary, Home (Political) Government of East Bengal, March 1948.

42. Home (Police) P 3I–4/50 (March 1951), 206–214.

43. Home (Police) P 5R–28/49 (August 1949), 8–9.

44. Home (Police) P 3I—4/50 (March 1951), 206–214.

45. Reid, "Recent Developments in Assam," 65.

46. CR IC–2/50.

47. CR 1A2–4/51 (March 1953), 1461–1467.

48. CR 3A–6/52 (August 1953), 103–109. For further allegations of trespassing, see CR 1B4–22/54 (January 1955), 1361–1364.

49. CR 1B4–5/52; CR 1B–2/50 (September 1954).

50. District Intelligence Branch, Mymensingh (22 January 1953), Memo 1046/100–2; Office of the Deputy Commissioner, Garo Hills, Confidential Branch, no. 61/C, Tura (10 March 1953).

51. Confidential memo 6/3, 4 May 1951, Com: XVII, 7–51; CR 6.MI–11.51 (July 1953), 161–173.

52. CR 3A–6/52 (August 1953), 103–109.

53. CR 6.MI–11.51 (July 1953), 161–173; CR 1B4–22/54 (January 1955), 1361–1364.

54. Government of Assam, Confidential Department, memo C/154/52/2, May 1952; CR.1262–1/52 (September 1953), 27–44; CR–12 C 2–1/52 (1465–1470, May 1953); D.O. no. EA/CAL/EB/37 pt. II, dated 9 April 1952, from Mr. D. M. Gupta, Deputy Secretary to the Government of India, Ministry of External Affairs, Calcutta, to Mr. K. M. Kaiser, Deputy Secretary to the Government of Pakistan, Ministry of Foreign Affairs and Commonwealth Relations, Camp Dhaka (December 1952); and CR 12 C2–1/52 (September 1953), 27–44.

55. *Hindustan Standard*, 8 May 1951.

56. CR 12C2–1/52 (September 1953).

57. On the history of the Catholic missions in Mymensingh see, Syiemlieh, "Catholic Missions Among the Garos of Mymesingh," 170–179; Bal, *They Ask If We Eat Frogs*.

58. Memorandum (1955), St. Elizabeth Church, Birohidakuni, Haluaghat, Mymensingh.

59. M. Majid, District Magistrate of Mymensingh, to Aziz Ahmad Esq. CSP, Chief Secretary to the Government of East Bengal, Dhaka (March 1953); memo 707, Mymensingh, 11 May 1952, copy of the report submitted by Court Inspector Sadar to the Superintendent of Police, ref: Haluaghat PS case 3, 11 January 1952, u/s 448/352 PPC.

60. CR 1 B4–59/54 (January 1955), 2161–2165.

61. van Schendel, *Bengal Borderland*, 96–97, 108.

62. Nasir's image of Assam does not correspond to current political maps. What he conceives as the hills of Assam have been located in the Indian state of Meghalaya since 1972. Since 1971, Mymensingh has been a district in Bangladesh.

63. On *ur*, which implies soil, and one's natal village and its relationship to personhood and character, as well as its distinct resonances and mobilizations in the lives of those displaced by the war in Sri Lanka, see Daniel, *Fluid Signs*, 102 and Thiranagama, *In My Mother's House*, 18–19.

64. "White Paper on Foreigners' Issue," Home and Political Department, Government of Assam, accessed 21 October 2014, http://online.assam.gov.in/web/homepol/whitepaper#1.5.

65. "White Paper on Foreigners' Issue."

66. Suranjan Das, "The 1992 Calcutta Riot in Historical Continuum," 287.

67. Hazarika, *Rites of Passage*, 61–62.

68. *Pakistan Observer*, 9 May 1964.

69. *Ranikhong Church Chronicles*, vol. 7, 1967–1970; Joseph's Church, Ranikhong, Netrakona, Bangladesh, 6 February 1964 and 23 February 1964.

70. *Ranikhong Church Chronicles*, vol. 7, 1967–1970, 29 January 1964.

71. *Ranikhong Church Chronicles*, vol. 7, 1967–1970, 15 March 1964.

72. *Ranikhong Church Chronicles*, vol. 7, 19 March 1964.

73. *Chronicles of Birohidakuni Mission from 15 August 1955–1993*, St. Elizabeth Church, Birohidakuni, Haluaghat, Mymensingh Birohidakuni, 25 August 1964.

74. Rajagopal, *The British*, 247.

75. Sengrang Sangma, *Bangladeshi Immigrants in Meghalaya*, 24.

76. Interview with T. Tojuu and M. Sangma, Ramchenga, Garo Hills, Meghalaya, India, 22 October 2007.

77. *Pakistan Observer*, 29 September 1964.

78. Bal, *They Ask If We Eat Frogs*, 188–189.

79. Interview, Netrakona, Bangladesh, 9 January 2008.

80. Malkki, "National Geographic," 37. For a definition of borderlands, see Baud and van Schendel, "Towards a Comparative History of Borderlands," 211–242.

81. Scott, *The Art of Not Being Governed*, 193, 219; van Schendel, "Geographies of Knowing," 647–668.

82. Duara, *Rescuing History from the Nation*; Ludden, "Presidential Address," 1057–1078.

83. I have written about this in greater detail in Sur, "Battles for the Golden Grain," 804–832.

84. Ohnuki-Tierney, *Rice as Self*, 3–5, 10, 132–134.

Chapter 3

1. A pair of Zebu cows bought for $350 to $400 in Assam in 2015 to 2016 (including transportation costs) can fetch twice the price in border villages in Bangladesh and be sold five to seven times the cost price during the festival of Eid, when cattle are slaughtered for ritual purposes. In the high-value Zebu trade, both Hindu and Muslim borderlanders are involved as investors, passage guarantors, traders, and brokers, whereas the "home *goru*" business is mostly conducted by small-scale Muslim traders and transporters.

2. Hindu notions of cattle's sacredness do not apply to states such as Meghalaya in Northeast India. In Meghalaya, BJP leaders have quit the party over issues relating to bans on beef consumption and cattle trade. *NDTV*, "Meghalaya BJP Leader Resigns."

3. The prohibition on beef exports is listed as item 0201 in the ITC (HS)—Classification of Export and Import Items of the EXIM Policy, 2002–2007, Department of Commerce, Government of India. However, India did export carabeef, which is buffalo meat.

4. Dhingra, "India's Beef Exports Rise Under Modi Govt Despite Hindu Vigilante Campaign at Home," The Print.in, 26 March, 2019.

5. I have intentionally been vague about the location of the border *chars* and the cattle markets in lower Assam and Bangladesh. I have mentioned the animal corridors in Kurigram district in Bangladesh, which is common knowledge, and the main market in Rowmari; I have provided pseudonyms for the *chars*.

6. Appadurai, *The Social Life of Things*, 22; Ralph, "Commodity," 79.

7. *Fang-fung* is Bengali. The Garo colloquial equivalent is *bung-bang*.

8. Hansen, "Sovereigns Beyond the State," 169–191.

9. Smart and Heyman, *States and Illegal Practices*, 1, 10–11; van Schendel and Abraham, *Illicit Flows and Criminal Things*.

10. Roitman, *Fiscal Disobedience*, 188–189.

11. In India, people who do not belong to tribal and indigenous communities often use the word "tribal" pejoratively. For a discussion on this, see McDuie-Ra, "Embracing or Challenging the Tribe?" 66–86.

12. Govindrajan, *Animal Intimacies*, 65–66. For a rich discussion on the relationships that people have with bovines as agentive beings and how these relationships disrupt the dichotomies of religion and economy, as well as legality and illegality that dominate the scholarship on cow protection, see Adcock and Govindrajan, "Bovine Politics in South Asia," 1095–1107.

13. Singh and Dave, "On the Killing and Killability of Animals," 232–245.

14. Between 2015 and June 2018, 61,297 cases of cattle smuggling were filed at the India-Bangladesh border. See Human Rights Watch, "India."

15. See Human Rights Watch, *"Trigger Happy,"* 42–44.

16. Roitman, "Productivity in the Margins," 222 and *Fiscal Disobedience*, 248–249.

17. Van Schendel, "Easy Come, Easy Go," 194–195 and *Bengal Borderland*, 172.

18. On the role of the Indian border forces in controlling and preventing cattle smuggling, as well as the ways in which Indian Muslim village headmen negotiate with them for cattle passage during Eid to Bangladesh, see Sahana Ghosh, *"Chor,* Police and Cattle," 1122–1123.

19. For instance, the electronic media in India make connections between cattle smuggling and terrorism. Often, such news coverage prompts the Indian Border Security Forces to conduct cattle seizures and arrest the people involved, while at the same time they admit that the rate of seizures does not match the volume of trade. Such reports also boast about the outcomes of media vigilance. See, for instance, one widely aired news channel's reporting on cattle smuggling: *NDTV,* "NDTV Impact."

20. Money transfers largely rely on brokers and exchangers in border villages who deal in both Indian and Bangladeshi currency. These transfers are known as *"taka* transfers" (*taka* means money in Bengali) and occur on the basis of secret code numbers between traders and brokers on either side of the border.

21. Van Schendel, "Easy Come, Easy Go," 199.

22. See Jason Cons's analysis of how the cattle ceiling imposed in Dhahagram, an enclave at the India-Bangladesh border, deeply entrenched the power of local politicians. Cons, *Sensitive Space*, 126–127.

23. Chalfin, "Border Zone Trade," 202.

24. The official website of the Border Guard Bangladesh (BGB) records cattle transactions in ambiguous ways. For instance, in March and April 2011, it reported cattle raids involving a total of twenty-seven head of cattle, without any mention of animal corridors (BGB website). In April 2018, on the BGB website, no statistics of cattle seizures were mentioned, but cattle did feature in small thumbnail images in the BGB picture gallery dated 3 April.

25. Press Trust of India, "Illegal Cattle Smuggling."

26. *Daily Star,* "BGB Won't Bar Cattle Coming thru' Proper Corridors."

27. In January 2020, the BGB website recorded that the total number of cattle seized and legalized in 2019 was 93,592,000.

28. Usually traded at numerous fairs, cattle were mentioned as an important commodity in the eastern borderlands in the records of British colonial cattle surveys in the early twentieth century. Records indicate that, in the late nineteenth and early twentieth centuries, cattle—both milch cows and bulls—were exported from Bihar to Bengal. See Blackwood, *A Survey and Census of the Cattle of Bengal.*

29. Robb, "The Challenge of Gau Mata," 289; Pinney, "The Nation (Un) Pictured?" 481–483.

30. Pinney, "The Nation (Un)Pictured?" 481–483.

31. Van der Veer, *Religious Nationalism in India*, 91; Hansen, *The Saffron Wave*.

32. On the restrictions of cattle as livestock, see the Indian Customs Act of 1962. The Indian Customs Act (1962) does allow cattle exports with a license; however, cattle remain categorized with camels and horses as "restricted items."

33. Government of East Bengal, Home (Political) CR 3A–10/52; Government of East Bengal, Home (Political) CR 1B4–49/54; Letter No c.18/54/227, Shillong, 9 August 1954; Government of East Bengal, Home (Political) CRI B4–25/54 B.

34. Government of East Bengal, Home (Political) CR 3A–10/52; Government of East Bengal, Home (Political) CR 1B4–49/54; Letter No c.18/54/227, Shillong, 9 August 1954; Government of East Bengal, Home (Political) CRI B4–25/54 B.

35. Khan, "Dogs and Humans," 245–264.

Chapter 4

1. Ranabir Samaddar refers to such border crossings as generative of everyday transnationality. I find this terminology especially useful and productive in the context of transborder labor and trade circulations in South Asia. See Samaddar, *Marginal Nation*, 19–21.

2. Baud and van Schendel, "Towards a Comparative History," 211–242; Cons, "Narrating Boundaries," 37–46. See also Cons and Sanyal, "Geographies at the Margins," 5–13.

3. Marshall Sahlins, "What Kinship Is," 14.

4. Carsten, "What Kinship Does," 245–251.

5. Veena Das, *Critical Events*, 63–64, 67.

6. Zamindar, *Long Partition*, 238.

7. On the Garo *Mahari* in Meghalaya, India, see Burling, *Rengsanggri*. Marak has mapped the changes in the role of the *Mahari* and the growth of associations in Meghalaya that function like NGOs. See Marak, "Role of the Mahari," 531–540. On the Garo *Maharis* in Mymensingh, Bangladesh, see Bal, *They Ask If We Eat Frogs*, 95–96. Bal's study suggests that the Bangladeshi Garos see themselves as a distinct ethnic group, with a distinct history from the Indian Garos. Life along the foothill and plain borderland that I explore in this chapter challenges this neat distinction.

8. Van Schendel, *Bengal Borderland*, 96–97.

9. Nowicka and Vertovec, "Comparing Convivialities," 342, 352.

10. Amin, *Land of Strangers*; Gilroy, *Multiculture in Times of War,* 27–45.

11. Nyamnjoh and Brudvig, "Conviviality and the Boundaries of Citizenship," 341, 343, 348.

12. Vigneswaran, "Protection and Conviviality," 484.

13. The Indian government deliberately does not allow mobile phone network coverage within three miles of the border. For outposts that were located within this range, the troops held weekly conversations with their family members mostly via public phone booths, unless in emergencies when the outpost was contacted through the official chain of command. Secretly, Indian troops also purchased Bangladeshi sim cards from traders for calling their family members.

14. I analyze such relationships in greater detail in Sur, "Danger and Difference," 846–873. See, also Thiranagama, "Civility of Strangers," 357–381.

15. Walker, *Legend of the Golden Boat*, 160–161; Lertchavalitsakul, "Shan Women Traders," 675–709; Harris, *Geographical Diversions* and "Cross-Border Commodities," 106–113;

Leungaramsri, "Women, Nation and the Ambivalence of Subversive Identification," 68–89; Sahana Ghosh, "Security Socialities," 349–450.

16. Walker, *Legend of the Golden Boat*, 111, 162.

17. I have written about Meghalaya's border haats in Sur, "Bamboo Baskets and Barricades," 127–150 and "Through Metal Fences," 70–89.

18. The Border Areas Development Department was created in 1973 to exclusively look after the implementation of various integrated schemes and developmental activities under the Border Areas Development Program. The focus of the program is primarily the building and maintenance of infrastructures. It was initially funded entirely by the central government of India, with the state government of Meghalaya now funding 10 percent. In 2020, the program covered 1,692 villages located within 10 kilometers of the India-Bangladesh border. See http://megbad.gov.in/history.html, accessed 10 February 2020.

19. Baruah, *Durable Disorder*, 42–43.

20. Karlsson, *Unruly Hills*, 46–49.

21. *Telegraph*, "Government Seeks More Men."

22. See Haokip, "Inter-Ethnic Relations," 302–316.

23. *Times of India*, "Six Border Haats."

24. Sturgeon, *Border Landscapes*, 9, 25.

25. Shneiderman, "Are the Central Himalayas in Zomia?" 292. Shneiderman, *Rituals of Ethnicity*, 34–36.

26. Raitapuro and Bal, "'Talking About Mobility,'" 393.

27. Sur, "Bamboo Baskets and Barricades," 144.

28. Subba and Wouters, "Northeast India," 194.

29. Vandenhelsken and Karlsson, "Fluid Attachments," 330–339.

30. Gellner, "Northern Asia's Diverse Borders," 19.

31. Karlsson, *Unruly Hills*, 158–159. For a detailed discussion on land holdings in the Garo Hills, see Parimal Chandra Kar, *Glimpses of the Garos*, 47–83.

32. See D'Costa, *Nation-Building*, 121–122, 125–126 and Mookherjee, *Spectral Wound*, 129–130, 157–158. Bangladesh valorized women whom the Pakistani armed forces had raped as "war heroines." Yet this official title did not entitle Bengali Muslim women to the same honor accorded to male freedom fighters. Families were reluctant to accept the women again, many refusing outright.

33. Bal, *They Ask If We Eat Frogs*, 193.

34. Bangladesh Garments Manufacturers and Exporters Association, "Trade Information," accessed 14 May 2018, http://www.bgmea.com.bd/home/pages/tradeinformation.

35. Kabeer and Mahmud, "Rags, Riches and Women Workers," 137–141.

36. Siddiqui, "Miracle Worker or Woman Machine?" L13.

37. Siddiqui, "Miracle Worker or Woman Machine?" L15.

Chapter 5

1. Nevins, *Operation Gatekeeper and Beyond*, 195.

2. Weizman, *Hollow Land*, 58.

3. Agamben, *State of Exception*, 3–9.

4. Scheper-Hughes and Bourgois, *Violence in War and Peace*.

5. Jeganathan, *Checkpoint*, 68.

6. See Vitebsky, *Reindeer People*; Jalais, *Forest of Tigers*.

7. The fear of elephants and the relationships that the Garos establish with the all-powerful elephants are specific to the foothill borderland between Meghalaya in Northeast India and Mymensingh and Netrokona in Bangladesh that I studied.

8. Sanatombi Sangma, "Shape-Shifting or Transformation Myth in Garo Culture," 77–79. See, also Brighenti, "Traditional Beliefs about Weretigers Among the Garos of Meghalaya."

9. My foothill Garo respondents and Garo Catholic priests explained the authority of maternal uncles in the following way. They conveyed that historically in Garo societies, the maternal uncle played an important role since his permission was required before selling land, and he had the right to demand that his sister's children marry his own children. Even today, such unions are based on considerations of property and lineage. Maternal uncles have affectionate and authoritative roles—the same attributes that are transplanted to elephants. The authority of maternal uncles has also changed over time and is also differentially experienced among the Garos, depending upon their location in Meghalaya and Mymensingh, and lineage.

10. India's fence construction has disrupted natural elephant corridors in the borderland. See Choudhury, "Impact of Border Fence," 27–30.

11. Foucault, *Discipline and Punish*, 201–202.

12. I have written about these changes in greater details in Sur, "Danger and Difference," 846–873.

13. Jones, "Geopolitical Boundary Narratives," 291–293.

14. Hage, *Waiting*; Kosravi, *Precarious Lives*; Andersson, "Time and the Migrant Other," 795–809; Janeja and Bandak, *Ethnographies of Waiting*.

15. Khosravi, *Precarious Lives*, 218–219.

16. O'Neill, *The Space of Boredom*, 43, 15–16.

17. Jeffrey, "Timepass," 466, 468.

18. I have written in more details about hunger and scarcity and changing notions of border times that small-scale Muslim workers such as Alibaba and their families face in Sur, "Time at Its Margins."

19. Netz, *Barbed Wire*.

20. Billé, "Skinworlds," 61–62.

21. I have written about these afflictions, including mine, in greater detail in Sur, "Dreaming Borders."

22. At a boundary group meeting, Bangladesh conveyed that it would not alter the boundary line and that a census or survey would not be permitted. Instead, it requested that India construct permanent pillars on the demarcated 3.5 kilometers in Boroibari near Rowmari in order. Source: Ministry of External Affairs, Government of India UO NO, I/ii/108/6/2005, 28 July 2006.

23. Taussig, "Terror as Usual," 3–20; I have written about Felani in "Divided Bodies," 31–35.

Chapter 6

1. Melkiganj is a fictitious name. Given the climate of official secrecy in India, it is extremely rare to be granted permission to sit and witness court proceedings. To protect the identity of the petitioners, the judges, and the staff, I have not revelated this town's location in my fieldwork map.

2. *Indian Express*, "Two Crore."

3. Roy, "Between Encompassment and Closure," 245. See also Kapur, "The Citizen and the Migrant," 537–570.

4. Jayal, *Citizenship and Its Discontents*, 52, 79.

5. Sur and Kumar, "India's Citizenship Act."

6. Reeves, "Clean Fake," 512. See Navaro-Yashin, *The Make-Believe Space*.

7. See Sadiq, *Paper Citizens*.

8. Kalir, Sur, and van Schendel, "Mobile Practices," 15.

9. Samaddar, *The Marginal Nation*, 19–21; Hazarika, *Rites of Passage*.

10. Fuller and Bénéi, *The Everyday State and Society in Modern India*.

11. Srivastava, "Duplicity, Intimacy, Community," 1–16; Anjaria, "Ordinary States," 58–72.

12. Sadiq, *Paper Citizens*, 82–85, 120–124.

13. Das and Poole, *Anthropology at the Margins of the State*, 10.

14. Van Schendel, *Bengal Borderland*, 212.

15. The data supplied by the Assam government to the state assembly are as follows. Until 2005, IMDT tribunals summoned 12,846 suspected Bangladeshis. The number of deportations reported was 1,547. See Jain, "Govt Slow in Deporting Illegal Bangladeshi Migrants."

16. See the Report on Illegal Migration to Assam, submitted to the President of India by Governor of Assam, 8 November 1998, D.O.No.GSAG.3/98, http://www.satp.org/satporgtp /countries/india/states/assam/documents/papers/illegal_migration.

17. Foreigners tribunals have clauses for imprisonment that may extend to five years and include a fine. Section 14 of the Foreigners Act (after amendment by Act No. 16 of 2004). See Bhairav Acharya, "The Controversy Surrounding the Supreme Court's Decision," 1–18.

18. Banerjee, *Borders, Histories, Existences*, 29–30.

19. *Sarbananda Sonowal v. Union of India (UOI) and Another*, No. 131 of 2000, India.

20. *Outlook India*, "Bangladesh Pact Signed."

21. Interview, Guwahati, Assam, 8 November 2007.

22. *Business Standard*, "In Assam, Does 'D' Stand for 'Doubtful' or 'Deprived' Voter?"

23. Karmakar, "Over 19 Lakh Excluded."

24. Barbora, "The Crisis of Citizenship in Assam." For the NRC on Assam's *char* regions and issues surrounding identity and climate change, see also Barbora, "National Register of Citizens," 3–28.

25. On immigration and conflicts in Assam, see Chandan Kumar Sharma, "The Immigration Issue in Assam," 287–309. For the history of the National Register of Citizens, see also Chandan Kumar Sharma, "Immigration, Indigeneity and Identity," 97–98.

26. Scott, *Seeing Like a State*, 23.

27. Hull, *Government of Paper*, 2016; Gupta, *Red Tape*.

28. Mathur, *Paper Tiger*, 5.

29. Tobias Kelly, "Documented Lives," 89–107.

30. Hull, "Ruled by Records," 505–506.

31. Tarlo, *Unsettling Memories*, 87.

32. Hull, *Government of Paper*, 88.

33. Hull, *Government of Paper*, 88–89.

34. Gupta, *Red Tape*, 146.

35. See Arunabh Saikia, "The Final Count."

36. Chaudhuri, "God Sent Opportunity?"

37. Sahana Ghosh has shown how interconnected layers of identification relate to and are made to match with the identities of people to live along the India-Bangladesh border. She argues that the documentary process, along with interceptive and discrete modes of policing

that accompany it, relates to the making of the "illegal Bangladeshi immigrant." See Ghosh, "Everything Must Match," 870–883.

38. Interview, Assam, 10 August 2007.

39. Gupta, *Red Tape*, 144–145.

40. Gupta, *Red Tape*, 145.

41. *Indian Express*, "Declared Foreigners by Tribunals."

42. Press Information Bureau, India BB/NK/PK/YS/2150.

43. Asad, "Where Are the Margins of the State?" 279–288.

BIBLIOGRAPHY

ARCHIVAL AND GOVERNMENT RECORDS

Assam Police Weekly Intelligence Reports (APWIR), 1947.

Border Areas Development Programme. Accessed 10 February 2020, www.megbad.gov.in.

Border Guard Bangladesh. Accessed 10 May 2011 and 13 April 2018, http://www.bgb.gov.bd /index.php?node=Node/Incidence.

Chronicles of Birohidakuni Mission from 15 August 1955-1993, St. Elizabeth Church, Mymensingh, Bangladesh.

Department of Commerce, Government of India. EXIM Policy, 2002-2007. Press Release, 7 December 2002, Ministry of Commerce and Industry, Government of India. Accessed 10 March 2011, http://commerce.nic.in/PressRelease/pressrelease_detail.asp?id=989.

General Administration Report of the Garo Hills for the Year 1875-1876, Assam State Archives, Dispur.

Government of East Bengal (East Pakistan), National Archives of Bangladesh, Dhaka.

Home (Police) Department, Branch Police, B. Proceedings (Pol), International Institute for Social History, Amsterdam.

Home (Political) Department, Branch C.R. (Confidential Records) B. Proceedings (CR), National Archives of Bangladesh, Dhaka.

Home (Political) Department, Branch Political, B. Proceedings (Plt), National Archives of Bangladesh, Dhaka.

Home and Political Department, Government of Assam, http://online.assam.gov.in Internal Memos, 2001-2007, Office of Land Records and Surveys, Guwahati.

Land Revenue Department, Branch Excluded Areas, B. Proceedings, National Archives of Bangladesh, Dhaka.

Ministry of Home Affairs, *Annual Report 2005-2006, Annual Report 2006-2007.*

Ranikhong Church Chronicles. St. Joseph's Church, Ranikhong, Netrakona, Bangladesh.

Regulation X of 1822. In Alexander Mackenzie, *The North-East Frontier of India.* New Delhi: Mittal Publications, 2005, 250-253.

Report of the Arbuthnot Commission. In *Unpublished Reports on Garo Affairs*, ed. Mihir N. Sangma. New Delhi: Scholar Publishing House, 1993.

Report on the Land Revenue Administration of Assam, 1901-1935, Assam State Archives, Dispur.

Resolution on the Land Revenue Administration of Assam for the Year 1933-1934, Shillong, 1934, Assam State Archives, Dispur.

South Asia Terrorism Portal. http://www.satp.org.
Weekly Confidential Report 1947 (Police Confidential Branch), Assam State Archives, Dispur.

BOOKS, ARTICLES, AND PAPERS

Acharya, Bhairav. "The Controversy Surrounding the Supreme Court's Decision to Strike Down the Illegal Migrants (Determination by Tribunals) Act." Unpublished paper, 1983.

Acharya, Jagat Mani, Manjita Gurung, and Ranabir Samaddar. "Chronicles of a No-Where People on the Indo-Bangladesh Border." SAFHR Paper Series 14. Kathmandu: South Asia Forum for Human Rights, Kathmandu, 2003.

Adcock, Cassie, and Radhika Govindrajan. "Bovine Politics in South Asia: Rethinking Religion, Law and Ethics." *South Asia: Journal of South Asian Studies* 42, no. 6 (2019): 1095–1107.

Agamben, Giorgio. *State of Exception*. Chicago: University of Chicago Press, 2005.

Ain-Salish, Kendra. "Reports on Border Violence." Accessed 7 March 2020, http://www.askbd.org/ask/category/hr-monitoring/border-violence/.

Alexander, Claire, Joya Chatterji, and Annu Jalais. *The Bengal Diaspora: Rethinking Muslim Migration*. London: Routledge, 2015.

Amin, Ash. *Land of Strangers*. London: Polity Press, 2012.

Anand, Nikhil. *Hydraulic City: Water and the Infrastructures of Politics in Mumbai*. Durham, NC: Duke University Press, 2017.

Anderson, Francis Philip. "The Effects of the Earthquake in 1897 on the Shaistaganj Division of the Assam-Bengal Railway." *Minutes of the Proceedings of the Institution of Civil Engineers* 141, no. 3 (1900): 258–261.

Andersson, Ruben. "Time and the Migrant Other: European Border Controls and the Temporal Economics of Illegality." *American Anthropologist* 116, no. 4 (2014): 795–809.

Andreas, Peter. *Border Games: Policing the U.S.-Mexico Divide*. Ithaca, NY: Cornell University Press, 2000.

Anjaria, Jonathan. "Ordinary States: Everyday Corruption and the Politics of Space in Mumbai." *American Ethnologist* 38 (2011): 58–72.

Anzaldúa, Gloria. *Borderlands/La Frontera: The New Mestiza*. San Francisco: Aunt Lute Books, 2007.

Appadurai, Arjun. *Modernity at Large: Cultural Dimensions of Globalization*. Minneapolis: University of Minnesota Press, 1996.

———. *The Social Life of Things: Commodities in Cultural Perspective*. Cambridge: Cambridge University Press, 1996.

Appel, Hannah, Nikhil Anand, and Akhil Gupta, eds. *The Promise of Infrastructure*. Durham, NC: Duke University Press, 2018.

Austen, H. H. Godwin. "On the Garo Hills." *Proceedings of the Royal Geographical Society of London* 17, no. 1 (1872): 36–40.

Asad, Talal. "Where Are the Margins of the State?" In *Anthropology in the Margins of the State*, ed. Veena Das and Deborah Poole, 279–288. Delhi: Oxford University Press, 2004.

Bagchi, Jasodhara, and Subhoranjan Dasgupta, eds. *The Trauma and the Triumph*. Kolkata: Stree, 2006.

Bagchi, Suvojit. "The Curious Case." *Hindu*, 1 December 2019.

Bal, Ellen. *They Ask If We Eat Frogs: Garo Ethnicity in Bangladesh*. Singapore: ISEAS, 2007.

Bal, Ellen, and Timour Claquin. "The Borders That Divide, the Borders That Unite: (Re)interpreting Garo Processes of Identification in India and Bangladesh." *Journal of Borderland Studies* 29, no. 1 (2014): 95–101.

Banerjee, Paula. *Borders, Histories, Existences: Gender and Beyond*. New Delhi: Sage, 2010.

Bangladesh Garments Manufacturers and Exporters Association (BGMEA). "Trade Information." Accessed 14 May 2018, http://www.bgmea.com.bd/home/pages/tradeinformation.

Barbora, Sanjay. "The Crisis of Citizenship in Assam." *India Forum*, 16 May 2019.

———. "National Register of Citizens: Politics and Problems in Assam Explorations." *Indian Sociological Society E-Journal* 3, no. 2 (October 2019): 3–28.

Barooah, Nirodh Kumar. *David Scott in North-East India, 1802–1831: A Study in British Paternalism*. New Delhi: Munshiram Manoharlal, 1970.

Baruah, Sanjib. "AFSPA: Legacy of Colonial Constitutionalism." *Seminar* no. 615 (2010). https://www.india-seminar.com/2010/615/615_sanjib_baruah.htm. accessed on March 1, 2020.

———. *Durable Disorder: Understanding the Politics of Northeast India*. New Delhi: Oxford University Press, 2007.

———. *India Against Itself: Assam and the Politics of Nationality*. Philadelphia: University of Pennsylvania Press, 1999.

———. "Nationalizing Space: Cosmetic Federalism and the Politics of Development in Northeast India." *Development and Change* 34, no. 5 (2003): 915–939.

———. "Reading Fürer-Haimendorf in Northeast India." In *Geographies of Difference: Explorations in Northeast Indian Studies*, ed. Mélanie Vandenhelsken, Meenaxi Barkataki-Ruscheweyh, and Bengt G. Karlsson, 17–30. New Delhi: Routledge, 2018.

Baud, Michiel, and Willem van Schendel. "Towards a Comparative History of Borderlands." *Journal of World History* 8, no. 2 (1997): 211–242.

Beaver, Janice Cheryl. "CRS Report for Congress." Accessed 12 May 2011, http://www.fas.org/sgp/crs/misc/RS21729.pdf.

Beteille, Andre. "The Concept of Tribe with Special Reference to India." *European Journal of Sociology* 27, no. 2 (1986): 297–318.

Beverley, Eric Lewis. "Frontier as Resource: Law, Crime, and Sovereignty on the Margins of Empire." *Comparative Studies in Society and History* 55, no. 2 (2013): 241–272.

Bhadra, Gautam. *Iman O Nishan: Unnish Satakey Banglar Krishakbridroher Ek Addhay*. Kolkata: Subararekha, 1993.

Biehl, João Guilherme. *Vita: Life in a Zone of Social Abandonment*. Berkeley: University of California Press, 2013.

Biehl, João Guilherme, and Peter Locke, eds. *Unfinished: An Anthropology of Becoming*. Durham, NC: Duke University Press, 2017.

Bigo, Dider. "The Mobius Ribbon of Internal and External Security (ies)." In *Identities, Borders and Orders: Re-Thinking International Relations Theory*, ed. Mathias Albert, David Jacobson, and Yosef Lapid, 91–116. Minneapolis: University of Minnesota Press, 2001.

Billé, Franck. "Skinworlds: Borders, Haptics, Topologies." *Environment and Planning D: Society and Space* 36, no. 1 (2018): 66–77.

Blackwood, J. R. *A Survey and Census of the Cattle of Bengal*. Calcutta: Bengal Book Deport, 1915.

Brighenti, Francesco. "Traditional Beliefs about Weretigers Among the Garos of Meghalaya, India." *eTropic* 16, no. 1 (2017): 96–111.

Brown, Wendy. *Walled States, Waning Sovereignty*. New York: Zone Books, 2010.

B'Tselem: The Israeli Information Center for Human Rights in the Occupied Territories. "Statistics." Accessed 18 May 2011, http://www.btselem.org/separation_barrier/statistics.

Burling, Robbins. *Rengsanggri: Family and Kinship in a Garo Village*. Philadelphia: University of Pennsylvania Press, 1963.

Business Standard (India). "In Assam, Does 'D' Stand for 'Doubtful' or 'Deprived' Voter?" *Business Standard*, 7 April 2016. Accessed 26 October 2016, http://www.business -standard.com/article/news-ians/in-assam-does-d-stand-for-doubtful-or-deprived-voter -116040700772_1.html.

Carey, William. *The Garo Jungle Book*. Philadelphia: Hudson Press, 1919.

Cartsen, Janet. "What Kinship Does—and How." *HAU: Journal of Ethnographic Theory* 3, no. 2 (2013): 245–251.

Chakrabarty, Bidyut. *The Partition of Bengal and Assam, 1932–1947*. London: Routledge, 2004.

Chakraborty, Gorky. *Assam's Hinterland: Society and Economy in the Char Areas*. New Delhi: Akansha Publishing House, 2009.

Chalfin, Brenda. "Border Zone Trade and the Economic Boundaries of the State in North-East Ghana, Africa." *Journal of the International African Institute* 71, no. 2 (2001): 202–224.

Chandra, Uday. "Going Primitive: The Ethics of Indigenous Rights Activism in Contemporary Jharkhand." *South Asia Multidisciplinary Academic Journal (SAMAJ)* 7 (2013). https://doi .org/10.4000/samaj.3600. Accessed January 26, 2015.

Chatterjee, Partha. *The Nation and Its Fragments*. Princeton, NJ: Princeton University Press, 2010.

Chatterji, Indrani. *Forgotten Friends: Monks, Marriages and Memories of Northeast India*. New Delhi: Oxford University Press, 2013.

Chatterji, Joya. "The Fashioning of a Frontier: The Radcliffe Line and Bengal's Border Landscape, 1947–52." *Modern Asian Studies* 33, no. 1 (1999): 185–242.

Chaudhuri, Sujit. "God Sent Opportunity?" *Seminar* 510 (2002). Accessed 9 May 2018, http:// www.india-seminar.com/2002/510/510%20sujit%20chaudhuri.htm.

Choudhury, Anwaruddin. "Impact of Border Fence Along India-Bangladesh Border on Elephant Movement." *Gajah* 26 (2007): 27–30.

Cons, Jason. "Narrating Boundaries: Framing and Contesting Suffering, Community, and Belonging Along the India-Bangladesh Border." *Political Geography* 35 (2013): 37–46.

———. *Sensitive Space: Fragmented Territory at the India-Bangladesh Border*. Seattle: University of Washington Press, 2016.

Cons, Jason and Romola Sanyal. "Introduction: Geographies at the Margins." *Political Geography* 35 (2013): 5–13.

Cornelius, Wayne A. "Death at the Border: Efficacy and Unintended Consequences of US Immigration Control Policy." *Population and Development Review* 27, no. 4 (2001): 661–685.

Cresswell, Tim. "Towards a Politics of Mobility." *Environment and Planning D: Society and Space* 28, no. 1 (2010): 17–31.

Daily Star. "BGB Won't Bar Cattle Coming thru' Proper Corridors." *Daily Star*, 3 August 2017. Accessed 13 April 2018, http://www.thedailystar.net/backpage/bgb-wont-bar-cattle -coming-thru-proper-corridors-1442962.

———. "BSF Agrees to Put Off Fencing Within 150 Yards of Border: Coordinated Patrolling with India Soon." *Daily Star*, 14 April 2005. Accessed 12 June 2011, http://www.thedailystar .net/2005/04/14/d5041401033.htm.

Dalakoglou, Dimitris. "The Road: An Ethnography of the Albanian–Greek Cross-Border Motorway." *American Ethnologist* 37, no. 1 (2010): 132–147.

Dalton, Edward T. *Descriptive Ethnology of Bengal*. Calcutta: Office of the Superintendent of Government Printing, 1872.

Daniel, Valentine. *Fluid Signs: Being a Person the Tamil Way*. Berkeley: University of California Press, 1984.

Das, Suranjan. "The 1992 Calcutta Riot in Historical Continuum: A Relapse into 'Communal Fury'?" *Modern Asian Studies* 34, no. 2 (2000): 281–306.

Das, Veena. *Critical Events: An Anthropological Perspective on Contemporary India*. New Delhi: Oxford University Press, 1995.

———. *Life and Words: Violence and Descent into the Ordinary*. Berkeley: University of California Press, 2007.

Das, Veena, and Deborah Poole, eds. *Anthropology at the Margins of the State*. New Delhi: Oxford University Press, 2004.

D'Costa, Bina. *Nation-Building, Gender and War Crimes in South Asia*. London: Routledge, 2011.

De Genova, Nicholas, and Nathalie Mae Peutz. *The Deportation Regime: Sovereignty, Space, and the Freedom of Movement*. Durham, NC: Duke University Press, 2010.

De León, Jason. *The Land of Open Graves: Living and Dying on the Migrant Trail*. Berkeley: University of California Press, 2015.

Deleuze, Gilles. *Nietzsche and Philosophy*. New York: Columbia University Press, 2006.

Dev, Bimal J., and Dilip Kumar Lahiri. *Assam Muslims: Politics and Cohesion*. New Delhi: Mittal Publications, 1985.

Dhingra, Sanya. "India's Beef Exports Rise Under Modi Govt Despite Hindu Vigilante Campaign at Home," The Print .in, 26 March, 2019. Accessed 1 February 2020, https://theprint .in/economy/indias-beef-exports-rise-under-modi-govt-despite-hindu-vigilante-cam paign-at-home/210164/

Dirks, Nicholas B. "The Policing of Tradition: Colonialism and Anthropology in Southern India." *Comparative Studies in Society and History* 39, no. 1 (1997): 182–212.

Donnan, Hastings, and Thomas M. Wilson. *Borders: Frontiers of Identity, Nation and State*. Oxford: Berg Publishers, 1999.

Duara, Prasenjit. *Rescuing History from the Nation: Questioning Narratives from Modern China*. Chicago: University of Chicago Press, 1995.

Dzuvichu, Lipokmar. "Roads and the Raj: The Politics of Road Building in Colonial Naga Hills, 1860s–1910s." *Indian Economic and Social History Review* 50, no. 4 (2013): 473–494.

Economic Times. "Electronic Surveillance of Indo-Bangla Border to Begin Tuesday." *Economic Times*, 4 March 2019. Accessed 30 March 2020, https://economictimes.indiatimes.com /news/defence/electronic-surveillance-of-indo-bangla-border-to-begin-tuesday /articleshow/68254084.cms?from=mdr.

Elden, Stuart. *The Birth of Territory*. Chicago: University of Chicago Press, 2013.

Eliot, John. "Observations on the Inhabitants of the Garrow Hills, Made During a Public Deputation in the Years 1788 and 1789." *Asiatick Researches* 3 (1794): 21–45.

Financial Express (New Delhi). "Dutch Bangladesh Bank Limited Builds First Bridge in Kurigram." *Financial Express*, 16 January 2012.

Flynn, Donna K. "'We Are the Border': Identity, Exchange, and the State Along the Bénin-Nigeria Border." *American Ethnologist* 24, no. 2 (1997): 311–330.

Foucault, Michel. *Discipline and Punish: The Birth of the Prison*. London: Penguin, 1991.

Fuller, Christopher J., and Véronique Bénéï, eds. *The Everyday State and Society in Modern India*. New Delhi: Social Science Press, 2009.

Gellner, David. "Introduction. Northern South Asia's Diverse Borders, from Kachchh to Mizoram." In *Borderland Lives in Northern South Asia*, ed. David Gellner, 1–24. Durham, NC: Duke University Press, 2013.

Ghosh, Kaushik. "Between Global Flows and Local Dams: Indigenousness, Locality, and the Transnational Sphere in Jharkhand, India." *Cultural Anthropology* 21, no. 4 (2006): 501–534.

———. "A Market for Aboriginality: Primitivism and Race Classification in the Indentured Labour Market of Colonial India." In *Subaltern Studies*, ed. Gyan Prakash, Gautam Bhadra, and Susie Tharu, vol. 10, 8–48. New Delhi: Oxford University Press, 1997.

Ghosh, Sahana. "*Chor*, Police and Cattle: The Political Economies of Bovine Value in the India-Bangladesh Borderlands." *South Asia: Journal of South Asian Studies* 42, no. 6 (2019): 1108–1124.

———. "Everything Must Match: Detection, Deception and Migrant Illegality in the India-Bangladesh Borderlands." *American Anthropologist* 121, no. 4 (2019): 870–883.

———. "Security Socialities: Gender, Surveillance and Civil-Military Relations in India's Eastern Borderlands." *Comparative Studies in South Asia, Africa and the Middle East* 39, no. 3 (2019): 349–450.

Giersch, Charles Patterson. *Asian Borderlands: The Transformation of Qing China's Yunnan Frontier*. Cambridge, MA: Harvard University Press, 2006.

Gilroy, Paul "Multiculture in Times of War," *Critical Quarterly* 48, no. 4 (2006): 27–45.

Govindrajan, Radhika. *Animal Intimacies: Interspecies Relatedness in India's Central Himalayas*. Chicago: University of Chicago Press, 2018.

Green, Linda. "Fear as a Way of Life." *Cultural Anthropology* 9, no. 2 (1994): 227–256.

Gregory, Christopher. "Exchange and Reciprocity." In the *Companion Encyclopaedia of Anthropology: Humanity, Culture and Social Life*, ed. Tim Ingold, 911–939. Hoboken, NJ: Taylor and Francis, 2013.

Guangmao, Xie. "Women and Social Change Along the Vietnam-Guangxi Border." In *Where China Meets Southeast Asia: Social and Cultural Change in Border Regions*, ed. Grant Evans, Christopher Hutton, and Kuah Khun Eng, 321–337. Singapore: ISEAS, 2000.

Guha, Amalendu. *Planter Raj to Swaraj: Freedom Struggle and Electoral Politics in Assam, 1826–1947*. New Delhi: Tulika, 2006.

Guha-Thakurta, Meghna, Hameeda Hussain, and Malini Sur. *Freedom from Fear? Freedom from Want? Rethinking Security in Bangladesh*. New Delhi: Rupa, 2010.

Gupta, Akhil. *Red Tape: Bureaucracy, Structural Violence, and Poverty in India*. Durham, NC: Duke University Press, 2012.

Hage, Ghassan, ed. *Waiting*. Melbourne: Melbourne University Press, 2009.

Haines, Chad. "Colonial Routes: Reorienting the Northern Frontier of British India." *Ethnohistory* 51, no. 3 (2004): 537–539.

Hansen, Thomas Blom. *The Saffron Wave: Democracy and Hindu Nationalism in India*. Princeton, NJ: Princeton University Press, 1999.

———. "Sovereigns Beyond the State." In *Sovereign Bodies: Citizens, Migrants, and States in the Postcolonial World*, ed. Thomas Blom Hansen and Finn Stepputat, 169–191. Princeton, NJ: Princeton University Press, 2001.

Hansen, Thomas Blom, and Finn Stepputat, eds. *Sovereign Bodies: Citizens, Migrants, and States in the Postcolonial World*. Princeton, NJ: Princeton University Press, 2001.

Haokip, Thongkholal. "Inter-Ethnic Relations in Meghalaya." *Asian Ethnicity* 15, no. 3 (2014): 302–316.

Harris, Tina. "Cross-Border Commodities: Processual Histories, Commodity Chains, and the Yak Tail Trade." In *Routledge Handbook of Asian Borderlands*, ed. A. Horstmann, M. Saxer, and A. Rippa, 106–113. London: Routledge, 2018.

———. *Geographical Diversions: Tibetan Trade, Global Transactions*. Athens: University of Georgia Press, 2013.

Hartley, Arthur Coulton. *Final Report on the Rangpur Survey and Settlement Operations 1931–1938*. Calcutta: Bengal Government Press, 1940.

Harvey, Penny, and Hannah Knox. "The Enchantments of Infrastructure." *Mobilities* 7, no. 4 (2012): 1–16.

Hazarika, Sanjoy. *Rites of Passage: Border Crossings, Imagined Homelands, India's East and Bangladesh*. New Delhi: Penguin, 2000.

Heyman, Josiah McC. *Life and Labor on the Border: Working People of Northeastern Sonora, Mexico 1886–1986*. Tucson: University of Arizona Press, 1991.

Hull, Matthew S. *Government of Paper: The Materiality of Bureaucracy in Urban Pakistan*. Berkeley: University of California Press, 2016.

———. "Ruled by Records: The Expropriation of Land and the Misappropriation of Lists in Islamabad." *American Ethnologist* 35, no. 4 (2008): 501–518.

Human Rights Watch. "India: Vigilante 'Cow Protection' Groups Attack Minorities," 18 February 2019. Accessed 14 January 2020, https://www.hrw.org/news/2019/02/18/india -vigilante-cow-protection-groups-attack-minorities.

———. *"Trigger Happy": Excessive Use of Force by Indian Troops*. New York: Human Rights Watch, 2010.

Hunter, William Wilson. *Imperial Gazetteer*. Vol. 5. London: Trübner and Co., 1885.

———. *A Statistical Account of Assam*. Vol. 2. London: Trübner & Co., 1879.

Hussain, Delwar. *Boundaries Undermined: The Ruins of Progress on Bangladesh-India. Border*. London: Hurst, 2013.

Ibrahim, Farhana. *Settlers, Saints and Sovereigns: An Ethnography of State Formation in Western India*. New Delhi: Routledge, 2009.

Indian Express. "Declared Foreigners by Tribunals, over 38,000 Bangladeshi Infiltrators Missing in Assam." *Indian Express*, 3 March 2015. Accessed 19 April 2018, http:// indianexpress.com/article/india/india-others/declared-foreigners-by-tribunals-over -38000-bangladeshi-infiltrators-missing-in-assam/.

———. "Two Crore Illegal Bangladeshis Living in India: Government." *Indian Express*, 16 November 2016. Accessed 24 April 2018, http://indianexpress.com/article/india/india -news-india/two-crore-illegal-bangladeshis-living-in-india-government-4379162/.

International Organization for Migration. *United Nations World Migration Report 2020*. Geneva: International Organization for Migration, 2020. Accessed 12 March 2020, https:// www.un.org/sites/un2.un.org/files/wmr_2020.pdf.

Iqbal, Iftekhar. "Towards an Environmental History of Colonial East Bengal: Paradigms and Praxis." *Journal of the Asiatic Society of Bangladesh* 2, nos. 1–2 (2005): 501–518.

Ispahani, Mahnaz. *Roads and Rivals: Politics of Access in the Borderlands of Asia*. London: Tauris, 1989.

Jain, Bharti. "Govt Slow in Deporting Illegal Bangladeshi Migrants." *Economic Times*, 1 November 2008. Accessed 17 November 2011, http://articles.economictimes.indiatimes.com /2008-11-01/news/27729987_1_illegal-bangladeshi-migrants-foreigners-act-imdt-act.

Jalais, Annu. *Forest of Tigers: People, Politics and Environment in the Sundarbans*. New Delhi: Routledge, 2010.

Janeja, Manpreet K., and Andreas Bandak, eds. *Ethnographies of Waiting: Doubt, Hope and Uncertainty*. London: Bloomsbury, 2019.

Jayal, Neerja Gopal. *Citizenship and Its Discontents: An Indian History*. Cambridge, MA: Harvard University Press, 2013.

Jeffrey, Craig. "Timepass: Youth, Class, and Time among Unemployed Young Men in India." *American Ethnologist* 37, no. (2010): 465–481.

Jeganathan, Pradeep. "Checkpoint: Anthropology, Identity and the State." In *Anthropology at the Margins of the State*, ed. Veena Das and Deborah Poole, 67–80. New Delhi: Oxford University Press, 2004.

Jones, Reece. "Agents of Exception: Border Security and the Marginalization of Muslims in India." *Environment and Planning D: Society and Space* 27, no. 5 (2009): 879–897.

———. *Border Walls: Security and the War on Terror in the United States, India and Israel*. London: Zed Books, 2012.

———. "'Geopolitical Boundary Narratives, the Global War on Terror and Border Fencing in India." *Transactions of the Institute of British Geographers* 34, no. 3 (2009): 290–304.

———. "Sovereignty and Statelessness in the Border Enclaves of India and Bangladesh." *Political Geography* 28, no. 8 (2009): 373–381.

———. "Spaces of Refusal: Rethinking Sovereign Power and Resistance at the Border." *Annals of the Association of American Geographers* 102, no. 3 (2011): 685–699.

Jusionyte, Ieva. *Savage Frontier: Making News and Security on the Argentine Border*. Oakland: University of California Press, 2015.

Kabeer, Naila, and Simeen Mahmud. "Rags, Riches and Women Workers: Export-Oriented Garment Manufacturing in Bangladesh." In *Chains of Fortune: Linking Women Producers and Workers with Global Markets*, ed. Marilyn Carr, 133–164. London: Commonwealth Secretariat, 2004.

Kalir, Barak, Malini Sur, and Willem van Schendel. "Mobile Practices and Regimes of Permissiveness." In *Transnational Flows and Permissive Polities: Ethnographies of Human Mobility in Asia*, ed. Barak Kalir and Malini Sur, 11–25. Amsterdam: Amsterdam University Press, 2012.

Kapur, Ratna. "The Citizen and the Migrant: Postcolonial Anxieties, Law, and the Politics of Exclusion/Inclusion." *Theoretical Inquiries in Law* 8, no. 2 (2007): 537–570.

Kar, Bodhisattva. "When Was the Postcolonial: A History of Policing Impossible Lines." In *Beyond Counter-Insurgency: Breaking the Impasse in Northeast India*, ed. Sanjib Baruah, 25–49. New Delhi: Oxford University Press, 2009.

Kar, Parimal Chandra. *British Annexation of the Garo Hills*. New Delhi: Navbharat Publishers, 1970.

———. *Glimpses of the Garos*. Tura: Meghalaya Book Depot, 1982.

———. *Garos in Transition*. New Delhi: Cosmo Books, 2003.

Karlsson, Bengt G. "Anthropology and the 'Indigenous Slot': Claims to and Debates about Indigenous Peoples' Status in India." *Critique of Anthropology* 23, no. 4 (2003): 403–423.

———. *Unruly Hills Nature and Nation in India's Northeast*. New Delhi: Social Science Press and Orient Blackswan, 2011.

Karmakar, Rahul. "Over 19 Lakh Excluded from Assam's Final NRC." *Hindu*, 31 August 2019. Accessed 9 January 2020, https://www.thehindu.com/news/national/over-19-lakh -excluded-from-assams-final-nrc/article29307099.ece.

Kelly, John. "Co-Existence: Nehru's Anthropology, Bandung, and the Fate of Highland Asia." Paper read at the Department of Anthropology, Johns Hopkins University, 10 September 2013.

Kelly, Tobias. "Documented Lives: Fear and the Uncertainties of Law During the Second Palestinian Intifada." *Journal of the Royal Anthropological Institute* 11, no. 1 (2006): 89–107.

———. *Law, Violence and Sovereignty Among West Bank Palestinians*. Cambridge: Cambridge University Press, 2006.

Kerr, Ian J. *Engines of Change: The Railroads That Made India*. Westport, CT: Praeger, 2007.

Khan, Naveeda. "Dogs and Humans and What Earth Can Be: Filaments of Muslim Ecological Thought." *HAU: Journal of Ethnographic Theory* 4, no. 3 (2017): 245–264.

Kosravi, Shahram. *Precarious Lives: Waiting and Hope in Iran*. Philadelphia: University of Pennsylvania Press, 2017.

Krishna, Sankaran. "Cartographic Anxiety: Mapping the Body Politic in India." *Alternatives* 19, no. 4 (1994): 507–521.

Kumar, Sanjeeva. "State 'Simplification': Garo Protest in Late 19th and Early 20th Century Assam." *Economic and Political Weekly* 40, no. 27 (2005): 2941–2947.

Lahiri-Dutt, Kuntala, and Gopa Samanta. *Dancing with the River: People and Life on the Chars of South Asia*. New Haven, CT: Yale University Press, 2013.

Larkin, Brian. "The Politics and Poetics of Infrastructure." *Annual Review of Anthropology* 42 (2013): 327–343.

Lertchavalitsakul, Busarin. "Shan Women Traders and Their Survival Strategies Along the Thai-Myanmar Border." *Sojourn: Journal of Social Issues in Southeast Asia* 30, no. 3 (2015): 675–709.

Leungaramsri, Pinkeau. "Women, Nation and the Ambivalence of Subversive Identification Along the Thai-Burmese Border." *Sojourn: Journal of Social Issues in Southeast Asia* 21, no. 1 (2006): 68–89.

Ludden, David. "The First Boundary of Bangladesh on Sylhet's Northern Frontiers." *Journal of the Asiatic Society of Bangladesh* 48, no. 1 (2003): 1–49.

———. "Presidential Address: Maps in the Mind and the Mobility of Asia." *Journal of Asian Studies* 62, no. 4 (2003): 1057–1078.

———. "Where Is Assam?" *HIMAL SouthAsia*, 15 January 2013. Accessed 7 June 2018, http://m.himalmag.com/where-is-assam/.

Mackenzie, Alexander. *The North-East Frontier of India*. New Delhi: Mittal Publications, 2005.

Magnier, Mark. "Where Is the Beef? Indians Don't Want to Know." *Los Angeles Times*, 2 May 2010. Accessed 14 May 2010, http://www.latimes.com/news/nationworld/world/la-fg -india-cows-20100503,0,7142346.story.

Malik, Bela. "The 'Problem' of Shifting Cultivation in the Garo Hills of North-East India, 1860–1970." *Conservation and Society* 1, no. 2 (2003): 287–315.

Malkki, Liisa. "National Geographic: The Rooting of Peoples and the Territorialization of National Identity Among Scholars and Refugees." *Cultural Anthropology* 7, no. 1 (1992): 24–44.

Marak, Caroline R. "The Role of the Mahari in A'chik Society: Change and Continuity." *South Asia: Journal of South Asian Studies* 30, no. 3 (2007): 531–540.

Mardsen, Magnus, and Madeleine Reeves. "Marginal Hubs: On Conviviality Beyond the Urban in Asia: Introduction." *Modern Asian Studies* 53, no. 3 (2019): 755–775.

Martinez, Oscar J. *The Border People: Life and Society in the U.S.-Mexico Borderlands*. Tucson: University of Arizona Press, 1994.

Masquelier, Adeline. "Road Mythographies: Space, Mobility, and the Historical Imagination in Postcolonial Niger." *American Ethnologist* 29, no. 4 (2002): 829–831.

Massey, Doreen. "Power-Geometry and a Progressive Sense of Place." In *Mapping the Futures: Local Cultures, Global Change*, ed. Jon Bird, Barry Curtis, Tim Putnam, George Robertson, and Lisa Tickner, 59–69. London: Routledge, 1993.

Mathur, Nayanika. *Paper Tiger Law, Bureaucracy and the Developmental State in Himalayan India*. Delhi: Cambridge University Press, 2016.

McDuie-Ra, Duncan. "Embracing or Challenging the Tribe? Dilemmas in Reproducing Obligatory Pasts in Meghalaya." In *Landscape, Culture, and Belonging Writing the History of Northeast India*, ed. Neeladri Bhattacharya and Joy L. K. Pachuau, 66–86. New Delhi: Cambridge University Press, 2019.

———. "Fifty-Year Disturbance: The Armed Forces Special Powers Act and Exceptionalism in a South Asian Periphery." *Contemporary South Asia* 17, no. 3 (2009): 255–270.

———. "Violence Against Women in the Militarized Indian Frontier: Beyond 'Indian Culture' in the Experiences of Ethnic Minority Women." *Violence Against Women* 18, no. 3 (2012): 322–345.

M'Cosh, John. *Topography of Assam*. Calcutta: Bengal Military Orphan Press, 1932.

Menon, Ritu, and Kamla Bhasin. "Recovery, Rupture, Resistance: Indian State and Abduction of Women During Partition." *Economic and Political Weekly* 28, no. 17 (April 1993): WS2–WS11.

Mezzadra, Sandro, and Brett Neilson. *Border as Method, or, the Multiplication of Labor*. Durham, NC: Duke University Press, 2014.

Michaud, Jean. "Zomia and Beyond." *Journal of Global History* 5, no. 2 (2010): 187–214.

Misra, Sanghamitra. *Becoming a Borderland: The Politics of Space and Identity in Colonial Northeastern India*. New Delhi: Routledge, 2011.

———. "Law, Migration and New Subjectivities: Reconstructing the Colonial Project in an Eastern Borderland." *Indian Economic and Social History Review* 44, no. 4 (2007): 425–461.

———. "The Sovereignty of Political Economy: The Garos in a Pre-conquest and Early Conquest Era." *Indian Economic and Social History Review* 55, no. 3 (2018): 345–387.

Mitchell, Timothy. "The Limits of the State: Beyond Statist Approaches and Their Critics." *American Political Science Review* 85, no. 1 (1991): 77–96.

Mookherjee, Nayanika. *The Spectral Wound: Sexual Violence, Public Memories, and the Bangladesh War of 1971*. Durham, NC: Duke University Press, 2015.

Navaro-Yashin, Yael. *The Make-Believe Space: Affective Geography in a Post-War Polity*. Durham, NC: Duke University Press, 2012.

NDTV. "Meghalaya BJP Leader Resigns from Party in Protest Against the Centre's Cattle Trade Rule." *NDTV*, 1 June 2017. Accessed 29 January 2020, https://www.ndtv.com/india-news/meghalaya-bjp-leader-resigns-from-party-in-protest-against-centres-cattle-trade-rule-1706678.

———. "NDTV Impact: Crackdown on Cattle Smuggling." *NDTV*, 10 May 2009. Accessed 18 July 2012, http://www.ndtv.com/video/player/news/ndtv-impact-crackdown-on-cattle-smuggling/74098.

Netz, Reviel. *Barbed Wire: An Ecology of Modernity.* Middletown, CT: Wesleyan University Press, 2004.

Nevins, Joseph. *Operation Gatekeeper and Beyond: The War on "Illegals" and the Remaking of the U.S.-Mexico Boundary.* New York: Routledge, 2010.

Nietzsche, Friedrich. *The Will to Power.* New York: Penguin, 2017.

Nowicka, Magdalena, and Steven Vertovec. "Comparing Convivialities: Dreams and Realities of Living-with-Difference." *European Journal of Cultural Studies* 17, no. 4 (2014): 341–356.

Nyamnjoh, Francis B., and Ingrid Brudvig. "Conviviality and the Boundaries of Citizenship in Urban Africa." In *The Routledge Handbook on Cities of the Global South,* ed. Susan Parnell and Sophie Oldfield, 341–356. New York: Routledge, 2014.

Ohnuki-Tierney, Emiko. *Rice as Self: Japanese Identities Through Time.* Princeton, NJ: Princeton University Press, 1993.

Oldham, Richard. D. *Memoirs of the Geological Survey of India,* vol. 24. Calcutta: Government of India, 1902.

O'Neill, Bruce. *The Space of Boredom: Homelessness in the Slowing Global Order.* Durham, NC: Duke University Press, 2017.

Outlook India. "Bangladesh Pact Signed Without People's Approval." *Outlook India,* 8 September 2011. Accessed 2 November 2011, http://news.outlookindia.com/items.aspx?artid =734066.

Pinney, Christopher. "The Nation (Un)Pictured? Chromolithography and 'Popular' Politics in India, 1878–1995." *Critical Inquiry* 23, no. 4 (1997): 834–867.

Playfair, A. *The Garos.* 1909. Reprint, Guwahati: Spectrum Publishers, 1998.

Portes, Alejandro, Luis E. Guarnizo, and Patricia Landolt. "The Study of Transnationalism: Pitfalls and Promise of an Emergent Research Field." *Ethnic and Racial Studies* 22, no. 2 (1999): 217–237.

Prakash, Gyan. *Another Reason: Science and the Imagination of Modern India.* Princeton, NJ: Princeton University Press, 1997.

Press Information Bureau, India. BB/NK/PK/YS/2150. Accessed 20 March 2020, https://pib .gov.in/newsite/PrintRelease.aspx?relid=177455.

Press Trust of India. "Illegal Cattle Smuggling from India Harming Bangladeshi Economy: BGB." *Business Standard,* 15 July 2017. Accessed 13 April 2018, http://www.business -standard.com/article/current-affairs/illegal-cattle-smuggling-from-india-harming -bangladeshi-economy-bgb-117071500374_1.html.

Raitapuro, Minna, and Ellen Bal. "'Talking About Mobility': Garos' Aspiring Migration and Mobility in an 'Insecure' Bangladesh." *South Asian History and Culture* 7, no. 4 (2016): 386–400.

Rajagopal, P. V., ed. *The British: The Bandits and the Bordermen, from the Diaries and Articles of K. F. Rustamji.* New Delhi: Wisdom Tree, 2009.

Rajaram, Prem K., and Carl Grundy-Warr, eds. *Borderscapes: Hidden Geographies and Politics at Territory's Edge.* Minneapolis: University of Minnesota Press, 2007.

Ralph, Michael. "Commodity." *Social Text* 27, no. 3 (1999): 78–84.

Reeves, Madeleine. "Clean Fake: Authenticating Documents and Persons in Migrant Moscow." *American Ethnologist* 40 (2013): 508–524.

Reid, John. E. "Recent Developments in Assam." *Royal United Services Institution Journal* 97, no. 585 (1952): 57–68.

Robb, Peter. "The Challenge of Gau Mata: British Policy and Religious Change in India, 1880–1916." *Modern Asian Studies* 20, no. 2 (1986): 285–319.

Roitman, Janet. "Productivity in the Margins: The Reconstitution of State Power in the Chad Basin." In *Anthropology at the Margins of the State*, ed. Veena Das and Deborah Poole, 191–224. New Delhi: Oxford University Press, 2004.

———. *Fiscal Disobedience: An Anthropology of Economic Regulation in Central Africa.* Princeton, NJ: Princeton University Press, 2005.

Roy, Anupama. "Between Encompassment and Closure: The 'Migrant' and the Citizen in India." *Contributions to Indian Sociology* 42, no. 2 (2008): 219–248.

Sadiq, Kamal. *Paper Citizens: How Illegal Immigrants Acquire Citizenship in Developing Countries.* New Delhi: Oxford University Press, 2009.

Sahlins, Marshall. "What Kinship Is (Part One)." *Journal of the Royal Anthropological Institute* 17, no. 1 (2011): 2–19.

Sahlins, Peter. *Boundaries: The Making of France and Spain in the Pyrenees.* Berkeley: University of California Press, 1989.

———. "State Formation and National Identity in the Catalan Borderlands During the Eighteenth and Nineteenth Centuries." In *Border Identities: Nation and State at International Frontiers*, ed. Thomas M. Wilson and Hastings Donnan, 31–62. Cambridge: Cambridge University Press, 1998.

Saikia, Arunabh. "The Final Count: Tracking the National Register of Citizens." The Scroll .in. https://scroll.in/topic/56205/the-final-count accessed 2 January 2020.

Saikia, Arupjyoti. *A Century of Protests: Peasant Politics in Assam Since 1900.* New Delhi: Oxford University Press, 2013.

———. *Forests and Ecological History of Assam 1826–2000.* New Delhi: Oxford University Press, 2011.

Samaddar, Ranabir. *The Marginal Nation: Transborder Migration from Bangladesh to West Bengal.* New Delhi: Sage, 1999.

Sangma, Mihir N. *Unpublished Reports on Garo Affairs.* New Delhi: Scholar Publishing House, 1993.

Sangma, Sanatombi K. "Shape-Shifting or Transformation Myth in Garo Culture." *Dialogue: A Journal Devoted to Literary Appreciation* 12, no. 1 (2016): 77–79.

Sangma, Sengrang N. *Bangladeshi Immigrants in Meghalaya.* Kolkata: Ansah, 2005.

Scheper-Hughes, Nancy, and Philippe I. Bourgois, eds. *Violence in War and Peace.* Oxford: Blackwell, 2004.

Schiller, Nina Glick, Linda Basch, and Cristina Szanton Blanc. "From Immigrant to Transmigrant: Theorizing Transnational Migration." *Anthropological Quarterly* 68, no. 1 (1995): 48–63.

Scott, James C. *The Art of Not Being Governed: An Anarchist History of Upland Southeast Asia.* New Haven, CT: Yale University Press, 2009.

———. *Seeing Like a State: How Certain Schemes to Improve the Human Condition Have Failed.* New Haven, CT: Yale University Press, 1998.

Sharma, Chandan Kumar. "Immigration, Indigeneity and Identity: The Bangladeshi Immigration Tangle in Assam." In *Unheeded Hinterland: Identity and Sovereignty in Northeast India*, ed. Dilip Gogoi, 89–113. New Delhi: Routledge, 2016.

———. "The Immigration Issue in Assam and Conflicts Around It." *Asian Ethnicity* 13, no. 3 (2012): 287–309.

Sharma, Jayeeta. *Empire's Garden: Assam and the Making of India.* New Delhi: Permanent Black, 2012.

Shewly, Hosna. "Abandoned Spaces and Bare Life in the Enclaves of the India-Bangladesh Border." *Political Geography* 32 (2013): 23–31.

Shneiderman, Sara. "Are the Central Himalayas in Zomia? Some Scholarly and Political Considerations Across Time and Space." *Journal of Global History* 5, no. 2 (2010): 289–312.

———. *Rituals of Ethnicity: Thangmi Identities Between Nepal and India.* Pennsylvania: University of Pennsylvania Press, 2015.

Siddiqui, Dina M. "Miracle Worker or Woman Machine? Tracking (Trans)national Realities in Bangladeshi Factories." *Economic and Political Weekly* 35, nos. 21–22 (2000): L11–L17.

Singh, Bhrigupati. "Anthropological Investigations of Vitality: Life-Force as a Dimension Distinct from Space and Time." *HAU: Journal of Ethnographic Theory* 8 no. 3 (2018): 550–563.

Singh, Bhrigupati, and Naisargi Dave. "On the Killing and Killability of Animals: Nonmoral Thoughts for the Anthropology of Ethics." *Comparative Studies of South Asia, Africa and the Middle East* 35, no. 2 (2015): 232–245.

Sivaramakrishnan, Kalyanakrishnan. "British Imperium and Forested Zones of Anomaly in Bengal, 1767–1833." *Indian Economic and Social History Review* 33, no. 3 (1996): 243–282.

———. *Modern Forests: Statemaking and Environmental Change in Colonial Eastern India.* Stanford, CA: Stanford University Press, 1999.

Skaria, Ajay. *Hybrid Histories: Forests, Frontiers and Wildness in Western India.* Delhi: Oxford University Press, 1998.

Smart, Alan, and Josiah McC. Heyman, eds. *States and Illegal Practices.* Oxford: Berg, 1999.

Smith, Susan J., and Rachel Pain, eds. *Fear: Critical Geopolitics and Everyday Life.* London: Ashgate, 2008.

Srivastava, Sanjay. "Duplicity, Intimacy, Community: Of Identity Cards, Permits and Other Fake Documents in Delhi." *Thesis Eleven* 113, no. 1 (2012): 1–16.

Stewart, Kathleen. *Space on the Side of the Road: Cultural Poetics in an "Other" America.* Princeton, NJ: Princeton University Press, 1996.

Stoler, Laura Ann. *Along the Archival Grain: Epistemic Anxieties and Colonial Common Sense.* Princeton, NJ: Princeton University Press, 2006.

Sturgeon, Janet C. *Border Landscapes: The Politics of Akha Land Use in China and Thailand.* Seattle: University of Washington Press, 2005.

Subba, T. B., and J. J. P. Wouters. "Northeast India: Ethnography and Politics of Identity." In *The Modern Anthropology of India: Ethnography, Themes and Theory,* ed. P. Berger and F. Heidemann, 193–207. London: Routledge, 2013.

Sundar, Nandini and T.N. Madan, eds. 2016. *The Scheduled Tribes and Their India: Politics, Identities, Policies, and Work.* New Delhi: Oxford University Press, 2016.

Sur, Malini. "Bamboo Baskets and Barricades: Gendered Landscapes at the India-Bangladesh Borderlands." In *Transnational Flows and Permissive Polities: Ethnographies of Human Mobility in Asia,* ed. Barak Kalir and Malini Sur, 127–150. Amsterdam: Amsterdam University Press, 2012.

———. "Battles for the Golden Grain: Paddy Soldiers and the Making of the Northeast India–East Pakistan Border, 1930–1970." *Comparative Studies in Society and History* 58, no. 3 (July 2016): 804–832.

———. "Dreaming Borders: On Cats and Trauma." *Somatosphere,* 19 February 2019.

———. "Divided Bodies: Crossing the India-Bangladesh Border." *EPW* 49, no. 13 (29 March 2014): 31–35.

———. "Danger and Difference: Teatime at the Northeast India–Bangladesh Border." *Modern Asia Studies* 53, no. 3 (May 2019): 846–873.

———. "In the Name of Indian Citizenship? Criminalizing Statelessness at the India-Bangladesh Border." Blog post. Accessed 27 March 2020, https://www.law.ox.ac.uk/research-subject -groups/centre-criminology/centreborder-criminologies/blog/2020/02/name-indian.

———. "Spiral." In *Volumetric Sovereignty Series Part Three: Turbulence, Society and Space*, ed. Frank Bille, 17 March 2019. Accessed 4 April 2020, https://www.societyandspace.org /articles/spiral.

———. "Through Metal Fences: Material Mobility and the Politics of Transnationality at Borders." *Mobilities* 8, no. 1 (2013): 70–89.

———. "Time at Its Margins: Cattle Smuggling Across the India-Bangladesh Border." *Cultural Anthropology*, 35, no. 4 (2020): 546–574.

Sur, Malini, and Rakesh Kumar. "India's Citizenship Act: Has PM Modi Bitten Off More Than He Can Chew?" *Globe Post*, 2 January 2020.

Syiemleih, David R. "Catholic Missions Among the Garos of Mymensing: Some Reflections of Its Early History 1909–1942." In *Readings in the History and Culture of the Garos: Essays in Honour of Milton S. Sangma*, ed. Mignonette Momin, 170–179. New Delhi: Regency Publications, 2003.

———. *On the Edge of Empire: Four British Plans for North East India 1941–1947.* New Delhi: Sage, 2014.

Tarlo, Emma. *Unsettling Memories: Narratives of the Emergency in Delhi.* Berkeley: University of California Press, 2001.

Taussig, Michael. "Terror as Usual: Walter Benjamin's Theory of History as a State of Siege." *Social Text* 23, no. 1 (1989): 3–20.

Telegraph (India). "Government Seeks More Men to Guard Check Posts." *Telegraph*, 21 February 2011. Accessed 15 July 2011, http://www.telegraphindia.com/1110221/jsp/northeast /story_13610277.jsp.

Thiranagama, Sharika. "The Civility of Strangers? Caste, Ethnicity, and Living Together in Postwar Jaffna, Sri Lanka." *Anthropological Theory* 18, nos. 2–3 (June 2018): 357–381.

———. *In My Mother's House: Civil War in Sri Lanka.* Philadelphia: University of Pennsylvania Press, 2011.

Times of India. "Six Border Haats to Come up Soon." *Times of India*, 6 August 2019. Accessed 14 February 2020, https://timesofindia.indiatimes.com/city/shillong/six-border-haats-to -come-up-soon/articleshow/70767318.cms.

Torpey, John. *The Invention of the Passport: Surveillance, Citizenship and the State.* Cambridge: Cambridge University Press, 2000.

Trouillot, Michel-Rolph. *Silencing the Past: Power and the Production of History.* Boston: Beacon Press, 1995.

Van der Veer, Peter. *Religious Nationalism in India.* Berkeley: University of California Press, 1994.

Van Schendel, Willem. *The Bengal Borderland: Beyond State and Nation in South Asia.* London: Anthem Press, 2005.

———. "Easy Come, Easy Go: Smugglers on the Ganges." *Journal of Contemporary Asia* 23, no. 2 (1993): 189–213.

———. "Geographies of Knowing, Geographies of Ignorance: Jumping Scale in Southeast Asia." *Environment and Planning* 20, no. 6 (2000): 647–668.

——. *A History of Bangladesh*. Cambridge: Cambridge University Press, 2009.

——. "The Invention of the 'Jummas': State Formation and Ethnicity in Southeastern Bangladesh." *Modern Asian Studies* 26, no. 1 (1992): 95–128.

——. "Madmen of Mymensingh: Peasant Resistance and the Colonial Process in Eastern India, 1824 to 1833." *Indian Economic Social History Review* 22, no. 2 (1985): 139–73.

——. "Stateless in South Asia: The Making of the India-Bangladesh Enclaves." *Journal of Asian Studies* 61, no. 1 (2002): 115–147.

——. "The Wagah Syndrome: Territorial Roots of Contemporary Violence in South Asia." In *Violence and Democracy in India*, ed. Amrita Basu and Srirupa Roy, 36–82. London: Berg, 2007.

——. "Working Through Partition: Making a Living in the Bengal Borderlands." *International Review of Social History* 46 (2001): 393–421.

van Schendel, Willem, and Itty Abraham, eds. *Illicit Flows and Criminal Things: States, Borders, and the Other Side of Globalization*. Bloomington: Indiana University Press, 2005.

van Schendel, Willem, and Md. Mahbubar Rahman. "'I Am Not a Refugee': Rethinking Partition Migration." *Modern Asian Studies* 37, no. 3 (2003): 551–584.

Vandenhelsken, Melanie, and Bengt G. Karlsson. "Fluid Attachments in Northeast India: Introduction." *Asian Ethnicity* 17, no. 3 (2016): 330–339.

Vas, J. A. *Eastern Bengal and Assam District Gazetteer, Rangpur*. Allahabad: Pioneer Press, 1911.

Vigneswaran, Darshan. "Protection and Conviviality: Community Policing in Johannesburg." *European Journal of Cultural Studies* 17, no. 4 (2014): 471–486.

Vila, Pablo. *Ethnography at the Border*. Minneapolis: University of Minnesota Press, 2003.

Vitebsky, Piers. *Reindeer People: Living with Animals and Spirits in Siberia*. London: Harper-Collins, 2005.

Walker, Andrew. *The Legend of the Golden Boat: Regulation, Trade and Traders in the Borderlands of Laos, Thailand, Burma and China*. Richmond: Curzon Press, 1999.

Watson, Archibald. *Memoir of the Late David Scott*. Calcutta: Baptist Mission Press, 1832.

Weizman, Eyal. *Hollow Land: Israel's Architecture of Occupation*. London: Verso, 2007.

Winichakul, Thongchai. *Siam Mapped: A History of the Geo-Body of a Nation*. Honolulu: University of Hawaii Press, 1994.

Xaxa, Virginius. "Tribes as Indigenous People of India." *Economic and Political Weekly* 34, no. 51 (1999): 3589–3595.

Yang, Anand A. "Sacred Symbol and Sacred Space in Rural India: Community Mobilization in the 'Anti-Cow Killing' Riot of 1893." *Comparative Studies in Society and History* 22, no. 4 (1980): 576–596.

Yuval-Davis, Nira. *Gender and the Nation*. London: Sage, 1997.

Zamindar, Vazira Fazila-Yacoobali. *The Long Partition and the Making of Modern South Asia: Refugees, Boundaries, Histories*. New Delhi: Viking, 2008.

Zolberg, Aristide. "Matters of the State: Theorising Immigration Policy." In *Handbook of International Migration: The American Experience*, ed. C. Hirschman, P. Kasinitz, and J. De Wind, 71–93. New York: Russell Sage Foundation, 1999.

Zutshi, Chitralekha. "Rethinking Kashmir's History from a Borderlands Perspective." *History Compass* 8, no. 7 (2010): 594–608.

INDEX

abandoned harvests, 63, 64

Adibashi, 15, 105; Adibashistan, ix; Adivasi, 175n45

Agamben, Giorgio, 121, 183n3

All Assam Students Union (AASU), 16, 150

Amin, Ash, 97, 182n10

Andreas, Peter, 10, 174n34

animals, 1, 10, 28, 35, 75, 87, 90, 121, 126, 129, 137, 138, 144, 172, 181n12; animal corridors, 68, 72, 83, 85–89, 180n5, 181n24; distraught animals, 3, 129; exhausted animals, 83; intelligent animals, 126; large animals, 126; noise of animals, rabbit, 140; 125; sheltered animals, 93; tradeable animals, 83; weak animals, 87

annexation, 176n20, 176n22, 176n25, 177n37, 177n53

Anzaldúa, Gloria, 21, 174n17, 176n54, 176n55

archives, 15, 19, 25, 34, 43, 177n33, 177n34

Assam, x, 1, 9, 13–17, 24–26, 45, 57, 61, 63, 68, 75, 78, 93, 135, 140, 145, 172, 173n3, 173n7, 174n14, 174n49, 176n15, 176n16, 176n18, , 177n33, 177n35, 117n1, 177n6, 177n7, 178n9, 178n11, 178n12, 178n21, 178n26, 178n30, 178n31, 178n37, 179n45, 179n54, 179n64, 180n1, 180n2, 180n5, 185n15, 185n16, 185n21, 185n22, 185n24, 185n25, 185n38; Kingdom of Assam, ix, 30; Assamese, 16, 17, 40, 45–49, 59–61, 151, 160, 166; Assam Movement, ix, 16, 148, 150, 168

Assam Provincial Congress Party, 48

Bal, Ellen, 15, 112, 175n46, 175n47, 178n17, 179n57, 180n78, 182n7, 183n26, 183n33

Bangladesh, ix, x, 1–4, 6, 8, 9–21, 23, 24, 27, 38, 40, 42, 44, 47, 64, 67–69, 71, 72, 77, 79, 80, 82–89, 91, 93–95, 97–100, 103–107, 109–112, 114, 119, 121–125, 127–132, 134, 136, 137, 139–151, 153, 154, 156–161, 163–165, 168, 170–172, 173n3, 173n5, 173n7, 174n28, 175n42, 175n44, 175n45, 175n49, 175n50, 176n1, 177n5, 179n62, 179n69, 180n79, 180n1, 180n5, 181n14, 181n18, 181n22, 181n24, 182n7, 183n18, 183n32, 183n34, 184n7, 184n22, 185n37

Bangladeshi citizens, 42, 109, 112, 173n5

Bangladeshi citizenship, 46

Bangladeshi foreigners, 148, 150, 167

Banglar manush, 105, 106, 107

barbed wire, 3, 9, 10, 20, 21, 119, 123, 124, 130, 137, 138, 140, 143, 144

Barbora, Sanjay, 151, 185n24

barricades, 9, 21, 40, 65, 128, 143, 183n17

Baruah, Sanjib, 103, 183n19, 173n7, 174n8, 177n48, 178n22, 183n19

belonging, 5, 6, 12, 31, 35, 48, 95, 97, 168, 172, 174n 17

Bengal Boundary Commission, 51

Bengali, 13–18, 28–30, 32, 39, 40, 45, 46, 48, 50, 52, 55, 60, 74, 75, 94, 105, 108–111, 116, 122, 127, 148, 151, 160, 163, 166

Beverley, Eric, 7, 174n15

Bharatiya Janata Party (BJP), x, 20, 68, 70, 80, 150, 151, 180n2

Biehl, João, 8, 174n19, 174n20

Billé, Franck, 138, 184n20

binoculars, 21, 199

bonded labor, 26, 34, 39. *See also* conscription
borders, 2, 12, 13, 15, 25, 29, 30, 36, 40, 58, 73, 75, 79, 80, 102, 114, 121, 151, 164, 172. *See also* nations and police
border brokers, 69, 76
border camps, 18
border commanders, 72, 73, 80, 82, 91, 100, 102, 116, 142
border communities, 90, 101
border crossers, 10, 104, 115, 120, 121, 132–134, 136
border crossings, 7, 10, 12, 17, 52, 87, 94, 102, 104, 106, 108, 109, 117, 127, 132, 134, 171
border development, 72, 97, 103
border disputes, 28–30
border enforcement, 10, 121, 128
border fences, 3, 10, 25, 69, 77, 124, 136, 170
Border Guard Bangladesh (BGB), 18, 110, 111, 137, 159, 175n50, 181n24, 181n26, 181n27
border guards, 57, 58, 62, 63, 80, 82, 91, 115, 142
border haats, 50, 103, 104, 170, 183n17, 183n23
border markets, 103, 104
border militarization, 2, 7, 9, 10, 98, 112
border outposts, 18, 19, 58, 99, 106, 122, 126, 128, 144
border patrols, 53, 63, 96
border security, 73, 89
Border Security Forces (BSF), 68, 110, 111, 116, 117, 128, 173n5, 175n50
border societies, 2, 3, 5–7, 12–14, 75, 100, 117, 118, 144, 175n44
border villages, 3, 19, 20, 24, 46, 53, 55, 59, 78, 82, 91, 99, 101, 109, 116, 122, 180n1, 181n20
border walls, 9, 10, 20, 172, 175n41
border zones, 70, 87, 173n3.
borderi, 1, 12, 17, 172
Boroibari, ix, 141–142, 184n22
British East India Company, 13, 25, 28, 30
British India, ix, x, 13, 25, 29, 36, 38, 89, 150, 160, 176n4, 176n12
brokerage, 69, 76
Brown, Wendy, 9, 174n32
bulls, 24, 35, 67–73, 75, 78–83, 86, 87, 89, 91, 173n2, 181n28

camouflage, 3, 20, 94
capital, 9, 34, 49, 69, 79, 80
Carsten, Janet, 95, 182n4
cattle, 2, 6, 7, 16, 35, 48, 49, 54, 57, 135
cattle flows, 81, 88, 91, 135
cattle raids, 76, 90, 181n24
cattle seizures, 69, 72, 80, 81, 82, 87, 181n19, 181n24
cattle smuggling, 68, 79, 80, 82, 87, 88, 181n14, 181n18, 181n19, 181n24
cattle traders, 69, 85, 86, 91
cattle transactions, 86, 91, 181n24
cattle transport, 71, 83, 87
Chalfin, Brenda, 87, 181n23, 175n37
chars, 1, 6, 9, 12, 14, 23, 25, 38, 43, 50, 53, 54, 61, 78, 79, 81–83, 86–93, 120, 122, 133, 137, 140, 142, 144, 170, 173n3, 174n14, 180n5
checkpoints, 5, 8, 9, 71, 80, 85, 104
citizenship, 3, 5, 7, 9, 14, 15, 46, 70, 95, 96, 111, 145–148, 151, 152, 155, 157–162, 168, 169, 171, 172; Citizenship Amendment Act (CAA), x, 147–151, 171; boundaries of citizenship, 148, 169, 182n11; citizenship certificate, 16–162; citizenship claims, 152, 168; citizenship documents, 147; citizenship through paperwork, 146, economic citizenship, 70; Muslim citizens, 59; national citizenship, 3, 6, 7, 95, 96, 148; *See also* nations and nationalism
climate, 6, 29, 170, 170, 184n1, 185n24
conflicts, 2, 5, 13, 97, 172, 175n50, 185n25; ethnic conflicts 14, 104; intercommunity conflicts 27; land conflicts 49, 148
conscription, 19, 27, 35. *See also* bonded labor
conviviality, 14, 95, 97, 98, 182n11, 182n12
cows, 67–71, 75, 76, 78, 79, 82, 83, 86, 87, 89, 90, 170, 173n2, 181n28
cow-protection, 68, 79, 79, 80, 181n12
cross-examinations, 156, 161, 162

Dalton, Edward, 35, 117n36
danger, 6, 8, 20, 70, 80, 124, 127, 132, 133, 135, 171
Das, Veena, 95, 96, 148, 182n5
Das, Veena and Poole, Deborah, 148, 175n36, 185n33
De Castro, Viveiros, 95 182n3
De León, Jason, 10, 174n35
death, 5, 8, 17, 20, 27, 57, 80, 120, 121, 133, 134, 142, 144, 172, 173n5

Deleuze, Gilles, 7, 174n18
deportation, 45, 46, 55, 60–63, 146, 148, 150, 167
displacement, 13, 46, 48, 63, 65, 66, 108, 118
dissidents, 13, 18, 103, 106, 117, 125, 129, 131, 145
du nombori bebsha, 17, 87
duplicity, 7, 12, 69, 80, 83, 158, 185n11

earthquakes, 6, 26, 30, 37, 38
East Pakistan, ix, 13, 15, 19, 45, 52–60, 62–66, 90, 96, 107, 108, 117, 160, 168
ecologies, 6, 7, 10, 13, 171, 174n28. See also forests, river, chars and natural disasters
elephant nation, 128, 131
elephants, 3, 20, 29–31, 122, 126–132, 137, 184n7, 184n9
enclave, 28, 145, 181n22
environment, 70, 105
espionage, 45, 57, 58, 108
ethnicity, 14, 15, 21, 48, 55, 61, 64, 105, 117, 124, 125, 151, 170, 183n25; ethnic identities, 66; ethnic minorities, 13, 27, 66, 110, 175n45
evictions, ix, 168
exclusion, 49, 50, 97, 116, 151

Fang-Fung, 12, 67–72, 76, 80, 82, 85–87, 91, 180n7
fear, 5, 8, 17, 20, 22, 50, 106, 109, 114, 119–122, 126, 127, 129, 131, 133, 134, 140, 141, 143, 144, 147, 168, 171, 172, 184n7. See also fieldwork, violence and torture
feast, 76, 99, 119, 170
Felani, x, 143
fieldwork, 1–3, 15, 16, 18–20, 24, 71, 74, 93, 122, 124, 125, 140, 170, 173n3, 175n48, 175n49, 175n50, 184n1; dreams, 20, 126, 138; trauma, 19, 20, 138
files, 19, 47, 151–153, 155, 156, 161, 164, 165, 167. See also papers
fires, 6, 21, 26, 30, 47
floods, 3, 4, 6, 20, 43, 45, 47, 66, 70, 83, 140
force, 7, 25, 30, 50, 60, 61, 63, 66, 89, 119, 121, 135, 153
force of life, 6, 12, 206; life force, 5, 8, 21, 171, 174n25
foreigners, ix, x, 15, 16, 61, 103, 108, 144, 145, 148, 150–152, 158, 159, 166, 167, 175n48, 179n64, 185n17, 186n41

Foreigners Act of India, ix, 150
Foreigners Tribunals, x, 15, 16, 61, 145, 151, 166, 175n48, 185n17
forests, 3, 6, 13, 20, 21, 29, 30, 34, 39, 44, 45, 61, 64, 106, 11, 115, 119, 122, 124, 128, 137, 144, 178n9
Foucault, Michel, 131, 184n11
frontiers, 7, 13, 25–27, 59

garments, 7, 12, 94, 97, 98, 104, 112–114, 116, 117, 183n34; textiles, 117
Garo, 14, 15, 21, 23, 24, 26, 27–33, 35, 38–40, 42, 45, 46, 50, 52, 53, 55–59, 62–64, 90, 94, 96–99, 103–110, 113, 117, 126, 127, 132, 177n46, 177n50, 179n57, 182n7, 183n31, 184n7, 184n9
Garo Hills, 13, 15, 25, 26, 28–36, 38, 39, 42, 47, 50, 54, 59, 64, 68, 71, 73, 82, 89, 90, 93, 104, 107, 110, 111, 176n22, 176n23, 176n25, 177n33, 177n35, 177n37, 177n43, 117n53, 177n1, 179n50, 180n76, 183n31
Gellner, David, 107, 183n30
gender, 21, 110, 152, 167, 173n2, 174n17; gendered banter, 170; gendered border crossings 104; gendered costs, 98; gendered gradations of Indian citizenship, 159; gendered hierarchies, 61; gendered identities, 12; gendered transborder livelihoods, 98; gendered values, 96
Gilroy, Paul, 97, 182n10
goats, 67, 82, 92, 99
gossip, 152, 155
Govindrajan, Radhika, 79, 181n12
grazing grounds, 128, 144
Great Wall of China, 3, 119
guns, 17, 19, 20, 24, 57, 120, 131, 132, 134, 137, 142, 143
Gupta, Akhil, 155, 166, 174n30, 185n27, 185n34, 185n39

Hajong, 50, 56, 57, 64
Hansen, Thomas Blom, 70, 175n36, 180n8, 182n31
haze, 26, 30, 31
head hunting, 28, 32
heliotrope, 21, 31, 36, 37
home goru, 67, 70, 80, 180n1
Hull, Matthew, 155, 185n27, 185n30, 185n32
humans and animals, 121, 122, 138, 144, 92. See also animals

hunger, 47, 77, 79, 11, 134, 136, 138, 184n18
hurmuri jatras, 5, 45, 62

illegal migration, ix, 147, 148, 158, 185n16
Illegal Migration (Determination by
  Tribunals) Act (IMDT), ix, x, 148–150,
  185n15; immigrants, ix, 10, 48, 54, 61,
  146–148, 150, 171, 178n30, 180n75
Immigrants (Expulsion from Assam) Act,
  ix, 54, 178n30
immigration, 16, 51, 125, 148, 150, 178n11,
  185n25
income, 74, 81, 89, 105, 113
India, 1–4, 6, 9–21, 23, 25, 27–30, 32, 35–38,
  40, 42, 44–48, 50, 52–66, 68–73, 75, 79,
  80, 82–91, 93–111, 115–117, 119–125,
  127–131, 134, 135, 138–148, 150, 151, 153,
  156, 157–160, 165, 167, 170–172, 173n7,
  174n8, 174n14, 174n28, 175n42, 175n44,
  175n45, 176n4, 176n9, 176n12, 176n14,
  176n19, 177n31, 177n38, 177n48, 178n22,
  178n37, 179n54, 180n76, 180n2, 180n3,
  181n11, 181n14, 181n19, 181n22, 181n25,
  182n31, 182n7, 183n18, 183n23, 183n28,
  184n7, 184n22, 184n1, 185n10, 185n16,
  185n19, 185n20, 185n37, 186n42
India-Pakistan War, ix, 63
Indian citizens, 15, 55, 112, 146, 148, 160,
  162, 163, 168
Indian citizenship, x, 14, 111, 146, 147,
  148, 151, 152, 155, 157–160, 162, 168,
  169, 172
infiltration, ix, 54, 61, 104, 106, 147, 148
infrastructures, 5–7, 9, 10, 40, 69, 74, 87,
  120, 121, 139, 170, 171, 183n18; border
  infrastructures, 2, 5, 6, 74, 139, 171
  See also borders
inner lines, 34
insularity, 5
intelligence, 18, 47, 49, 50, 51, 53, 54, 56, 115,
  116, 122, 124, 165, 179n50
intelligence agents, 18, 49, 50, 51, 53, 54, 115,
  124
intelligence files, 47
intelligence officers, 18, 50, 122, 124
intelligence reports, 49, 50, 51 54, 56,
  178n12
interrogations, 18, 20, 21, 115, 116, 125.
  See also police interrogation reports
Israel, 2, 8, 173n4

Jayal, Neerja Gopal, 147, 184n4
Jeganathan, Pradeep, 121, 183n5
Jones, Reece, 134, 174n16, 174n28, 175n41,
  175n42, 184n13
judicial trials, 21, 61, 146, 151, 161, 163
"jungle passports," 3, 5, 93, 94, 97, 100, 105,
  110, 113–115, 117, 118, 170

kacha bebsha pakka bebsha, 17
Kader Bahini Rebellion, ix, 112
Kar, Bodhisattva, 34, 177n29
Karlsson, Bengt, 103, 175n45, 177n51,
  183n20, 183n29, 183n31
Khan, Naveeda, 92, 173n3, 182n35
kinship, 5, 7, 12, 14, 93–98, 100, 107–111,
  113, 117, 118, 171, 182n3, 182n4; kinship
  authority, 114; kinship boundaries, 109;
  kinship structures, 110; kinship ties, 56,
  94, 103, 108; matrilineal kinship, 108;
  transborder kinship, 108
Krishna, Sankaran, 9, 174n33
Kurigram, 2, 11, 15, 43, 44, 71, 84, 134,
  173n3, 180n5

landscape, 2, 3, 14, 19, 24, 28, 35, 36, 67, 70,
  72, 83, 101, 105, 108, 122, 124, 125, 127,
  128, 130, 133, 137, 144
life worlds, 5, 92, 96, 105, 147
"line-clear," 3, 17, 71
"line-cuts," 71, 73
livelihood, 2, 5, 6, 7, 70, 90, 94, 105, 110, 120,
  127, 129
loyal subjects, 13
Ludden, David, 19, 176n52, 180n82

Mahari, 94, 98, 99, 105, 106, 110, 127, 132,
  170, 182n7
Malkki, Liisa, 65, 180n80
mama, 127, 128
maps, 6, 12, 13, 19, 21, 25, 26, 40, 46, 54, 58,
  65, 122; area maps, 58; local maps, 58; old
  maps, 6, 12, 19, 21, 65; political maps,
  179n62; secret maps, 54; stolen maps, 46
margins, 5, 8, 20, 21, 43, 44, 65, 70, 95, 96,
  110, 116, 137, 148, 175n36, 175n38, 177n2,
  181n36, 182n2, 184n38, 185n13, 186n43
markets, 12, 16, 18, 23, 24, 28, 29, 50, 56,
  67–69, 75, 80, 83, 85, 86, 88, 89, 91, 101,
  103–106, 108, 110, 112, 114, 135, 144,
  177n32, 180n5

Martinez, Oscar, 40, 177n54
Masquelier, Adeline, 27, 176n6
Mathur, Nayanika, 153, 185n28
Meghalaya, 2–4, 9, 13, 15, 17, 42, 68, 75, 93,
    100, 101, 119, 123, 129, 139, 141, 173n7,
    175n49, 179n62, 180n75, 180n76, 180n2,
    182n7, 183n18, 184n7, 184n9
migrants, ix, 5, 9, 14, 18, 27, 40, 48, 49, 51,
    93, 122, 145, 147, 148, 150, 158, 159, 161,
    163, 164, 167, 170, 172, 185n15
migration, ix, 1, 3
militarization, 2, 7, 9, 10, 17, 18, 32, 45, 70,
    98, 112, 173n7
mobility, 3, 5, 6, 8, 10, 12, 19, 21, 27, 34, 35,
    46, 58, 65, 66, 69, 93, 101, 102, 117, 120,
    133, 136, 160, 170, 172, 183n26; animal
    mobility, 10; anxious mobility, 133;
    human mobility, 19, 120; military
    mobility, 58; motif of mobility, 144;
    political topographies, 5; protected
    mobility, 136; regimes of mobility, 3
money, 66, 70, 75, 83, 86, 88, 106, 109, 134,
    169, 181n20
Muslim cattle workers, 2, 70, 80, 135
Muslim League, 48–51, 54
Mymensingh, 14, 15, 47–50, 58, 62–64, 93,
    98–100, 112, 122

nationalism, 5, 7–9, 12, 22, 27, 65, 172,
    182n3; gendering of nationalism 110;
    religious nationalism, 182n31; sub-
    nationalism, 2, 173n7. See also gender
    and religion
nations, 2, 5, 9, 13, 20, 65, 66, 96, 107, 118,
    120, 121, 128, 172
nation building, 5, 9, 12, 21, 42, 53, 94, 96,
    97, 108, 110, 112, 170, 172, 183n32;
    nation-state, 6, 9, 13, 46, 91, 96, 107, 109
National Register of Citizens, x, 24, 146–151,
    159, 185n24, 185n25
natural disasters, 26, 30, 38. See also
    ecologies
Netrokona, 2, 15, 93, 94, 100, 184n7
Netz, Reviel, 138, 184n19
Nevins, Joseph, 121, 183n1
Nietzsche, Friedrich, 174n18
Nodi bhanga manush, 23, 74
nokma, 100, 107
Northeast India, 2–4, 6, 10, 12, 14, 15, 17, 18,
    23, 25, 27, 40, 42, 45, 52, 66, 79, 95, 97,

    100, 101, 103, 107, 111, 120–123, 131, 144,
    170–172, 173n7, 175n44, 180n2, 183n28,
    184n7

officials, 25, 26, 28, 29, 30, 32, 38, 45, 54, 55,
    58–60, 62, 81, 83, 101, 102, 166; British
    officials, 26, 30, 38; customs officials, 83;
    district officials, 55, 62; East Pakistani
    officials, 62; Indian officials, 45; visiting
    officials, 10
official circular, 56
official correspondence, 19, 57, 59, 90
official histories, 45
official letters, 59, 90
official mandates, 10, 102
official memorandum, 58
official records, 17, 26–28, 38, 45, 55, 90
official restrictions, 78, 81
Ohnuki-Tierney, Emiko, 66, 180n84

Palestine, 2, 8, 121, 173n4
panoptic, 168, 171; panopticon, 131
papers, 6, 19, 77, 148, 152, 153, 155–158,
    160–163, 166, 168, 169, citizenship papers,
    160; fake papers, 148; identity papers, 6,
    146, 148, 152, 155–157, 168; land papers,
    162; legal papers, 77; newspapers, 19, 24,
    54, 59, 163; property papers, 168;
    registration papers, 152. See also files
partition, 49, 96, 148, 162, 168, 175n40,
    177n7, 182n6; partition of Bengal (British
    India), ix, 40; partition of the Indian
    subcontinent 13, 51, 52, 90, 95, 160
pillars, 1–3, 9, 10, 24, 65, 83, 119, 121–124,
    129, 130, 133, 137, 143
plantation, 34, 48
police, 51–62, 76, 77, 86, 96, 104, 106, 108, 111,
    145, 146, 149, 151, 152, 154–168, 178n39,
    179n59, 181n18; Assam Border Police, 150,
    152, 157, 159, 162, 163, 165, 166; border
    police, 17, 50, 53, 55–59, 61, 96, 108, 145,
    146, 158, 159, 161, 164; British police, 51;
    confessions, 132, 161, 162; East Pakistani
    police, 56; Indian police, 53, 57, 58; police
    battalions, 32; police force, 60, 61, 30; police
    interrogation reports, 152, 161, 164, 167;
    police outpost, 32; police records, 51; police
    report, 19, 152; police stations, 61, 82, 148;
    police surveys, 151, 155, 164, 168, 171
political subjects, 6, 8, 9, 160

poverty, 14, 114, 117, 135, 173n3
power, 6–9, 12, 20, 21, 28, 40, 44, 48, 54, 65,
    82, 86, 87, 97, 103, 113, 121, 126, 127, 131,
    132, 138, 150, 181n22; sovereign power, 7,
    9; territorial power, 28; state power, 8, 82,
    87, 131, 132. See also state and sovereignty
proto-nation, 90, 131
pushback, 18, 159, 176n51

race, 21, 25, 26, 29, 32, 38, 174n17
Rangpur, 16, 28, 43, 47, 74, 89
reciprocity, 5, 7, 95–97, 102, 117
Reeves, Madeleine, 147, 185n6
refugees, 5, 9, 18, 51, 55, 59, 62, 64, 108, 109,
    147, 148, 151, 160, 163, 172
Regulation X, ix, 28, 176n12
religion, 14, 48, 51, 61, 76, 90, 94, 97, 107,
    151, 170, 172, 181n12
reverence, 119, 126–128, 144, 171
rice, 1–3, 7, 20, 21, 35, 36, 42, 44–51, 53–55,
    57–66, 76, 90, 119, 122, 124, 128, 129, 131,
    132, 135, 136, 140, 142, 144, 168, 170,
    180n84
rice cultivation, 45, 48, 53
rice cultivators, 45, 46, 50, 51, 54, 55, 57, 65, 66
rice harvests, 3, 21, 45, 55, 57, 58, 59, 63
rice paddy, 46, 60, 122, 131
rice raids, 57, 58, 168
rice smuggling, 51, 53, 54, 60
rice wars, 42, 46, 51, 66, 90
riots, 61–63, 90, 108, 160; Hindu Muslim
    rioting, ix, 61
risk, 8, 12, 67, 71, 79, 133, 144
rivers, 11, 47, 111, 123, 140, 158, 171, 173n3;
    Brahmaputra River, 1, 51, 67, 78, 81, 91;
    Jinjiram River 23, 36; Ronkha River 124,
    127, 137
roads, 3, 6, 17, 18, 20, 25–27, 30, 31, 34–36,
    39–41, 51, 83, 88, 89, 104, 128, 129
Roitman, Janet, 70, 175n38, 180n10, 181n16
routes, 3, 6, 10, 12, 25, 53, 69, 71–73, 85, 91,
    102, 109, 122, 136, 164, 176n3
Rowmari-Tura road, 14, 20, 21, 23, 25–27,
    34, 40, 42, 43, 50, 52, 53, 65, 73, 89, 93,
    141, 143, 144
Roy, Anupama, 147, 184n3
rumors, 3, 48, 61, 131, 142, 154, 155, 158

sacred, 12, 68–70, 73, 75, 78–80, 83, 86, 89, 90
Sahlins, Marshall, 95, 97, 182n3

Sangma, Sonaram R., 39, 177n51
Scott, James C., 65, 185n26, 180n81
Sharma, Jayeeta, 48, 177n8, 177n30,178n10,
    178n11, 185n25
Shneiderman, Sara, 105, 183n25
Siddiqui, Dina, 113, 183n36, 183n37
Singh, Bhrigupati, 8, 174n21
Singh, Bhrigupati and Dave, Naisargi, 79,
    181n13
sirens, 20, 125, 166
Sivaramakrishnan, Kalyanakrishnan, 29,
    176n17
smuggling, 1, 3, 6, 10, 12, 17, 18, 45, 51, 53,
    54, 60, 67, 68–71, 73, 75–77, 79–81, 83, 87,
    88, 91, 93, 94, 102, 171, 175n50, 181n13,
    181n18, 181n19, 181n25
Sonowal, Sarbananda, 50, 185n19
sovereignty, 7–9, 70, 96, 121, 138, 170, 171,
    174n17, 175n42, 176n10; national
    sovereignty, 9; 170; sovereign authority, 7;
    territorial sovereignty, 8. See also state
    and power.
space, 3, 7, 9, 12, 32, 35, 94, 102, 103, 109,
    111, 117, 147, 155, 174n17, 175n39, 175n41,
    181n22, 184n16
spies, 13, 46, 55, 58, 61, 108
state, 5–10, 12–14, 18–20, 23, 25, 27, 30,
    44–46, 49, 51, 53–61, 63, 65, 66, 68, 70–72,
    74, 78, 80–87, 90, 91, 93, 94, 96, 104, 105,
    107–110, 116, 121, 131, 132, 138, 142, 143,
    146, 147, 150, 152, 155–158, 160–162, 165,
    167, 174n17, 175n45, 177n50, 180n8,
    183n3, 185n10, 185n13, 185n15, 185n26,
    186n43
stateless, 5, 151, 168, 175n42
statelessness, 14, 175n42
state agents, 10, 18, 53, 55, 57, 7, 78, 81, 82,
    84, 86, 87, 91, 108, 131, 152, 165
state oppression, 49, 58
state prosecutors, 146, 155, 161
state repression 5, 59, 109, 110, 116. See also
    nations, power and sovereignty
Sturgeon, Janet, 105, 183n24
surplus, 3, 12, 94, 98, 110, 112, 113
surveillance, 2, 87, 104,131, 138,
    141,163,168,170,171, 174n14
survey, 29–32, 36, 37, 43, 47, 62, 155, 159,
    166, 177n38, 177n47, 181n28, 184n22
suspicion, 39, 51, 54, 58, 108, 151, 154, 164,
    168, 169

Tarlo, Emma, 153, 185n31
Taussig, Michael, 143, 184n23
tax, 47, 49, 61, 65, 84, 85, 87, 162
tea, 24, 34, 48, 75, 88, 94, 98, 99, 115, 116,
  125, 135, 136, 140, 166
torture, 27, 70, 80, 106, 120, 121, 134, 135.
  See also violence and fear.
traitors, 13, 59, 96, 107

unauthorized migration, 5, 9, 10, 91, 168.
  See also migration
U.S., 10, 129, 173n4
U.S.-Mexico border, 2, 10, 40, 121
"UT" (The Untraceable), 164, 165, 167

value, 68–71, 80–82, 92, 97, 102, 113, 168,
  180n1
van Schendel, Willem, 12, 174n26, 175n40,
  175n41, 175n42 178n16, 178n24, 178n25,

178n33 178n38, 179n61, 180n80, 180n81,
  180n9, 181n17, 181n21, 182n2, 182n8,
  185n8, 185n14
vibrant, 8,41
violence, 2, 8–10, 13, 27, 65, 66, 79, 97,
  117, 121, 135, 165, 174n10, 183n4;
  border violence, 7, 21, 134, 173n5;
  domestic violence, 72; state violence,
  5, 19, 45, 53, 80, 94, 96, 109, 143;
  tactility of violence, 20. *See also* torture
  and fear

Weizman, Eyal, 121, 183n2
Winichakul, Thongchai, 32, 176n28
wireless radio, 103, 125

Zebu cattle, 67, 69–72, 77–79, 81, 83, 84, 88,
  93. *See also* animals
Zomia, 65, 183n25

ACKNOWLEDGMENTS

In a house of women—where I lived with my great-grandmother, my grand-mother, my maternal aunt, and my mother—everyone hoped that one day I would travel far and write books. My home-schooled grandmother Rani did everything possible to send my aunt Anima and my mother Nilima to the university. They richly repaid her with their academic and professional ac-complishments. Every evening after her prayers, my great-grandmother Sara-jubala, a pious Hindu widow, would whisper in my ears, "You will travel very far to study." Dipali Adhikari held our family together, providing care for four generations and especially for me, after my father Pramatha's sud-den death. Their love for books and for reading and writing inspired me to cross many borders. *Jungle Passports* is a tribute to their dreams.

The generosity of the families I lived and traveled with in villages in Assam and Meghalaya in Northeast India, as well as Kurigram, Mymensingh, and Netrokona districts of Bangladesh, sustained me during long and difficult years of fieldwork. They showered me with endless affection and care, and took many risks to protect me. To Alibaba, Aladdin, Sister Mary, Shufola, Manik, Judge B., A. Bhattacharji, and Sujala Das and to Theo, Runa, Bijoy, Rezaul, Rahmuna, Khalamma, and Nanabhai, as they are known in this book, I give my heartfelt gratitude. In Rajshahi, I thank Mahbubur Rahman and Nepa Rahman. To the staff of the Ain-O-Salish Kendra (Dhaka), Assam State Archives (Dispur), British Library, National Archives of Bangladesh (Dhaka), Heritage Archives (Rajshahi), Land Records and Surveys (Guwahati), and the International Institute of Social History (Amsterdam), my appreciation for making possible a wealth of official documents at my disposal. In My-mensingh and Netrokona, I thank the Birohidakuni Catholic Mission and the Ranikhong Catholic Mission for making their archives available to me.

I thank Willem van Schendel for his guidance and encouragement in the project that became this book. I could not have asked for a better teacher. His book *The Bengal Borderland* continues to inspire my writing. For Willem's humor during all the challenges of fieldwork, writing, and life, I remain indebted forever.

Jungle Passports is a product of many years of intellectual mentoring and generous friendships across continents. I thank Itty Abraham for his valuable advice since my tenure at the Social Science Research Council (New York), where he headed the South Asia Program. Over the years, Partha Chatterjee and Hastings Donnan asked several critical questions that greatly improved this manuscript, and I thank them both. For conversations that sparked my critical imaginations as well as for vigorous criticism, I am indebted to Manan Ahmed, Paula Banerjee, Prathama Banerjee, Eric Beverley, Uday Chandra, Jason Cons, Bina D'Costa, Thomas Blom Hansen, Tina Harris, Martha Kaplan, John D. Kelly, Christopher Krupa, David Ludden, Annemarie Mol, Dina Siddiqui, Kalyanakrishnan Sivaramakrishnan, Sharika Thiranagama, Ranabir Samaddar, Andrew Shryock, Emrah Yildiz, Donna Young, and Alsi Zengin. Manan, Jason, and Uday have provided scholarly advice and critical readings on various chapters. From my early postdoctoral days, Jayeeta Sharma has offered guidance at every step of my academic career, and I thank her for her generosity. I have turned to George Jose and Bodhisattva Kar on innumerable occasions; their gentle criticism has helped me turn my embryonic ideas into shape. They have carefully read this manuscript and engaged with my work across time zones, often on very short notice. My conversations on life and loss with Sharika and Emrah have shaped this book. My intellectual debts to all of them are immense.

In Assam, Xonzoi (Sanjay) Barbora, Kazu Ahmed, and Xorot (Sarat) Phukhan made the impossible possible during my fieldwork. My sanctuary was 100 Kharguli Road in Guwahati, with a never-ending supply of Assamese and Naga delicacies and good cheer. Xonzoi and Kazu so generously looked out for me during my fieldwork in Assam, and Xorot Kai's phone calls to check on my well-being meant a lot. In Guwahati, I especially thank Achuyut Deka. Makiko Kimura and Dolly Kikon offered valuable suggestions during my fieldwork in Assam. Rashid and Chandra, as they are known in this book, accompanied me during my early fieldwork in Assam and Meghalaya, and I am grateful to them. In Dhaka, Sara Hossain, David Bergman, and Papreen Nahar asked important questions on borders and state violence and, above all, offered new ways to think about and work toward a more just world. In

Guwahati and Dhaka, Sanjib Baruah, Meghna Guhathakurta, and Hameeda Hossain shared their vast knowledge on citizenship, identity, and belonging. Their suggestions have shaped my writing. Sarada Hariharan's friendship, unfailing support, and sense of humor helped me cope with years of challenging fieldwork, loss, and more.

Initial ideas for this book were nurtured with friends at the University of Amsterdam, especially in engagement with endless intellectual debates at the Amsterdam School for Social Science Research. My ideas were refined in the company of Martin Boekelo, Maria Fernanda Olatre-Sierra, Nisa Fachry, Silke Heumann, Katharina Paul, Emily Yates-Doerr, Ward Berenschot, Julia Challinor, and Piet van Peter. Nienke Klopmaker showered endless warmth; it was all mine to ask. I remain grateful for all of our canal walks, bicycle rides, and discussions on refugees and the stateless. I am indebted to Annemarie Mol, for her ever willingness to read, debate, and go for long walks in the Dutch countryside. I thank all the members of the "Illegal but Licit" and the Moving Matters program groups at the University of Amsterdam. The Amsterdam School and especially Jose Komen provided institutional and moral support to cope with and recover from the lingering aftereffects of dangerous fieldwork. To Marianne Vysma, I remain ever indebted for helping me make sense of trauma.

My research was funded by the Netherlands Organization for Scientific Research (NWO),the Amsterdam Institute for Social Science Research, University of Amsterdam and the Asia Research Institute, National University of Singapore. At the Asia Research Institute, National University of Singapore, I am grateful to Prasenjit Duara, Chua Beng Huat, and Michael Feener's intellectual generosity and engagement. Brenda Yeoh's valuable advice on my research shaped this book. Her support in critical moments of writing and in balancing career advancement and family was precious and remains with me. Every conversation I have had with her has enriched my life. I thank all the members of the Asian Migrations Programme, of which I was a part. Nausheen Anwar, Bernardo Brown, Céline Coderey, Ashley Pack, Catherine Smith, Michiyo Vaughan, and Juan (Jessie) Zhang have asked me incisive questions and generously offered advice. Animated exchanges and critical debates with Philip Fountain, Tyson Vaughan, and Bernardo Brown helped in rethinking significant parts of this book. Eric Kerr spent hours listening and reading about regions and issues that were distant from his scholarly interests as a philosopher. His wise words, perceptive questions, and friendship have helped me beyond this book. Eli Elinoff generously read multiple versions of this manuscript. His close reading and willingness to debate in Singapore and Wellington have shaped my thinking and writing. Across the ridge, I thank Annu Jalais and Sidharthan Maunaguru from the South Asian Studies program for productive conversations on borders and the force of life. To Annu, Sid, and Céline, I am grateful for many extraordinary dinners. I give my appreciation forever to Sharon Ong and all the professional staff who made ARI such a super-efficient and fun place to work in.

At the Western Sydney University, where I completed the manuscript, I thank James Arvanitakis, Kevin Dunn, Paul James, Bob Hodges, and Brett Neilson. At the Institute of Culture and Society, Paul and Bob read every page of this manuscript. Their perceptive and generous commentaries have greatly improved this book. I remain indebted to Brett Neilson's constructive engagement and intellectual support for my work on borders; it is such an honor to be his colleague. Gay Hawkins has mentored me with care; she has raised important questions, and the introduction to this book is greatly improved due to her thought-provoking criticisms. Paul, Brett, and Terence Fairclough provided valuable advice during a rather tough phase of early parenting, and Gay and Katherine Gibson have generously taught me how to balance academic pursuits and parenting without compromises. I was very fortunate to be in the company of Louise Crabtree, Stephen Healey, and Liam Magee. They have engaged with this book and pointed me to new intellectual directions. At the School of Social Sciences, I sincerely thank Mary Hawkins for her close reading and critical engagement. Geir Henning Presterudstuen and Helena Önnudóttir warmly welcomed me to our new BA program in anthropology, and asked me important questions on borders, identity, and the uncanny. Simone Casey, Cheryl D'Cruz, Tulika Dubey, Terence Fairclough, Emily-Kate Ringle Harris, and Gillian Relph have made all the big and small things in my academic life possible; I thank them.

I presented chapters of this book at the Australian National University, Centre for Studies in the Social Sciences–Kolkata, Columbia University, Indian Institute of Technology–Guwahati, Jadavpur University, National University of Singapore, New York University, New Zealand India Institute, Nehru Memorial Library, Macquarie University, Sarah Lawrence College, Sydney University, University of Toronto, Western Sydney University, and Yale University. I thank the organizers and the audience for their engagement with my work. Parts of this book have been featured in *Comparative Studies of Society and History* and *Modern Asian Studies*, and *Cultural Anthropology*, I thank the journals for permissions.

At the University of Pennsylvania Press, I thank the editors of the Ethnographies of Political Violence series, Sharika Thiranagama, Tobias Kelley, and Danny Hoffman. Sharika has shepherded this project, and I remain indebted for all the important questions that she has posed. Peter A. Agree and Jerome Singerman at the University of Pennsylvania Press were the best editors I could ever ask for. I thank Jerome for guiding this project to its final form. To Kalyanakrishnan Sivaramakrishnan and Bengt G. Karlsson, I owe gratitude for their insightful and generous review of this manuscript. I have learned so much from them, and I remain indebted for their unwavering support.

An unexpected email from Shanti Robertson, a migration scholar I had yet to meet, provided the context of my sudden relocation to Australia. Shanti's research on international migration and its troublesome pathways in Australia continues to shape my thinking. Every conversation with her has pushed me to think about precarity and resilience.

In Sydney, I have found a home away from home in the Rozario-Samuel clan. Since the first week we landed in Sydney, Santi Rozario and Geoffrey Samuel have been unfailingly generous and intellectually supportive. Santi read chapters and discussed at great length women's changing roles and identities in Bangladesh, for which I remain grateful. My relocation to Australia reunited me with my lovely Irish Australian family Finbarr and Deborah, as well as my amazing nephew Kiran Lynch.

To Jayanti Bose, Barnita Bagchi, Dipanwita Mitra, Deep Purakayastha, Aprajita Sapra, Aveek Sen, and Vinita Suryanarayan, I owe years of intellectual exchanges and laughter. In San Francisco, I had many occasions to discuss this book with Janet and Wayne Vetach, and I especially thank Janet for all the wisdom and the joy. I have turned, time and again, to my most loving family, Basabi Das, B. K. Sen Choudhury, Atin, and Archana Das. I have also discussed this book at great length with Debjani Chowdhury; every intellectual discussion and gesture of sisterly affection has touched my life beyond words. My talented nieces Deboleena and Amrita fixed and collated maps and retrieved data; they have so lovingly responded to all my unreasonable demands on their time. Along with Jayeeta, Madhurima, and Sreetama, they are vital to my life.

Rakesh Kumar has been my partner in life and crime. He closely followed this book's journey across four continents, patiently reading and rereading every page of this manuscript. Rakesh has put up with my long absences during fieldwork and in the writing of this book. I thank him for lifting every cloud for me. I live in the hope that our son Neel, who turns four as this book goes to press, will one day turn these pages.